I0762479

TO LOVE
A COUNTRY

TO LOVE A COUNTRY

The Problem of Patriotism in America

DOMINIC ERDOZAIN

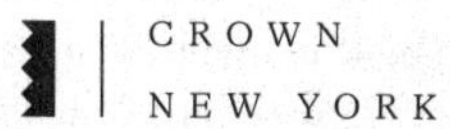
CROWN
NEW YORK

CROWN
An imprint of the Crown Publishing Group
A division of Penguin Random House LLC
1745 Broadway
New York, NY 10019
crownpublishing.com
penguinrandomhouse.com

Library of Congress Cataloging-in-Publication Data
is available upon request.

ISBN 979-8-217-08717-4
Ebook ISBN 979-8-217-08718-1

Editor: Kevin Doughten
Editorial assistant: Jess Scott
Production editor: Patricia Shaw
Text designer: Andrea Lau
Production: Jessica Heim
Proofreaders: Nicole Ramirez, Lisa Lawley, Andrea Peabbles, and Nancy Inglis
Indexer: Cathy Dorsey
Publicist: Elora Weil
Marketer: Mason Eng

Manufactured in the United States of America

1st Printing

First Edition

The authorized representative in the EU for product safety and compliance is Penguin Random House Ireland, Morrison Chambers, 32 Nassau Street, Dublin D02 YH68, Ireland, https://eu-contact.penguin.ie.

To a true friend and a true American,
Emanuele Di Lorenzo

The people I admire most in our history are the hell-raisers and the rabble-rousers, the apple-cart upsetters and plain old mumpish eccentrics who just didn't want to be like everybody else. They are the people who made and make the Constitution of the United States a living document—Tom Paine and Clarence Darrow, Mother Jones and Harriet Tubman, Margaret Sanger and Martin Luther King Jr., Brown of *Brown v. the Board of Education*, Joe Hill and Frederick Douglass, Sockless Jerry Simpson and Eleanor Roosevelt, John Henry Faulk and J. Frank Dobie, Saul Alinsky and Ralph Nader.

And I believe every word of the Declaration: I do hold these truths to be self-evident, that all men are created equal, that they are endowed by their Creator with certain unalienable Rights, that among these are Life, Liberty, and the pursuit of Happiness.

Let's celebrate it today, too.

—Molly Ivins, *Fort Worth Star-Telegram,* July 5, 1994

CONTENTS

TO LOVE A COUNTRY

PROLOGUE

Americanism or the American Promise?

> The distinction between past, present and future is only an illusion, however persistent.
>
> —ALBERT EINSTEIN

In June 1826, Thomas Jefferson penned his last-ever letter, an essay on the American project. He had been invited to attend a celebration in Washington, to mark the fiftieth anniversary of American independence, and he politely sent his regrets. Sickness now controlled him, but he applauded the sentiment, the fervor of commemoration, and offered his own thoughts on the American experiment. America was a nation built on an idea; an idea "pregnant" with "the fate of the world"; an idea that would drive tyranny and bondage from the earth. What was it? What was the secret of American felicity and prosperity? It was the scandal of equality, the brave assertion of human dignity: "the palpable truth, that the mass of mankind has not been born with saddles on their backs, nor a favored few booted and spurred, ready to ride them legitimately, by the grace of god." No. In America, every life is sacred, and nobody is born to rule. That was America's calling and its gift to the world.

Consciously or otherwise, Jefferson was quoting from a speech delivered by the English radical Richard Rumbold moments before he was executed for high treason in 1685. But the tables had turned. What was crime and delusion in the Old World was real and true in America. Patriots of Jefferson's generation had the dizzying sensation of learning from the pioneers while breaking free and building something new. America was first in freedom, a lamp and guide to the nations. "All eyes are opened, or opening, to the rights of man," he marveled. America's anniversary was a message to the world—"the Signal of arousing men to burst the chains under which monkish ignorance and superstition had persuaded them to bind themselves, and to assume the blessings & security of self-government."

Only Jefferson could turn a dinner invitation into a lecture on time and progress. Although he was famously skeptical in matters of theology, Jefferson's patriotism was untrammeled by doubt. Had he applied the same scrutiny to his political philosophy, he might have seen the irony of preaching equality from Monticello, a neoclassical mansion perched on a slave plantation in Virginia. Did America's grandeur excuse his own? Was the majesty of America's historical mission enough to forgive the indiscretions of the present? Jefferson wrote extensively on the evils of slavery, and he introduced bills for emancipation in Virginia, but in a crucial and telling disclaimer he averred that the problem would not be solved until Providence—"the power of a superior agent"—lifted the curse.

This nonchalant maneuver enables Jefferson to extol America as the seat and refuge of liberty over and against the contradictions of the hour. Indeed, the belief that America's destiny is larger than a troubled present assists the evasion. Like an Old Testament patriarch whose sins are absorbed in a greater story of redemption, America's identity as the apostle of liberty relieves it of the excesses of introspection. Certainly it were better that such a nation live than tear itself to pieces over the fate of the slave. Abraham Lincoln stated the principle when he declared, “Much as I hate slavery, I would consent to the extension of it rather than see the Union dissolved, just as I would consent to any GREAT evil, to avoid a GREATER one.”

Such is the problem of patriotism: a higher law that is really a lower law, because it substitutes a theory about America for the reality. It esteems the state above the person, the shell above the contents, in the hope that what is good for one will be good for the other. It has never worked that way. Where patriotism has meant exceptionalism—the belief that America was born to lead—it has wreaked havoc on the cause of democracy and fair dealing, at home and abroad.

America’s descent, on its 250th anniversary, to the demagoguery of an unapologetic nationalist is not the aberration many want it to be. It is the consummation of forces that have been latent from the start: a rumbling warfare between a political theory of equality and a more visceral urge for mastery. And while “America First” may represent a particularly abrasive form of the phenomenon, it cannot be isolated from a tradition that has long confused the strength of America with the substance of democracy. When the answer to Donald Trump is a renewed and refined patriotism, drawing on the example of Abraham Lincoln and a civil war that claimed nearly a million lives, it is clear that we need to go deeper.

Then, as now, patriotism had a way of hiding divisions under a glittering rhetoric of unity and, by doing so, perpetuating the fractures it professed to heal. To say that patriotism is always marked by falsehood would be unfair, but hyperbole is the time-honored idiom—as though one cannot be true to one’s country without drowning it in praise. Part of the faith, or superstition, of the patriot is that the end will justify the means: that the progress of the nation will deliver all that America stands for, even in war. It is patriotism, not economic or military necessity, that has propelled the nation into so many of its military adventures, flush with certainty that light will prevail against darkness and that we are the light. Far from being the antidote to our own age of nationalism, Lincoln's attempt to close America's sectional wounds in a "mighty contest" of war, to conjure a nation out of fire and blood, is the high-water mark of patriotic fantasy—something I am reminded of every time I see a "Sons of Confederate Veterans" license plate in the snarl of an Atlanta rush hour or a Confederate flag hanging in sullen defiance by the roadside. We are still fighting that war, still nursing those wounds, and the task of history is to find causes, not wallow in myths.

Jefferson, like every political philosopher of his time, was rightly concerned about "superstition" and government—those audacious and "interested" pieties that turn power into the will of God. He hated the falsity as much as the cruelty of the divine right of kings, with its grim conjecture that one family had been called to govern the rest. But patriotism reframed, rather than solved, the problem, achieving for Jefferson and his slaves something akin to what theology had done for kings.

My conviction, as a true believer in what the journalist Randolph Bourne called the "American promise," is that America needs to shed the conceit of exceptionalism to fulfill its democratic mandate. We must lose the myth of preeminence to see the world as it is. From foreign policy to health care, education to the environment, questions of freedom and justice have been lost in the mists of national pride: the still-religious intuition that we have already arrived. The paradox, as Bourne defined it during the nationalist frenzy of World War I, is that America will have to become less patriotic before it can recover what is true and beautiful in its creed.

There are so many areas in which America excels Europe, thought Bourne, but in patriotism we follow and regress. As the irrepressible Emma Goldman lectured a jury, as she defended herself against charges of conspiring against conscription, there are more kinds of patriotism than carnivals of self-regard.

"Gentlemen of the jury," she told a court in 1917, "we respect your patriotism. We would not, if we could, have you change its meaning for yourself. But may there not be different kinds of patriotism as there are different kinds of liberty? I for one cannot believe that love of one's country must needs consist in blindness to its social faults, to deafness to its social discords, of inarticulation to its social wrongs." "Our patriotism," she continued, "is that of the man who loves a woman with open eyes. He is enchanted by her beauty, yet he sees her faults." Goldman loved the American people, and the "great possibilities" of a free society, but she hated the "cant" of an Americanism that trampled on freedom and expected to be thanked for it: the misconceived idealism that deemed a flag more precious than a person. Patriotism, Goldman argued in an earlier essay, had become a "Moloch" and a "menace to liberty," a value that cheerfully "abrogates the principles of the Declaration of Independence." When a court could sentence a man to ninety days in prison for quoting the nation's founding document, in a manner supposedly subversive of the war, the crisis was complete.

Goldman's homily did not move the jury, who convicted her of conspiring against the war effort on the palest of evidence. Her case wound its way up to the Supreme Court, where she was duly exonerated, before that "terrible solidarity" of patriotism had the last word. Goldman was deported to Russia in the Palmer Raids of 1919—an undocumented immigrant, shipped to obscurity. But the question did not go away: Does patriotism help or hinder the democratic project? As the peace activist Devere Allen quipped in

1930, one "can analyze nationalism and live to tell the story; but woe be to that individual who undertakes in public to scrutinize the idea of patriotism with anything resembling scientific detachment." I make no profession of scientific detachment, but I agree with Allen that the distinction begins to crumble when patriotism means exceptionalism—an idea, as Tolstoy observed, that denotes not equality and brotherhood but the recognition of one nationality as superior to all the others. America is a revolution wrapped in a myth: an idea trapped in its own publicity. This book contests the myth in the name of the idea.

CHAPTER 1

Chosen: The Problem of Providence

> Faith gives man a peculiar sense of his own dignity and importance. The believer finds himself distinguished above other men, exalted above the natural man; he knows himself to be a person of distinction, in the possession of peculiar privileges; believers are aristocrats, unbelievers plebeians.
>
> —LUDWIG FEUERBACH, "THE CONTRADICTION OF FAITH AND LOVE"

America's founders, mused Harriet Beecher Stowe, were children of two very different eras. They got their politics from the seventeenth century, in the social contract theory of John Locke and the English Whigs. They got their theology from the sixteenth century, in the fervid Calvinism of the Protestant Reformation. One taught equality, compromise, and rational self-interest. The other taught inequality and division, imparting a hard and heroic element to the American character.

This strange union between liberty and dogma, freedom and fire, has defined the American experience. Those gusts of providence that drove the colonies into independence left a complex and unstable legacy: a vision of unity without the reality, and a burning sense of entitlement. Dynamic in war but uneasy in debate, the doctrine of providence brought strength and fragility to the American character in equal measure. It planted a seed of theocracy in the soil of a democracy.

I

The democratic tradition began as the assertion of the rights of "freeborn Englishmen" against the corruptions and usurpations of kings, tracing its origins to a golden age of Anglo-Saxon freedom, before the Norman Conquest of 1066. What better evidence of the artifice of monarchy, wondered Thomas Paine, than the foreignness of England's kings, and the fact that the English crown descended from William the Conqueror—a "French bastard landing with an armed banditti, and establishing himself king of England against the consent of the natives"? Democracy was doubt: the unmasking of prerogative as the vanity and conceit of ordinary men. England had known a few decent kings, Paine admitted, but had "groaned beneath a much larger number of bad ones." If nature intended one man to reign, why had it so often given us "an ass for a lion"? One honest man, wrote Paine, was worth more "than all the crowned ruffians that ever lived." For men like Paine, battered and bruised by an unforgiving class system, the assertion of human dignity required an attitude of aggression, a flash of native pride. If that purest blood, running through the royal family, could be shown to be foreign, so much the better.

To quibble with the divine right of kings was not to attack religion per se but a certain vision of the deity as a celestial enforcer. If there was a metaphysical foundation for popular sovereignty, it was the burning conviction that God has no favorites and is merciful to all—what one of Benjamin Rush's biographers has termed "the loving heresy of universal salvation." God is "no respecter of persons," proclaimed the Levellers, a radical sect who produced the first truly democratic manifesto of the early modern period. If God was just, the notion of prerogative, or special entitlement, savored of blasphemy. The consequence of this reasoning was to turn the world upside down: Monarchy was exposed as a profane and violent usurper, while the will of the people was dignified and empowered. "This thing called *prerogative,*" protested one of the Levellers, "flows meerly from the wills and pleasures of Robbers, Rogues, and Theaves." Monarchy was theft. Aristocracy was plunder. Democracy was a long struggle to pry the rights and liberties of the people "out of the pawes of those Kings, who by force had conquered the Nation, changed the lawes and by strong hand held them in bondage."

This was strong dissent, a radical inversion. But was there a danger of creating a new idol called "the people," or a new monarch called "the English nation"—commissioned to bring liberty to the world? Yes, thought the poet and philosopher John Milton, who wrestled with the idea of the chosen nation before rejecting it with chastened ferocity.

Had God singled out one nation to teach the others the ways of freedom? wondered Milton, like many Christian thinkers of his time. Perhaps so. Milton's early republicanism combined awesome statements of equality and human potential with almost comical pride in England as the happy locus of an exceptional nation. England is the nation that brings the devil to confusion, a land "mightier" than Satan's crafts: a strong people, inclined to liberty. Milton's tribute to the intellectual powers of the common people has been quoted so many times it is easy to miss the fact that he is talking about a certain kind of people—his own. England was a nation of prophets and sages, men "of a quick, ingenious and piercing spirit."

Milton's republicanism is nationalism: a belief that political equality is possible because English people are uniquely fitted to the task—a "nation chosen before any other." The idea soon appalled him.

Writing, five years later, in a work that arguably defined the democratic project, *The Tenure of Kings and Magistrates,* Milton repented of these boasts. Liberty moves in minds, not nations, he now declared. Faith in nations was wasted energy. There was, he insisted, "a mutual bond of amity and brotherhood between man and man over all the World." It is not distance or blood that makes enmity "but enmity that makes distance." Whoever "keeps peace with me," he writes, is my neighbor, whether he is "a Turk, a Sarasin, a Heathen." England's failed republic under Oliver Cromwell was a sad epiphany for Milton, showing that the English were courageous in war but not "over fertil" of wisdom and justice. Patriotism was a mistake and a distraction. Milton solemnly abandoned the notion of a unique and "covenanted" nation. "One's country," he wrote to a European correspondent in 1666, "is wherever it is well with one."

The eighteenth-century Enlightenment, which supplied so many of the ingredients of the American Revolution, fell somewhere in the middle of this dilemma. It hated nationalism, as an engine of bigotry and war, but it embraced the nation-state as a vehicle of democracy. The notion that one nation is inherently superior to others was repugnant to Enlightenment sensibility, with its fervent belief in natural equality and universal reason. But if humans were rational and capable of virtue, they were also creatures of passion, given to violence and war. Freedom demanded law, and laws required a political community in which values were shared and consensus was possible. As Europe lurched from Wars of Religion to a permanent condition of jealous rivalry, philosophers like Voltaire looked to America as the harbinger of a more peaceful future, and their ideas began to shape it.

There are few golden ages in history, wrote Voltaire, but William Penn's "holy experiment" in Pennsylvania was a sprightly contender. These "enemies of pomp," as he affectionately described the Quakers, had reinvented the art of government, showing that it was possible to live in peace with one another, and one's neighbors. Voltaire saw the Quakers, who "never bow to anybody" and treat "kings and cobblers alike," as pioneers of democracy, and a bracing model for a world drunk on status. Voltaire thought Penn the only governor who honored his treaties with the Native Americans, and he often threatened to move there himself, if he could handle the seasickness. "If I were forty," he told Benjamin Franklin, shortly before his death in 1778, "I should go and settle in your happy fatherland."

This was more than flattery. As Jill Lepore has observed, the seed of equality grew in the radicalism of eccentrics such as Benjamin Lay, a diminutive Quaker who registered his disgust for slavery by stretching his body across the entrance of houses of worship so that every member had to walk over him and ponder what it meant to own a human. The American Revolution, notes Lepore, did not begin in 1775. It began when people like Benjamin Lay trained a skeptical eye on the granite of caste and found that it was made of clay. It was a slow contagion, driven by self-interest as much as considerations of justice, but the change was palpable. As John Adams famously remarked, the war was not the revolution. The war was only the effect and consequence of the revolution, which occurred before a drop of blood was shed at Lexington. "The Revolution was in the Minds of the People."

Adams was no pacifist, but he knew that the principles of the revolution were larger than the passions of revolt, and in some ways opposed. The American political creed comprised a series of claims about natural rights, popular sovereignty, and the sanctity of the rule of law—a charter of transparency, building on decades of colonial self-government and centuries of English law. All power came from the people, filtered and refined through chambers of consent. Government was complex, with wheels within wheels, so that passion was always tempered by reason. As James Madison explained in *The Federalist Papers,* men are proud and slaves to self-love, always "contending for pre-eminence and power." Americans could not assume that their advantages of learning would shield them from these visceral propensities. "Enlightened statesmen will not always be at the helm."

Such was the prose, the practical philosophy of checks and balances. But the poetry was never far away: waiting to write the story of self-government as an epic of world redemption. "The eyes of all people are upon us," declared the Puritan statesman John Winthrop as he planted a colony in Massachusetts in 1630. "We shall be as a City upon a Hill." Madison said that government was for men, not angels, because angels are rarely found this side of heaven. Winthrop agreed, but made an exception for his own community, "the elect," who would burn like a candle in a darkened room. The national idea, inherited from Winthrop, and the rational philosophy, coursing through the Constitution, were at war from the start. And the struggle was not between the founders, between saints and philosophers; it was within them.

II

The problem was grace: an idea that sparkled with innocence but kicked like a mule. A Christian principle held that "mercy is greater than justice," and that God does not treat the sinner as his sins deserve. To be "saved by grace" was to be redeemed above and beyond what you have done or will do—a wonderful thought, easily abused.

The Protestant emphasis on grace was a reaction to a Catholic tradition that demanded virtue and charity to a point that seemed harsh and unrealistic. Discovering the secret of Christianity in faith, like the key to a lost inheritance, Protestants swung in the opposite direction, extolling a piety that was free from all expectations of perfection. A Christian, said Martin Luther, was someone who could "sin boldly," knowing that God had paid the price. In fact, one had to sin boldly to be sure that you were not trusting in your own goodness. Like many ideas, this was not improved in the heat of theological debate. Can I be a Christian and a sinner at the same time? Yes, said Luther. We are no less Christian, no less dear to God, "even though we commit fornication and murder a thousand times a day."

This was splendid nonsense from Luther, but the political implications were profound. As the philosopher (and recovering Lutheran) Ludwig Feuerbach observed, Protestant theology was so intoxicated by its release from the laws of natural morality it could be cavalier to the point of negligence on that ancient injunction, "Thou shalt not kill." "Preachers are the greatest of slayers," boasted Luther, as he recalled his part in suppressing the Peasants' Revolt in 1525. "But I pass it on to our Lord, who commanded me to speak thus."

What was brash and theatrical in Luther was cold and pitiless in the Calvinism that succeeded him. Here, there was more concern for moral living and obedience to law. But there was also, thanks to the doctrine of predestination, an even stronger sense of exoneration from the ordinary virtues of love and mutual esteem that endeared groups like the Quakers to Voltaire. This simple theological claim, that Christ had died for a tiny and preordained elect, was one of the most dangerous ideas in history, argued Voltaire, because it sanctified division and authorized hate. If American democracy was rooted in the former principle of universal love, its national identity drew on this far more pungent idea of predestination.

"By predestination," wrote John Calvin, "we mean the eternal decree of God by which he determined with himself whatever he wished to happen with regard to every man." For, he explains, "all are not created on equal terms, but some are preordained to eternal life, others to eternal damnation." Some are chosen; most are damned, regardless of how they live. On this chilling account of divine "freedom" rested the Puritan identity. To be in was to be in. To be out was to be cursed. This was a theology that could inspire superhuman fortitude, the very spirit of the pioneer, wrote Harriet Beecher Stowe. It could also inspire cruelty and contempt for those outside the circle of redemption. As Calvin said, all are *not* created equal.

"It is impossible to live in peace with people one believes to be damned," wrote Jean-Jacques Rousseau, with an elegant version of Voltaire's complaint. If one part of the revolution was William Penn and Benjamin Lay, another was Calvin and John Winthrop. The Puritans combined democratic structures of government with cosmic self-assurance. It was this certainty of being lifted above the contradictions of history—spared the fate of lesser nations—that threw America into some of its own.

The double standard was clear in Winthrop's iconic sermon of 1630, "A Modell of Christian Charity." The settlers were to love one another, as God loved them, but charity did not go beyond the family of faith. God had chosen the settlers by "a special overvaluing providence," beholding in them the image of "his beloved sonne." Theirs was a special and peculiar calling, and if they were equal to its demands, they would see their enemies scattered to the winds. "Wee shall finde that the God of Israell is among us, when ten of us shall be able to resist a thousand of our enemies." Winthrop passes from counsels of meekness to promises that God would go before them in battle. Love and war, peace and destruction, roll off the Puritan tongue.

The Puritans held with Calvin that there were two creations: those ordained for life and those "ordained for destruction." This placed them outside the economy of natural rights and equality before the law. A humorist expressed the reasoning with a cheerful précis of a Puritan town meeting: "Voted, that the earth is the Lord's and the fullness thereof; voted, that the earth is given to the Saints; voted, that we are the Saints." As a smallpox epidemic tore through the Native population in 1634, Winthrop thanked "the Lord" for clearing "our title to what we possess." A massacre of Pequot Indians at Fort Mystic in 1637 was another awesome deliverance—the burning bodies, "a sweet sacrifice" to the Lord, said New Plymouth's governor, William Bradford.

In an even more revealing comment on the power of religion to process guilt, one of the English captains described how readings from the Old Testament calmed the nerves of his militiamen as they prepared to attack the Pequots. Some of the men had hesitated, commiserating with a weak and defenseless enemy. But the passage, where King David "harrowes" and "sawes" a whole people at the Lord's command, settled the affair. "We had sufficient light from the word of God for our proceedings," reported the captain. "Every man being bereaved of pitty fell upon the worke without compassion." It was, he marveled, "as though the finger of God had touched both match and flint."

Providence was not hypocrisy. It was the outworking of an austere, yet manifestly practical, doctrine of predestination. The savagery of the English shocked their Narragansett allies, who said their mode of warfare was "too furious, and slaies too many men." But providence dissolved all responsibility, ascribing to a transcendent deity the all-too-human actions of men. As the Boston preacher Increase Mather reported on yet another remarkable deliverance, "God so disposed of the bullets" that not a single Englishman died.

Your lives, Mather's son Cotton told a company of anxious militiamen as they prepared to go into battle in 1689, are not in your hands. "No," he counseled, "they are in the Hands of that God, without whom not a Sparrow falls, and by whom every Bullet is directed."

The "sermon histories" of Puritan divines like Increase and Cotton Mather were vital sources of an emerging national identity, establishing the two enduring myths of American exceptionalism: the myth of innocence and the myth of invincibility. As Increase explained the logic, "The dealings of God with our Nation . . . and with the Nations of the World is very different." All nations experience suffering, but ours is never total. Where others are destroyed, we are only ever chastened. For we are "the Apple of God's eye," "dandled in the lap of his providence." The Lord may afflict, but never abandon, his beloved.

With unconditional love came an unworldly confidence—a belief that God *must* crown our endeavors, because his glory is bound up with ours. As a young Quaker wrote to a friend in London, during King Philip's War, "Our Rulers, Officers, and Councellors are like men in a maze, not knowing what to do: but the Priests spur them on, telling them the Indians are ordained for destruction." Yet the soldiers saw no miracles. They complained and said, with tears, "They see not God go along with them."

Providence was many things—vanity, hubris, division. At a more basic level, it was confusion: the serial misrepresentation of reality. When New England becomes "New Israel," and every enemy is a "Satan," history dissolves into typology: a jangle of stereotypes that dance before the eyes. Providentialist thought was inveterately dishonest, because it was always forcing the facts into the theory. After the humiliation of "Braddock's defeat," in 1755, the famed evangelist Jonathan Edwards urged authorities not to dwell on the tactical ineptitude that led to the loss of nearly a thousand men to a small and ragged enemy, because God was in charge. "If God be pleased to forsake a people," intoned Edwards, "defeat and confusion is like to be the consequence." This called for a fast, not an inquest, and Edwards disparaged the shallow and profane reasoning that would attribute a military disaster to human error. Providence was a metanarrative, a holiday for the senses.

Two forces helped to spread Puritan tenets across the disparate and varied colonies. One was the Great Awakening, a religious revival that swept across the English-speaking world in the 1730s and 1740s, building networks and challenging authority at every turn. The other was the French and Indian War, which rumbled across North America from 1754 to 1763, bringing victory to Great Britain and spelling doom for its empire. In 1759, newspapers rejoiced that the kind hand of providence had prospered "his Majesty's Arms" against a proud and insulting enemy. "GOD BE PRAISED! QUEBEC IS IN ENGLISH HANDS," screamed *The Pennsylvania Journal*. Six years later, a Stamp Act devised to pay for that war sent ripples across the colonies. Providence paused, looked up, and prepared to back a rebellion.

III

As the godly portion of a half-chosen people, the Puritans had always been a nation within the nation. Evangelical piety strengthened that sentiment, deepening the perception of the mother country as a faded and fallen land. England was "Leah," the plain and homely elder sister who brought forth Judah, wrote Jonathan Edwards. America was "Rachel," the ravishing younger sister who brought forth Joseph and Benjamin, "the beloved children," who outshone all the others. In the process of disenchantment, the conduct of English troops might have been as influential as the imposition of new taxes. Soldiers quartered in homes, Redcoats shooting civilians on the streets of Boston, were signals of a malaise. If England could not uphold the spirit of Magna Carta—its vaunted principles of equity—perhaps its time had come. This was where republican scruple and providentialist intuition came together.

"God pleads his own, and his people's cause by his providence," declared a typical sermon. Indeed, the whole of history, "from the creation of the world, [was] a series of wonderful interpositions in behalf of his elect." The writers of the Hebrew Scriptures, continued the preacher, hardly mentioned the affairs of any other nations, save those that were connected with his own. God loved his people "with a distinguishing love." He was gathering his elect and preparing to "burn up" the rest. In a widely quoted sermon titled "The Dominion of Providence over the Passions of Men," John Witherspoon, president of Princeton and one of the signers of the Declaration of Independence, argued that God was using the perfidy of the enemy to promote "the good of his chosen." David was mastering Goliath. "Has not the boasted discipline of regular and veteran soldiers been turned into confusion and dismay, before the new and maiden courage of freemen?" he marveled.

"Cousin America has run off with a Presbyterian parson!" groused Horace Walpole in London. But it wasn't just the parsons. The belief that God was peculiarly involved in America's struggle was an axiom among even the more secular patriots. When Franklin and Jefferson presented designs for a national seal to the Continental Congress in 1776, both drew on the biblical narrative. Franklin proposed an image of Pharaoh drowning in the Red Sea while Moses led the Israelites to safety; Jefferson suggested the children of Israel guided by pillar and cloud through the wilderness. And then there was Thomas Paine, whose barnstorming *Common*

Sense combined flawless Lockean argumentation with a messianic vision of America as a redeemer nation. No kings here, but every man a prophet. "We have it in our power to begin the world over again," he declared. The discovery of America at the dawn of the Reformation was no accident. It was "as if the Almighty graciously meant to open a sanctuary to the persecuted in future years." Now was the time. "The birthday of a new world is at hand."

By 1776, the Puritan idea of America as a "second, far more glorious Israel" was firmly wedded to the political and legal rationale for independence. It was a basic tenet of American patriotism. But it was an awkward union, a precarious bond. It imposed a sectarian idea on a welter of independent cultures, claiming a unity that was less than real.

The revolution, writes the historian David Hackett Fischer, was not a single struggle but "four separate Wars of Independence," some of them decidedly reluctant. The first was an insurrection in New England, a genuinely popular revolt in which most able-bodied males willingly served. That war was virtually over by 1776. The second was a "gentleman's war," fought by the Virginia gentry in the middle states and the coastal south, from 1776 to 1781, a patrician revolt for ancient liberties. The third was a rising of farmers in the Southern backcountry against British soldiers and American loyalists, who had invaded their region—a savage struggle feeding on old animosities between roughhewn backcountry settlers and a wealthy lowland elite. The fourth was a nonviolent economic war, led by Philadelphia elites and typified by the urbane diplomacy of Benjamin Franklin.

All of these struggles contributed to the American victory, but none of them resolved the volcanic tensions beneath the surface of patriotic bliss. "Join or Die" was the war cry, but distrust and mutual loathing was the modus operandi. The four major cultures of British America had never got on. Puritan New Englanders "detested the people of Virginia" as louche and lordly hedonists, as did the Quakers of Pennsylvania. The Virginians returned the compliment, despising the "saints" of New England as a joyless and persecuting people, whose religion was another word for gain. Washington called them "nasty people" as he struggled to manage the New England militias during the war. One of the few points of agreement between Anglican Virginians and Puritan New Englanders, writes Fischer, "was their common loathing of Quakers" as subversives and fanatics. The Quakers, for their part, had not forgotten how their ancestors had been tortured and executed by Puritans in Boston, and by Anglican clergy on both sides of the Atlantic. All of them, meanwhile, harbored an intense dislike for the rude and rugged people of Appalachia and the Southern backcountry, with their hard drinking, summary justice, and compulsive violence. A Pennsylvania Quaker called them "the Goths and Vandals of America." New Englanders called them "savages and barbarians." The colonies had been built on difference, forged in defiance. And that was before slavery took the problem to another level.

As Colin Woodard observes in a superb analysis of these nations within the nation, the planter aristocracy of the Deep South had no intention of taking up arms against the Crown until rumors of slave rebellions began to circulate. When Lord Dunmore issued his infamous proclamation of November 1775, offering freedom to any slave willing to assist the British army, attitudes changed overnight. Dunmore's decision to involve the slaves, wrote Edward Rutledge, a member of South Carolina's delegation to the Continental Congress, was the turning point in the war. This offer of freedom to the slaves, he wrote to a friend in London, seemed calculated "to force us into Independence"—something that had appeared distant and "chimerical" until then. Dunmore's proclamation promised "more effectually to work an eternal separation between Great Britain and the Colonies," he believed, "than any other expedient, which could possibly have been thought of."

Even then, the Southern commitment to independence was hardly total. In 1779, John Rutledge, Edward's brother and the newly elected governor of South Carolina, offered to declare the state's neutrality for the duration of the war, leaving it to be decided at the peace to whom it would belong. Of the 232,000 regulars enlisted in the Continental army, 68,000, or nearly a third, came from Massachusetts. South Carolina supplied 6,660, only slightly more than Rhode Island, the smallest of the original thirteen colonies. When Charleston was besieged, "its citizens did not rally to save it," noted the nineteenth-century historian Lorenzo Sabine. The "leaven" of the revolution, he added, was not widely "diffused" in the region.

In 1777, South Carolina's Thomas Lynch Jr. issued an ominous warning to Congress: Should that august body so much as speculate "whether their slaves are their property, there is an end of the confederation." A gag rule, in embryo. Georgia had been even slower to embrace the cause of independence, having refused any involvement in the First Continental Congress. When it did join the party, it was not exactly the life and soul. "A republican government is little better than a government of devils," sneered John Zubly, Georgia's delegate to the Continental Congress, in October 1775. As the abolitionist Charles Sumner remarked sardonically in 1860, "The cry from these States was then, 'We will not come in.' Ever since it has been, 'We will not stay in.'"

To one school of thought, this sudden convergence of "jarring interests" was a sign of providence, and grounds for hope that "a new and more perfect system" was in the making. It had to be God's will. "The real wonder," wrote Madison, "is that so many difficulties should have been surmounted, and surmounted with a unanimity almost as unprecedented as it must have been unexpected." It was, he ventured, "impossible for the man of pious reflection not to perceive in it a finger of that Almighty hand which has been so frequently and signally extended to our relief in the critical stages of the revolution." The reality was that patriotism had run ahead of its cause. There was nationalism before there was anything resembling a nation. The providentialist thesis had established a nationalist ideology in the absence of many of the traditional sources of national solidarity. It was one thing to win a war, quite another to build a political community where affection is real and consent is willing. The doctrine of exceptionalism did not assist the process. It sacrificed action and honesty to the romance of an idea.

The first draft of the Declaration of Independence contained a stunning rebuke of the transatlantic slave trade as a "cruel war against human nature" and the last word in royal tyranny, naming Britain's continuation of "this execrable commerce" among the grounds for separation. This clause, recalled Jefferson, "was struck out in complaisance to South Carolina and Georgia," whose minds, he later remarked, with fabulous understatement, "were not yet matured to the full abhorrence of that traffic." And just as soon as these offensive phrases had been removed, "these gentlemen continued their depredations on other parts of the instrument." As early as 1764, the Massachusetts lawyer James Otis had argued that the enslavement of human beings was incompatible with natural rights, and therefore grounds for colonial resistance. All humans were by the law of nature freeborn, he insisted. "Does it follow that tis right to enslave a man because he is black?" he wondered. Every dealer in slavery was "a tyrant," and tyranny was contagious. For Otis, the "ferocity, cruelty and brutal barbarity that has long marked the general character of the sugar-islanders" was enough to prove the point about the moral effect of slavery and to justify his disaffection from a government that supported it.

Antislavery sentiment was integral to the revolutionary ferment, as many historians have noted, and then it was quashed. An attempt by the Massachusetts House of Representatives to abolish slavery in 1777 was abandoned out of fear of alienating Southern partners in the war. Even John Adams spoke against it, for that reason. Ultimately, only Vermont went ahead and outlawed slavery, leaving the remainder of the new states frozen in a paradox. The Declaration of Independence, scoffed Thomas Hutchinson, former governor of Massachusetts, begins "with a false hypothesis, that the Colonies are one distinct people." There never had been one people in North America, still less a people united around a common cause. He was especially eager to ask "the Delegates of Maryland, Virginia, and the Carolinas, how their Constituents justify the depriving more than an hundred thousand Africans of their rights to liberty, and the pursuit of happiness and in some degree to their lives, if these rights are so absolutely unalienable." It's rare for historians to take someone like Hutchinson seriously, but this was the million-dollar question: How do you build a house on sand? Matters came to a head in Philadelphia.

IV

The old canard that history is written by the winners is occasionally true. Critics of the Constitution, as it emerged in its commanding clarity in 1787, are known to posterity as the "antifederalists"—men of little faith. Defending the Constitution's taut and "efficient" lines of command, Alexander Hamilton conjured a dazzling array of insults to position the antifederalists as men of "gloomy doctrines" and "distempered imaginations"—self-appointed experts "whose sagacity disdains the admonitions of experimental instruction." Their complaints were "airy phantoms"; their zeal for liberty "more ardent than enlightened."

Sometimes a man doth protest too much. The antifederalists were clearer thinkers and more consistent "federalists" than nationalists like Hamilton, who assumed the name. They saw the dangers of a premature union, contending with devastating prescience that the attempt to force thirteen independent colonies into a single, unitary republic would result in civil war. In the neatest summary of the intuition, "Agrippa" in Boston averred, "It is impossible for one code of laws to suit Georgia and Massachusetts." Government rests on trust and affection, argued the antifederalists, and where values and traditions are so divergent, affection will be elusive. The states will quarrel, and either war or despotism will be the outcome. "The plan of government now proposed is evidently calculated totally to change, in time, our condition as a people," wrote the "Federal Farmer," in New York. "Instead of being thirteen republics, under a federal head, it is clearly designed to make us one consolidated government." Whether such a change could be effected "without convulsions and civil wars," he seriously doubted. The best writers on government, such as Montesquieu, agreed that a healthy republic requires a degree of intimacy and mutual respect among the citizenry, which was conspicuous by its absence. "Different laws, customs, and opinions exist in the different states," he noted. Force them together, and the result will be war.

The elephant in the room was slavery, which was at the heart of the antifederalists' fear about a centralized militia. The Constitution gave the president authority to call out the militia in cases of invasion or insurrection. The prospect of being marched, like "Prussian soldiers," from New England or Pennsylvania to rivet "the chains of despotism" on runaway slaves in the Carolinas horrified many of the document's Northern critics. Under the new Constitution, men who hated and despised slavery might be forced to uphold it. And what adds to the evil, wrote the shrewd and penetrating "Brutus," was that the slave trade was going to continue, at least until 1808, so that "for every cargo of these unhappy people which unfeeling, unprincipled, barbarous and avaricious wretches may tear from their country . . . they are to be rewarded by having an increase of members in the General Assembly."

Luther Martin, representing Maryland at the Constitutional Convention, called it a "bargain with sin." Martin described a scene in which delegates from Georgia and South Carolina threatened to withdraw from any system that trespassed on their rights, and the Eastern states, "notwithstanding their aversion to slavery," willingly indulged them. "We scarcely had risen from our knees" from seeking God's blessing in forming a government on the principles of liberty, he reported, when we violated those principles by barring Congress from interfering with the slave trade—"even encouraging that most infamous traffic, by giving the states power and influence in the Union in proportion as they cruelly and wantonly sport with the rights of their fellow-creatures." All of this was done in a spirit of piety and self-congratulation. Far from any example to the nations, warned Martin, this decision would "render us contemptible to every true friend of liberty in the world."

Yet it was on precisely such grounds that Hamilton, Madison, and their co-author of *The Federalist Papers,* John Jay, defended the proposed Constitution: as a light to the world. "It seems to have been reserved to the people of this country," urged Hamilton, "by their conduct and example, to decide the important question, whether societies of men are really capable or not of establishing good government from reflection and choice, or whether they are forever destined to depend for their political constitutions on accident and force." America's situation was, "in many respects, the most interesting in the world." A failure on our part may "deserve to be considered as the general misfortune of mankind." This was essentially rhetorical. "Happily for America, happily, we trust, for the whole human race," perorated Madison in another essay, the patriots of 1776 did not take the road of submission. "They accomplished a revolution which has no parallel in the annals of human society. They reared the fabrics of governments which have no model on the face of the globe."

Time and again, Hamilton and Madison respond to their critics with statements about the "genius" of the American people and the uniqueness of the historical moment, warning that if this Constitution slips through America's fingers, republican government may be lost to the world. It was a secular version of the Puritan myth. "If it be asked what is to restrain the House of Representatives from making legal discriminations in favor of themselves and a particular class of the society," wrote Madison, "I answer, the genius of the whole system, the nature of just and constitutional laws, and above all the vigilant and manly spirit which actuates the people of America, a spirit which nourishes freedom, and in return is nourished by it." It will be all right on the night.

In another essay, Madison responds to the antifederalist concern that a strong federal government will denude Americans of their rights with what can only be termed flattery: Americans were "free and gallant citizens," not "the debased subjects of arbitrary power." It was an insult to suppose they would cave before the majesty of the state. Having explained their checks and balances as the remedy for the human disease of aggression, Madison and Hamilton fall back on patriotism to meet the charge that conflict might be the order of the day. They disavow virtue as a basis for planning, and then say that Americans are the most virtuous people in the world.

"Hearken not to the unnatural voice which tells you that the people of America, knit together as they are by so many cords of affection, can no longer live together as members of the same family," counsels Madison. Love will win. To the fierce contention that these states are not ready for consolidation, the federalists preach destiny. "This country and this people seem to have been made for each other," writes Jay, in Federalist No. 2, "and it appears as if it was the design of Providence, that an inheritance so proper and convenient for a band of brethren, united to each other by the strongest ties, should never be split into a number of unsocial, jealous, and alien sovereignties."

Brutus, for one, thought this was moonshine. These platitudes were like a stucco, hastily applied to a gravely flawed structure. "You may solace yourselves with the idea, that society, in this favored land, will fast advance to the highest point of perfection; the human mind will expand in knowledge and virtue, and the golden age be, in some measure, realized," he censured. But history cannot be forced. Where affection is lacking, popular sovereignty is a fiction. It was better to retain a degree of distance under a confederation than force a union under the boyish ardor of destiny. An unloved government, he warned, will have no recourse but "the bayonet."

Others objected to the appeal to heaven as a way of closing down debate. "A Plebeian" in New York reported that one gentleman in Philadelphia had pronounced, "in the ardour of his enthusiasm," that the men who drafted the Constitution "were as really under the guidance of Divine Revelation, as was Moses, the Jewish lawgiver." In Massachusetts, three writers complained that objections to the slave clauses had been hammered to gold leaf on the anvil of providence. It was said that "the adoption of this Constitution, would be ominous of much good, and betoken the smiles of Heaven upon the country," they reported. "But we view the matter in a very different light; we think this . . . lust for slavery portentous of much evil in America." No prayer could redeem the compromise or drown out "the cry of innocent blood."

Strong words, deftly ignored. Providential optimism won the day as the Constitution was confirmed and a national identity ushered into being. "The preservation of the sacred fire of liberty and the destiny of the republican model of government," asserted Washington in his first inaugural address, were "staked on the experiment entrusted to the hands of the American people." America was *the* temple of liberty—not one of many. Providentialist exultation became the mandatory framing of public discourse, with presidents serving as the high priests of this ancient-modern civil religion. In his first inaugural, Jefferson called the United States the "world's best hope," a living example to the nations. In his second, he invoked the blessing of the God "who led our forefathers, as Israel of old, from their native land, and planted them in a country flowing with all the necessaries and comforts of life; who has covered our infancy with his providence, and our riper years with his wisdom and power." Providence was the filter, the rose-tinted lens.

Madison was not far behind, contrasting a bleak and haggard Europe with the beaming felicity of America, for which he could only thank "that Divine Providence whose goodness has been so remarkably extended to this rising nation." As president, he gave sanction to the Puritan myth that God would always protect his chosen people in war. Madison, who believed so passionately in the separation of church and state, was making a church *of* the state. America was secure in the will of "that Almighty Being whose power regulates the destiny of nations." Predestination, an idea slowly dying in the churches, found a home in national pride.

Only John Adams, among the founders, could see the danger.

Born in Massachusetts, educated at Harvard, and fired by an

implacable ambition, Adams was the original New England overachiever. Like some of his generation, and many of the next, however, he turned Puritan zeal on Puritan theology. As a young man in his twenties, Adams shuddered at the Calvinist dogma of "unconditional Election," which held that "God elected a precious few . . . to Life eternal without regard to any foreseen Virtue, and reprobated all the Rest, without regard to any foreseen Vice." Such a gospel was "detestable," and one that the natives would reject with horror, should they grasp its hideous logic.

At the same time, Adams toyed with the political version of the doctrine, offering the conventional wisdom that America enjoyed a divine commission for the illumination of humankind. "America," he wrote in the heat of the revolution, "is the City, set upon a Hill," a vehicle of destiny. His inaugural address as second U.S. president, in 1797, made the usual noises about "an overruling Providence which had so signally protected this country from the first." But this was an homage to an idea he no longer believed. In a letter to Benjamin Franklin, appended to his *Defence of the Constitutions of Government of the United States of America* (1787), Adams stated what had for him become a settled conviction: "There is no special providence for Americans, and their natures are the same with that of others." The advantages we have over Europe, he advised Benjamin Rush, were chiefly geographical. It was dangerous to think that we have been cut from finer cloth.

Mercy Otis Warren remembered sharing a carriage with Adams, soon after his return from Europe in 1788, and how he startled her on the subject of national character. It would not do to talk of "the virtue of Americans," he told her, as they rolled through the streets of Cambridge. "We are like all other people, and shall do like other nations," he advised, as though revealing a diplomatic secret. More than twenty years later, Adams repeated his view to Rush: "There is no Special Providence for Us. We are not a chosen People. . . . We must and We Shall, go the Way of all the Earth."

These were more than the jaundiced thoughts of a seasoned curmudgeon. Each of these remarks came within a discussion of the political organization of the United States, and the dangers of sacrificing judgment to national pride—whether it be decisions of war and peace or the balance of the legislature. To be chosen was to be beyond the law—the high road to despotism.

When Jefferson voiced his despair over the descent of Europe, once again, into "an Arena of gladiators," in the early nineteenth century, Adams responded with a withering critique of the patriotic mind. Jefferson's query centered on the limits of Enlightenment: the miserable failure of an age of reason. It was one thing to see a brutal autocracy like Russia, or a rising power like Prussia, brawl over a neighbor, noted Jefferson—carving up Poland like a wedding cake. But why did the civilized peoples of France and England—"so great, so dignified, so distinguished by science & the arts"—acquiesce in such crimes? Why did cultured and learned nations act on the principle that "power [makes] right"?

Well, returned Adams, learning and morality are no match for the passions, and there is no passion like love of country, which is really love of self. Patriotism was to law what egoism was to reason: an able seducer. It was the same in late antiquity, when Rome laid the world in ashes in the name of its own brand of peace, and patriot historians waved it on through. "The Morality of Tacitus," counseled Adams, "is the Morality of Patriotism, and Britain & France have adopted his Creed; i.e. that all things were made for Rome." So it was in ancient Greece, and in France, under Napoleon. "All things were made for my Use," cries the preening patriot—the vanity of the "Pampered Goose." Even the philosophers had succumbed to the contagion. Of course "Jesus despized and condemned this Patriotism," noted Adams, with a jolt of excitement. But his ideas, like loving your enemy, were mostly honored in the breach. Patriotism was the religion of the age: power, with an easy conscience.

A no less remarkable version of this unsettling thesis was "An Oration on the Extent and Power of Political Delusion," delivered by the fiery Jeffersonian Abraham Bishop in 1800. "A nation which makes *greatness* its polestar can never be free," he submitted; "beneath national greatness sink individual greatness, honor, wealth and freedom." A bold contention. With nationalism comes militarism, he reasoned, which brings "passive obedience" and gawping subservience to the state. The people stand in awe while mighty battleships slide gracefully onto the ocean, and there goes their self-respect. "A few more such delightful launches," suggests Bishop, "will launch this country from liberty to slavery, from a republican to a monarchical government." Of all delusions, few were more effective in getting people to "lend a helping hand in putting on their own fetters and rivetting their own chains" than the adoring raptures of the patriot. A true republican could never be reconciled to the stony idol of national greatness.

Adams and Bishop anticipate a number of modern thinkers on the processing power of mythology: the ability to turn black into white, because God or History has declared it so. A myth, wrote the critic and philosopher Roland Barthes, "naturalizes" something that is unnatural. It simplifies complexity and purifies power. Myths can be benign, when they propose the best of a situation and inspire a response—like a married couple, living in trust. They're dangerous when they soothe and extenuate power. Barthes likened the effect to "inoculation"—protection from unwelcome thoughts.

Patriotism was essential to the revolution and the creation of a new political community. There would have been no freedom without a vision of a new nation, called out of bondage to Britain. Yet the nature of this patriotism, nursed on the Puritan conceit of unconditional election, was pregnant with danger. It grafted a singular worldview onto a sea of schism, pronouncing intelligent dissent a failure of faith. The Puritan ethos was unrealistic in what it claimed and unreasonable in the way it did so. The simple intuition that slavery and freedom could not live together was brushed away with a prayer.

The big idea of representative democracy was popular sovereignty, drawing on a prior belief in human equality. Popular sovereignty meant representation, which was the cause and catalyst of the war against Britain. But that very demand for authentic representation was imperiled by the Constitution that aimed to consolidate it. It subjected diverse cultures and divergent ideas of liberty to a unitary authority, and it stamped the deal with destiny. Criticism was infidelity; union, the will of God. Providence not only buried the dilemmas of confederation under a billowing garment of fate: It infused American discourse with the cosmic entitlement that had enabled Britain to play the tyrant in the first place.

Nobody was more caustic on the hubris and inhumanity of the Calvinist credo than Thomas Jefferson, yet few embraced its political incarnation with more gusto. Hamilton excoriated the European powers for their arrogance and aggression, pluming themselves on delusions of preeminence, but the doctrine of the New Israel ensured that the remedy contained more than traces of the disease. The self-image of a chosen people left little room for that beginning of all political wisdom: doubt. The divine right of kings was transferred, not destroyed. It should surprise no one, wrote the historian Edward McNall Burns, that "a strongly developed sense of mission should blind a people to numerous realities." This was an understatement. There was a mission before there was a people.

As the Yale historian Edmund Morgan has mischievously proposed, Madison's doctrine of national sovereignty was actually an invention—in some ways, a "more fictional fiction than the divine right of kings." After all, "a king, however dubious his divinity might seem, did not have to be imagined." But that is what this audacious project required: an imagined community; less a city on a hill than a city stretched across a continent. "Madison," writes Morgan, "was inventing a sovereign American people to overcome the sovereign states"—those engines of autonomy that threatened anarchy on all sides. Could the idea be made real? Nationalism had won a war and drafted a constitution. Could it build the nation it proclaimed: one out of many? That was a question for the nineteenth century.

CHAPTER 2

Who Were Your Daddies?: Patriotism and the Color Line

PATRIOT, n. One to whom the interests of a part seem superior to those of the whole. The dupe of statesmen and the tool of conquerors.

—AMBROSE BIERCE, *THE DEVIL'S DICTIONARY*

We now want a country in which the obligations of patriotism shall not conflict with fidelity to justice and liberty.

—FREDERICK DOUGLASS

What is freedom? In the early stages of the American Revolution, merchants in Boston agreed to a boycott of British goods, in protest against the Townshend Revenue Act, which imposed punishing duties on imported wares. The Daughters of Liberty began spinning yarn and making clothes, and substitutes were found for the compulsion to drink tea. But not everyone entered into the spirit. A number of merchants decided to ignore the boycott, continuing to trade with the British, prompting a furious response from one of its architects. "Pray gentlemen," raged Samuel Adams in *The Boston Gazette*. "Have you not a right if you please, to set fire to your own houses, because they are your own, tho' in all probability it will destroy a whole neighbourhood, perhaps a whole city!"

This selfish, private liberty, fulminated Adams, was death to the patriot cause: "Where did you learn that in a state or society you had a right to do as you please? And that it was an infringement of that right to restrain you?" Such restraints, he insisted, are the substance of freedom and the condition of membership in the society "with which you are joined." Whoever despises law despises liberty.

Adams was not engaging in a debate. He was asserting one of the core principles of the American political creed: liberty as law, liberty as common good. The idea was as old as government, assuming a revolutionary quality only in the context of Britain's high-handed treatment of the colonies. The revolution was the overthrow of Parliament and the Crown. Liberty itself enjoyed a degree of continuity, as colonial charters were redrafted as state constitutions, and the rights of freeborn Englishmen morphed into an American vernacular. Liberty, writes the historian Bernard Bailyn, was a "contagion," a dynamic principle, and it displayed a remarkable cohesion across the revolutionary mind—the right to vote, the right to worship without harassment, and the cluster of protections later enshrined in the Bill of Rights.

That was true. But where was the revolutionary mind? Not everyone who participated in the revolution embraced its principles. "If slavery be thus fatally contagious," wrote the essayist and lexicographer Samuel Johnson, in response to a revolutionary dogma, "how is it that we hear the loudest yelps for liberty among the drivers of negroes?" These "lords of themselves, these kings of ME, these demigods of independence," were no better than their colonial masters. The anomaly was felt on both sides of the ocean. It was with "a very ill grace," thought the Connecticut pastor Levi Hart, that we plead for freedom "when *we* are the tyrants." Liberty was "freedom from force": the ability to live and move "without constraint, or fear of punishment." Slavery was the antithesis: an "atrocious violation" of the law of nature. "Who can count us the true friends of liberty as long as we deal in, or publicly connive at slavery?" he submitted. As Abigail Adams chided her husband in 1774, "It always appeared a most iniquitous Scheme to me—fight ourselves for what we are daily robbing and plundering from those who have as good a right to freedom as we have. You know my mind upon this Subject."

Historians have explained, if not resolved, the paradox by elucidating the variety of impulses sheltering under that pregnant word "liberty." In Virginia, liberty meant honor and dignity, a right to govern based on birth and blood. In Appalachia and the border country, it meant something more primal: a right to defend one's person and property; a willingness, even a hunger, to fight. Only in New England, and the Quaker civilization of Pennsylvania, did freedom entail a transfer from natural to civil liberty, with a conscious surrender of the brutal prerogatives of "the state of nature." Samuel Adams's lecture, in other words, would have meant little to the Scotch-Irish settlers of the backcountry, or the imperious planters of the Carolinas. Liberty for them was the very "egoism" or self-assertion that political philosophers wanted to temper and tame in a social contract.

Early modern thinkers, from Hobbes to Rousseau, expended a vast amount of energy trying to reason away the glitter of honor as a relic of barbarism and a motor of war. But nobody told Kentucky. A nineteenth-century blood feud between two clans in the Bluegrass State, which resulted in more than twenty murders and many more injuries, began over the theft of a pig. Frontier ethics, imported wholesale from the Scottish borders, smiled at vengeance and laughed at compromise. When Patrick Henry issued his iconic battle cry, "Give me liberty or give me death!" he was not thinking of the reciprocal duties of the social contract. He was speaking as a planter and a warrior. His concept of liberty, writes David Hackett Fischer, was an impulse, "drawn from the political folkways of the border culture in which he grew up." In these contexts, liberty was honor, of the kind that inspired the old Scottish motto *Nemo me impune lacessit*—"no one provokes me with impunity." Or in the American translation: "Don't Tread on Me."

The causes of conflict, wrote James Madison, are "sown in the nature of man." They were also sown in the regional cultures of the United States: the building blocks of an exemplary nation. Could patriotism, as Rousseau and George Washington variously proposed, transcend the problem: turning love of self into love of country? Or would it coddle and comfort the old vices? as John Adams feared. Race was the test, the measure of measures.

I

Had the civil religion centered on equality or the human texture of liberty, the outcome might have been different. But the doctrines of providence and "manifest destiny," as it came to be known, centered on the prestige of the nation and the glory of the experiment, reducing slavery and the fate of Native peoples to negotiable anomalies. As abolitionists and Native Americans perceived a link between the buoyancy of the national myth and the miseries unfolding beneath it, they attacked the myth with startling ferocity.

The problem was as old as the decision to amend the Declaration of Independence to mollify the South. The revolution combined surges of egalitarian zeal with icy pragmatism and nervous extenuation. The myth proclaimed a new nation and a temple of liberty. The history was a lumpier affair. Connecticut and Rhode Island outlawed the slave trade in 1774, declaring that any enslaved person brought into their jurisdiction would be instantly free. Pennsylvania taxed the trade out of existence and established the continent's first antislavery society, and Massachusetts finally got over the line in 1783, when its highest court ruled that slavery was incompatible with the state constitution's declaration that "all men are born free and equal." But the revolution, as we have seen, made way for the Constitution.

The Constitution forbade any attempt to abolish the slave trade for twenty years, and it included a fugitive slave clause, which required citizens of free states to assist in the return of runaways—a radical departure. If that were not enough, the agreement that slaves could be held as property yet counted as persons (or almost persons) in the apportionment of the franchise essentially surrendered Congress to the South. This was more than appeasement; it was courtship. Madison explained the policy like an engineer unveiling a new device. "Another clause secures us that property which we now possess," he told the Virginia ratification convention, with unsuppressed enthusiasm:

> At present, if any slave elopes to any of those states where slaves are free, he becomes emancipated by their laws. For the laws of the states are uncharitable to one another in this respect. But in this constitution, "no person held to service, or labor, in one state, under the laws thereof, escaping into another, shall in consequence of any law or regulation therein, be discharged from such service or labor; but shall

> be delivered up on claim of the party to whom such service or labor may be due." This clause was expressly inserted to enable owners of slaves to reclaim them. This is a better security than any that now exists.

Madison admits that slavery was imperiled by the legal patchwork of the Confederation: Slaves could run away, and there was no mechanism for catching them. He sells *his* Constitution as relief for that perennial headache of absconding "property." This nonchalant rendering of the old arrangement as "uncharitable" to the slave states, followed by the assurance that slaves will be more secure under the new government, might be the most damning single comment of the constitutional debate, and it came from the architect. Was this the new "science of politics"? as he and Hamilton liked to call it. Or was it, as John Quincy Adams charged, "the art of committing the lamb to the tender custody of the wolf"?

The cold truth of the three-fifths clause, protested Gouverneur Morris in New York, was that the slave lord of Georgia or South Carolina who goes to Africa, and "tears away his fellow creatures from their dearest connections and damns them to the most cruel bondages, shall have more votes in a Government instituted for protection of the rights of mankind, than the Citizen of Pennsylvania or New Jersey who views with a laudable horror, so nefarious a practice." The final absurdity was that the new Constitution could compel the free states to "march their militia for the defence of the Southern States; for their defence against those very slaves of whom they complain."

No wonder the planters thought they'd won the lottery. As Charles Pinckney reported in triumph to the South Carolina state convention, "We have obtained a right to recover our slaves in whatever part of America they may take refuge, which is a right we had not before." "We have a security," he exulted, "that the general government can never emancipate them." The result of these decisions, wrote the abolitionist Wendell Phillips, was that slave owners owned the republic for sixty years—from the White House to the Supreme Court; from wars of conquest in Mexico to gag rules and vigilante codes that made it impossible to oppose slavery "without trembling for bread or life." From 1788 until 1860, only two opponents of slavery held the nation's highest office, both called Adams. Slave owners led the nation for fifty of those seventy-two years. "Our Revolution," said Phillips, "earned us only *independence*." On that altar, liberty was sacrificed.

Native Americans fared little better under the glare of national destiny. None of the founders took up the cause of Indian rights, and the doctrine of providence proved as fatal in the age of revolution as in the time of the Pilgrims. When Jefferson, as governor of Virginia, authorized a military expedition against British-held posts in the Northwest Territory, he was somewhere between casual and ruthless on the status of the "Northern Indians," whom he described as "thorns in our sides." He left it with his general, George Rogers Clark, to determine whether "the end proposed should be their extermination, or their removal beyond the lakes or Illinois river." "The same world," he mused with pallid profundity, "will scarcely do for them and us."

Even Benjamin Franklin, who condemned violence against Indian settlements and lambasted his own government for failing to prevent it, was not immune to the providential bromide. His remarks on alcohol addiction within the Iroquois Nation recall Winthrop on the happy effects of smallpox. "If it be the design of Providence to extirpate these savages in order to make room for cultivators of the earth," he wrote, "it seems not improbable that rum may be the appointed means. It has already annihilated all the tribes who formerly inhabited the sea-coast."

All of this was normal for the children of the morning. In 1783, the president of Yale, Ezra Stiles, preached a sermon on the "glory and honor" of the American republic, and God's intention to make it first among the nations. In the same breath, he calmly predicted that the aboriginal "Indians, as well as the million Africans in America . . . may gradually vanish." By so doing, the stain of an "unrighteous slavery may at length, in God's good providence, be abolished and cease in this land of liberty." Cleansed of the sin, America's example would blaze back to Europe, Asia, and Africa "and illumine the world."

Honor had always been a question of status and reputation. Here in nationalist guise, prestige is again the criterion. The worry is not what slavery is doing to its victims but the damage to our standing among nations. And while Stiles commends no force, no schemes of removal, the idea that a million Africans, and untold numbers of Indians, are destined to "vanish" from the continent announces a logic. Preaching about liberty was the best way of denying it. Patriotism was the shield and protection against what Mary Wollstonecraft once called the "wild wish" of equality.

Even the Fourth of July became a weapon. When the Presbyterian minister Robert Finley established the American Colonization Society in 1816, he found that patriotism was his unfailing friend. More than a quarter of a million free Blacks were living in the United States, and the idea of moving them to Africa was a staggering presumption, but Finley cast the scheme within the drama of providence and quickly gained an audience. Independence Day orations became the society's major source of funding, and thousands of Americans became "accustomed to hearing the redemption of Africa as the latest chapter in America's providential story," notes the historian Nicholas Guyatt. One Independence Day orator offered a three-stage history, from the Crucifixion of Jesus to the signing of the Declaration of Independence to the regeneration of Africa by Liberian colonists.

African colonization became "the most popular and respectable solution to the problem of racial diversity in America," backed by most of the political giants of the day, including Henry Clay, Andrew Jackson, and James Monroe. In 1820, the society persuaded the Monroe administration to purchase the new colony of Liberia, and in 1824 three of the four presidential candidates supported the society's mission to relocate African Americans, John Quincy Adams being the sole dissenter. In 1833 the ACS acquired its most illustrious recruit: An eighty-two-year-old James Madison became the organization's president, sealing his commitment with a substantial bequest. The only problem was that few of the unwanted "Africans" wanted to travel. As the Methodist minister William J. Watkins wrote to the abolitionist William Lloyd Garrison in 1831, "We [would] rather die in Maryland, under the pressure of unrighteous and cruel laws, than be driven, like cattle, to the pestilential clime of Liberia, where grievous privation, inevitable disease, and premature death, await us in all their horrors."

Garrison, who had initially wondered whether colonization might be a solution, rallied. These policies laughed in the face of the American theory of liberty, he protested. Their spring and source were not benevolence but "this wicked distinction of color in our land." If blood and soil were going to be the tests of citizenship, warned Garrison, nobody was safe. He was only half joking when he proposed that the ACS vice president and New Jersey senator, Theodore Frelinghuysen, be sent "back" to Holland, in fidelity to his creed. "The American Colonization Society," wrote Garrison, "stands in the same attitude to our colored population, as Georgia does to the Cherokees. It willfully disregards their earnest, unequivocal and reiterated desires; pretending at the same time to be actuated by the most disinterested and benevolent motives; promising to remove them to Africa only with their own consent; yet determining by every artifice to render their situation so intolerable here, as to compel them to emigrate."

Advocates of colonization seemed to agree with Garrison on the political heresy. "Shall we put [Black people] on a footing with ourselves, and accord to them equal rights?" wondered a lawyer and future governor of New Jersey, in an address to the American Colonization Society. "Strict justice and the spirit of our free institutions would seem to require it," he acknowledged. Yet racial equality "was utterly out of the question." Only fanatics thought of it. "The consequence," he confessed, "is we are driven to the most absurd inconsistencies, and compelled to do violence to our dearest political principles." Here was a frank admission that racial prejudice was anathema to the American political creed, yet a problem that only zealots like Garrison were willing to confront. The answer: emigration. The rationale: providence. Indeed, the greater the challenges facing the quixotic scheme of colonization, the more fervently it was anchored to destiny. God has "called us to colonize Africa, as significantly as he called our fathers to colonize at Plymouth," declared Lyman Beecher, Harriet Beecher Stowe's father and a dancing prophet of exceptionalism. Only occasionally did the mask of benevolence slip. A writer in *The African Repository,* house journal of the ACS, marveled that the United States will soon be "liberated from her black population."

The tranquilizing effects of exceptionalism were no less apparent in the politics of Indian removal, a policy more controversial within the white majority. For the Cherokees of Georgia—settled, stable, and armed with a U.S.-style constitution—the notion of an involuntary exodus was preposterous. The states of Georgia and Alabama had long demanded the clearing of Indian settlements, to make way for the true "cultivators of the earth," and the arrival of Andrew Jackson in 1829 was the golden opportunity. As Jackson made Indian removal a priority, providence once again held the coats and calmed the nerves. These noble savages, sighed a lawmaker in Georgia, were destined to melt away "like snow beneath the beams of the sun." The fact that they were protected by laws, treaties, and decades of legal precedent was immaterial to the higher law of God's design.

Even Joseph Story, a Supreme Court justice who joined Chief Justice John Marshall in ruling against Georgia's plans to drive the Cherokees off their land in 1832, succumbed to the narrative. In a speech celebrating the bicentennial of the founding of Salem in Massachusetts, Story offered a flawless account of American providentialism, in which the colonists were blameless in their treatment of the natives, who fade away like "the withered leaves of autumn." Was this the law of nature? Had God willed their demise? "It may be so," responded Story; "perhaps, in the wisdom of Providence, it must be so."

With friends like this, who needed enemies? William Apess, a Methodist preacher and Pequot Indian, felt that history, no less than bullets, was destroying his people. Apess was a child of broken homes who ran away from indentured servitude in Connecticut at the age of fifteen to join a militia in New York. He fought in the War of 1812, before returning to his family in Massachusetts and reclaiming his Pequot identity. Converting to Christianity and discovering a gift for preaching, Apess enjoyed a period of celebrity in New England, publishing a well-received autobiography and several important lectures. His target was Andrew Jackson and the hated policy of Indian removal. His method was a sparkling revision of nationalist history.

The seeds of Apess's skepticism were sown during his dismal experience in the War of 1812, where he witnessed the execution of several troops for mutiny and desertion. Apess described how the men, "clothed in white with bibles in their hands," were forced to kneel on their coffins alongside newly dug graves. A chaplain spoke to them, and shots were fired. When one of the condemned was spared, in a display of imperious mercy, the man wept like a child and had to be carried to his quarters. Apess wondered what kind of world he had entered. "Death never seemed so awful," he recalled. Patriotism never seemed less plausible.

Apess was writing at a time when providential narratives were dominating the public square. On December 22, 1820, the two-hundred-year anniversary of the Plymouth landing, Daniel Webster made an electrifying speech on the Pilgrims as pioneers of civilization and a model for the young nation. Six years later, a young scholar called George Bancroft delivered a Fourth of July oration that became the nucleus of his epic *History of the United States,* which set the tone of historical scholarship in America, and defined the national mission for several presidents, including Lincoln. This was history as heroism: the past as glistening future. Bancroft described how "the elect martyrs" of the revolution had saved Liberty from a fading Albion, holding her for "a more beautiful maturity" in America. There would be no bigotry, militarism, or state-sanctioned religion under American skies. America's moral condition was superior to that of the Old World, and destined to invigorate that benighted continent. In the American Revolution, "the dearest interests of mankind were entrusted to our country," declared Bancroft. And "the nations of the earth turned towards her as to their last hope."

These were no innocent boasts, thought Apess. They offered an ancestry to intolerance. They clothed violence in destiny. Bancroft portrayed New England of 1620 as an unproductive waste peopled by "a few scattered tribes of feeble barbarians," to whom the "axe and the ploughshare were unknown." The soil, he falsely reported, was languishing "in magnificent but useless vegetation," until the Pilgrims descended like industrious angels. Apess saw his people being erased: his ancestors, reduced to a prelude. "The doctrines of the pilgrims ha[ve] grown up with the people," he lamented. Now as then, there were those who thought the Indians were marked for oblivion. These inherited dogmas were like "burning elements," carrying a cruel past into an uncertain present. Freedom would be found not in fawning homage to "our fathers," as Webster and Bancroft proposed, but in breaking the spell.

Apess made his point in a dashing *Eulogy on King Philip,* delivered at the Odeon in Boston, in January 1836. Apess took Philip, the archenemy of the New England Puritans, a figure "cursed" and reviled by the Mathers as a troubler of Israel, and defended him as "the greatest man that ever lived upon the American shores." Not that Apess approved of war as the means of "civilizing the world," but when patriot histories cast his people as villains, questions of valor acquired urgency. "Now let us see who the greatest savages were," he coolly proceeded. In his bicentenary address, Webster had established a splendid dichotomy between the purity of the Pilgrims and the cruelty of the Spanish, who descended on the New World like a vulture on its prey. Where Spain came in fire and blood, these humble Protestants came in dignity and peace, planting liberty in a virgin soil. Theirs, said Webster, were "the first footsteps of civilized man" on the American continent.

Was there a fragment of truth in this unctuous parable? No, rejoined Apess. His people were degraded, not improved, by contact with the colonizers. The Pilgrims came armed and ready for conquest. They returned kindness with showers of lead, and they made slaves of a proud people, easing their consciences with the belief that the Indians had been "made" for destruction—"a most sorry and wretched doctrine." The pious settlers "professed to be a free and humane people," but they killed without mercy and sold "a part of my tribe" to the Spaniards in Bermuda. Bodies were dismembered and "exhibited in savage triumph" in Plymouth and Boston, and all of this was said to be "the design of God." Apess could only hope that "God understood his work better than this." With mordant allusion to the custom of praying "bullets through people's hearts," he drolly submitted, "I hope they will not pray for me."

Why the bitterness? Why the reopening of old wounds? Because the battle was not over, Apess insisted. More than a century after King Philip's War, people still thought of Native Americans as "red Canaanites," trespassing on their promised land. To honor the Pilgrims was to perpetuate their sins. "Let the children of the Pilgrims blush," admonished Apess. And "let every man of color wrap himself in mourning, for the 22d of December and the 4th of July are days of mourning and not of joy."

The brilliance of this analysis was that it transcended personal prejudice or private loathing. His point was that Native Americans were condemned by an idea and a story, regardless of individual sympathies. A modern historian assures us that Jackson's Indian removal policy was "not overly malevolent," and that Jackson was a child of his times. Apess would not have been encouraged. It was an idea that was killing his people, quite as much as individual men. Neither Webster nor Bancroft was a white supremacist, pining for pure Anglo-Saxon blood. They didn't need to be for their history to point in the same direction.

It is fashionable for scholars to distinguish a good and healthy patriotism, centering on the Constitution, from a toxic and nativist strain, centering on birth and blood. But the distinction is overdrawn when the implications were virtually the same. Whether the three-fifths clause represented racism or realpolitik, in the final analysis, the patriotism that hovered around it like a guardian angel was no less problematic for those who would heal the wound. That was why the abolitionists confronted the civil religion with no less vigor than William Apess.

II

The antislavery movement was buoyantly internationalist from the start: a conspiracy of justice, reaching across borders. "The democratic idea," wrote William J. Watkins, one of the leading Black voices of the age, was that of "the unity of the race." He did not mean color. Garrison saw the American cause as part of a larger struggle for liberation, and the first edition of his iconic journal, *The Liberator,* declared a stance: "Our Country is the World, Our Countrymen are All Mankind." The illustrated masthead, which appeared three months later in April 1831, placed a slave auction and a whipping post in painful juxtaposition to the U.S. Capitol, where an oversized flag fluttered with the word "Liberty." Garrison did not go in for subtlety. He wanted to stir the American conscience from a fog of self-appreciation. And he was a follower as much as a leader in that bracing ministry.

"America! America! awake from thy suicidal slumbers, and thy wild, delusive dreams of perpetual peace and safety," thundered Watkins in a typical address. The sins of "this *soi disant* Republic," this "practically atheistic nation," could not be erased by "the magic wand of rhetoric." Indeed the rhetoric was the sin, the "hypocritical hallelujahs" of Fourth of July orators, who cry peace when there is no peace. Patriotism was denial: a glorious evasion of the fact that here, in the United States of America, the "living and the dead [are] chained together in one habitation."

It seemed harsh to spurn the festivities, confessed the prominent Black freeman William H. Newby, "but patriotism may be a vice." To celebrate a country "built upon our sweat and blood" was "to make ourselves ridiculous." It was to volunteer a degree of servility and to trivialize the open wound of slavery. "God knows I speak advisedly," he ventured, but "I would hail the advent of a foreign army upon our shores, if that army provided liberty to me and my people in bondage." Others were no less candid, renouncing allegiance to a country that "treats us like dogs."

The Mexican War put the matter in sharp relief. Here, patriotism seemed like another word for slavery, as the United States pursued a war of conquest precipitated by the migration of slave owners to the Mexican region of Texas. Mexico had abolished slavery in 1829. Seven years later, American settlers staged a revolt and reinstated slavery in their self-proclaimed republic, then lobbied for annexation to the United States. A seminal article of July 1845, drawing on the work of George Bancroft, declared it "our manifest destiny" to receive Texas into the republic, within the plan "allotted by Providence for the free development of our yearly multiplying millions." Annexation of a slaveholding territory the size of about five existing states threatened disaster to the delicate balance of free and slave states that was holding the Union together by a thread. The subsequent war redrew the map of North America and made an empire of a republic.

How could a Christian people countenance such crimes? Because their true religion was patriotism, thundered Garrison. This was a war for "the extension and preservation of slavery," sanctioned by that "diabolical motto, 'Our country, right or wrong.'" The war was declared against the moral convictions of most Americans. But once the wheels began to turn, those convictions turned to dust. Opposing the invasion "subjects us to great odium, and brings down upon our heads the heavy charge of 'treason,'" Garrison told his nephew. But the real treason, the real failure, was with those who sacrificed their conscience to their country.

For all his pacifism, Garrison loved a fight. It was as if he, and the entire abolitionist movement, were inventing a new masculinity, a fellowship of dissent. In *Civil Disobedience,* Henry David Thoreau developed a theory of conscientious revolt in which freedom surfaces as the ability to say no to a blundering state. "When a sixth of the population of a nation which has undertaken to be the refuge of liberty are slaves, and a whole country is unjustly overrun and conquered by a foreign army," he challenged, "I think that it is not too soon for honest men to rebel and revolutionize. What makes this duty the more urgent is the fact that the country so overrun is not our own, but ours is the invading army." Thoreau's decision to go to jail, rather than contribute to the war chest, struck friends as an overreaction. But this was his point about patriotism and virtue. Everyone had morality, it seemed, but few possessed courage. There were, he contended, "nine hundred and ninety-nine patrons of virtue to one virtuous man." And deep in the malaise, holding conscience in stony abeyance, was the desiccating religion of the flag.

Patriotism created wars and made killers of rational men, freezing their faculties in docile obedience to the state. "Now, what are they? Men at all? or small movable forts and magazines, at the service of some unscrupulous man in power?" inquired Thoreau. In war, men served the state "not as men mainly, but as machines." They "put themselves on a level with wood and earth and stones." They exercised no more judgment, no more freedom of will, than "horses and dogs." Yet in our peculiar inversion of values, these plodding conformists are considered the best of citizens.

As Thoreau argued in *Walden,* his hymn to rural solitude, published five years later, patriots were followers, not thinkers; proud, yet strangely lacking in self-respect. "Patriotism," he asserted, with a certain violence of his own, "is a maggot in their heads." Thoreau thought there was more glory in a sugar maple, displaying its "annual splendor" in October, than in all the flags and banners the world had ever seen. Even if the state were virtuous, patriotism would be a problem for Thoreau. In the context of slavery and conquest, it was a disaster. "This people must cease to hold slaves, and to make war on Mexico," he submitted, "though it cost them their existence as a people."

Frederick Douglass had been saying something similar for years. Douglass brought a lighter touch and a sharper wit to the same problem: chronic injustice, wrapped in a flag. His critique of providence and the prostitution of religion to power recalls the satire of Voltaire. In a classic account of slaveholding religion, he told the story of a pious lady who said she had been to heaven in a dream. After she described her excursion in fabulous detail, someone asked if she saw any Black folks in heaven. "Oh," she replied. "I didn't go in the kitchen." This brought the house down every time.

"Do not misunderstand my railing," pleaded Douglass; "do not identify me with the infidel." Douglass wanted to break "the charm" of the slaveholder's religion, and satire was the weapon of choice. He performed a similar move on the civil religion, turning the icons of the revolution upside down. Patriotism had blinded Americans to the fact that their Constitution was a "radically and essentially slaveholding" document, he argued in a barnstorming oration of 1847. Americans loved to extol their virtue and their freedom from the despotisms of Europe, he observed: "Yet the damning fact remains, there is not a rood of earth under the stars and the eagle on your flag, where a man of my complexion can stand free.... Wherever waves the star-spangled banner there the bondman may be arrested and hurried back to the jaws of Slavery."

Having relished a moment of unity, as his jokes about Southern religion reduced his Yankee audience to an ecstasy of mirth, Douglass turned and jabbed them in the ribs, exchanging the "we" and "our" of the antislavery cause for an accusing "you" and "your," as he addressed the stupefactions of national pride. "This is your 'land of the free,' your 'home of the brave,'" he thundered. From Lexington and Bunker Hill to all the holiest sites of the revolution, men of color languished in fear. "I never knew what freedom was till I got beyond the limits of the American eagle," he sternly reported. "When I first rested my head on a British Island, I felt that the eagle might scream, but from its talons and beak I was free, at least for a time." There, nobody could insult him, still less enslave him. But back in republican, Christian America, he had to scan every room and parse every sentence, knowing it might be his last. Douglass was aware of how offensive such observations were to those who "are called patriots." A certain religious journal had recommended that he be hanged as a traitor. The prophet was unrepentant. He could not be a traitor to a nation that had already excluded him. "No, I make no pretension to patriotism," he maintained. Not until he had a country to call his own.

The new Fugitive Slave Law, passed as part of the Compromise of 1850, drove Douglass to new heights. In a landmark oration titled "The Meaning of July Fourth for the Negro," Douglass condemned the racism that scarred the nation, and the patriotism that covered its tracks. "This Fourth of July is yours, not mine," he submitted. "You may rejoice, I must mourn." The English writer Sydney Smith had written that "men seldom eulogize the wisdom and virtues of their fathers, but to excuse some folly or wickedness of their own," and this was the story of America. Just as the Pharisees of the first century had hidden their crimes under their status as the descendants of Abraham, "the traders in the bodies and souls of men shout—'We have Washington to our father,'" as if pedigree were a substitute for justice.

Confirming his own release from the emasculations of filial piety, Douglass returned to his favorite rhetorical device: *your* country, *your* republicanism, *your own* Thomas Jefferson. "What, to the American slave, is your 4th of July?" he pondered. "To him, your celebration is a sham; your boasted liberty, an unholy license; your national greatness, swelling vanity; your sounds of rejoicing are empty and heartless; your denunciation of tyrants, brass fronted impudence; your shouts of liberty and equality, hollow mockery."

The following month, Douglass went further, excoriating the founders as men of small hearts and cramped vision. "It has been said that our fathers entered into a covenant for this slavecatching," he noted, as if the history determined the policy. "Who were your daddies?" he responded, to roars of laughter. "I take it they were men, and so are you." So perhaps it was time to move on. With shades of Thomas Paine's remark that government "is for the living, and not the dead," Douglass urged Americans to grow up and cast off the chains of tradition. The founders were deeply flawed actors who overstepped their limits when they established a right to hold their brothers and sisters as property. The crowd burst into song.

History mattered in 1854. How you thought about the founders and the Constitution determined whether the nation's wounds demanded surgery or patience and prayer. Douglass decried the sanctimony of those who shifted the problem onto the shoulders of providence and then washed their hands. The irony was that a superficial belief in America's excellence held the nation in tragic mediocrity, scraping around for compromises when courage was the need of the hour.

In November 1854, George Bancroft, now enjoying the status of a national bard, gave a lecture in New York on the "necessity" and "promise" of human progress, in which America played the starring role. Drawing on the mystical idealism of Hegel, Bancroft described a nation that had absorbed the disparate forces of history, achieving a unity and grandeur unparalleled in human experience. "Our country," declared Bancroft, "is bound to allure the world to freedom by the beauty of its example."

Douglass responded by publishing a blistering editorial in his weekly paper, titled "Our Influence Abroad," written by William J. Watkins. It was normal, "in the course of human events, to be compelled to listen to such rhetorical flourishes on the Fourth of July, when everybody knows that Truth has taken leave of absence," he began, in sarcastic homage to the Declaration of Independence. But November was no month for this kind of "claptrap." "Where has Mr. Bancroft been living?" Watkins was curious to know. Was he aware of the Fugitive Slave Law? Wincing at Bancroft's phrase about the beauty of our example, Watkins suggested an alteration: "In order that it may speak the truth, it should read, 'Our country is bound to allure the world to *Slavery!*' " That was where the nation was heading. "Is there anything very beautiful in whipping women, burning them with red hot irons, setting bloodhounds upon their track, tearing their infant children from them, and selling them with horses and other cattle?" he protested. This was a nation that authorized murder, sexual violation, and all the "black catalogue of American slavery," while punishing with fines and imprisonment those who would feed or clothe the desperate fugitive.

There was, raged Watkins, a criminal folly in boasting about freedom when "the great object of this Government, *as developed in its policy*, is the extension, the consolidation, and the perpetuity of a system of robbery, and plunder, and oppression, aptly characterized the vilest that ever saw the sun." Until three and a half million men, women, and children are emancipated from their chains, "all our nonsensical rhodomontade about free thought, and free discussion, and free institutions—all the unmeaning twaddle of Fourth of July orators concerning the 'beauty of our example'—will be regarded by the 'world' . . . as a sounding brass, and a tinkling cymbal."

The sermon ended, but the question remained: Could the Union be recovered? Could the experiment be redeemed?

III

All of these critics agreed on the complicity of patriotism in the crimes of slavery and caste. They saw a working relationship, a fatal bond, between exceptionalism and exclusion. There perhaps the similarities ended. Watkins gave up and moved to Canada. For Garrison, the problem was deeper than a failure to live up to the ideal of equality. The Constitution was fatally flawed. When the founders of the republic offered a home to tyrants, he wrote in one of the first issues of *The Liberator*, they "trampled beneath their feet their own solemn and heaven-attested Declaration, that all men are created equal." Under the terms of this "infamous bargain," politics was a losing game. Disunion was the only road to freedom. The South knew that its only security "lies in northern bayonets," and it had "repeatedly taunted the free States with being pledged to protect her." So why not let them go?

It was sobering to reflect, he argued in another editorial, "that it is solely by the authority of the free states slavery is tolerated in our land." The only thing holding the hated edifice together was "OUR PHYSICAL FORCE." Garrison noted the panic with which Southern congressmen reacted to a petition to dissolve the Union, read by John Quincy Adams in 1842. Some called for the former president to be hanged for treason. Joseph R. Underwood, of Kentucky, delivered a calmer but more revealing speech, proving everything the abolitionists had always suspected. "Just so soon as the bonds of this Union are dissolved," Underwood warned those of his colleagues who welcomed the idea, "just as soon as Mason and Dixon's line and the Ohio river become the boundary between two independent nations, slavery ceases in all the border States." Currently, he observed, "our slaves escape into Canada and write insulting letters to their former masters" from that distant land. Imagine, "if instead of having to travel hundreds of miles to reach the land where they cannot be arrested, we, by dissolving the Union, bring that land so near them that a single step, a mile, or a night's journey, will enable hundreds and thousands of them to place their feet upon it? Sir, it is too obvious to require argument or illustration, that to dissolve the Union is to dissolve the bonds of slavery in all the border States." Sooner or later, he continued, the process would extend farther south, rendering slave labor so precarious and uncertain that it could not be depended upon. Slaves would be worth nothing, and all discipline would evaporate. "The Constitution, as it now stands on the subject of slavery," maintained Underwood, "is the only safeguard to the institution."

This was music to abolitionist ears, and something that Madison privately admitted when threats of secession began to surface in the 1820s and 1830s. "What madness in the South, to look for greater safety in disunion," he wrote to Henry Clay in June 1833. "It would be worse than jumping out of the frying pan into the fire. It would be jumping into the fire from a *fear* of the frying pan." Such talk was excited by nothing more than "pride and resentment." Everyone knew that the slave states needed the Union for their survival.

The release of Madison's notes on the Constitutional Convention in 1840 was a moment of clarity for the abolitionists. Here, in jotted fragments of expediency, was the indifference of the founders laid bare. The Constitution, concluded Wendell Phillips, was no grudging alliance of freedom and force. It was "a Pro-Slavery Compact," designed and structured to hold slaves. The abolitionist movement had begun with moral suasion, and the belief that public opinion could be inspired to end the curse. The Madison Papers, and the violence visited upon opponents of slavery, including the murder of the journalist Elijah Lovejoy in 1837, made separation seem the wiser path. An article in *The Liberator* wondered why there was so much hate for abolitionists among the self-styled patriots of the Liberty Party. Could they not see that loyalty to a "blood-cemented union" was acquiescence in tyranny?

At the tenth anniversary meeting of the American Anti-Slavery Society, in May 1844, members agreed by a vote of nearly three to one that it was "impractical for tyrants and the enemies of tyranny to coalesce and legislate together for the preservations of human rights." The banner of freedom would now bear the words "NO UNION WITH SLAVEHOLDERS," a phrase grafted onto the masthead of *The Liberator*. Gag rules and Fugitive Slave Laws were the fruits of the tree. Nothing more or less than could be expected from "a covenant with death" and "an agreement with hell," as Garrison cheerfully termed the Constitution. "You know, and we all know, that the Union of these States has been a curse," argued the Ohio abolitionist James W. Walker at the New England Anti-Slavery Convention of 1850, "a curse from the beginning." "Whoever strengthens the American Union," asserted Phillips with devastating simplicity, "strengthens the chain of the American slave."

This was more than the petulance of dreamers, notes the historian Melinda Lawson. It was based on a shrewd historical consciousness, encapsulated in Phillips's advice that runaways need not be ashamed of fleeing to Canada. At a time when fugitives were being encouraged to stay and fight, Phillips urged caution. "There is no safety for you here; there is no law for you here," he said. "The hearts of the judges are stone, the hearts of the people are stone." Violence was suicide. Had John and Samuel Adams announced their revolution in 1765, rather than 1775, he reasoned, "their journey would have ended at the scaffold," because public opinion was not ready. The same was true now. If the North was ripe for reform, one had to be realistic about the epicenter: a land of tyranny and torture. Phillips still thought of himself as an American, even a patriot of sorts. Yet only in disunion did the American promise stand a chance. "If I am to love my country," he once told a crowd, "it must be loveable."

Garrison made the case in his signature statement, "No Compromise with Slavery." The patriotism of the North was carte blanche to the slave owners, who knew that lachrymose orators like Daniel Webster would do anything to preserve their fancied Elysium. Every year the terms of the deal stiffened. "The reason why the South rules," explained Garrison, "is simply this: With the South, the preservation of Slavery is paramount to all other considerations. . . . With the North, the preservation of the Union is placed above all other things—above honour, justice, freedom, integrity of soul, the Decalogue and the Golden Rule"—above "the Infinite God himself." Each of these things came second to national pride, which polished and policed the hierarchy with nervous alacrity. It was "the most terrible form of idolatry." But there was a failure of judgment, as well as of conscience, in the cult of the indivisible union: an attempt to cheat the laws of "cause and effect."

None of the virtues that men like Webster and Clay wanted to see in their exemplary republic was possible in union with men who called equality a "self-evident lie," and believed "that personal freedom and free institutions are a calamity and a curse." Garrison gave eager notice, in the pages of *The Liberator,* to the work of Southern intellectuals such as George Fitzhugh, to make his point about the folly of compromise. In bestselling works of 1854 and 1857, Fitzhugh pronounced the entire development of the "Free Society" a colossal failure, and he condemned the politics of consent as an affront to the natural hierarchy established by God. In a subsequent article, Fitzhugh called John Locke a "presumptuous charlatan" and Jefferson a "thoughtless, half-informed" plagiarist, and he scoffed at the "pompous inanities of the Declaration of Independence." These delusions of equality were "engines of destruction," he said: "silly" and incendiary. The fathers of the republic built their house on these "powder-cask abstractions," and it had been downhill from there.

Garrison welcomed the candor. Fitzhugh said nothing that John C. Calhoun hadn't declared openly in the U.S. Senate, where the godfather of states' rights railed against "the dangerous error . . . that all men are born free and equal," and bemoaned Jefferson's decision to grant it "a place in the declaration of our independence." The toxin of equality was now bearing "its poisonous fruits," scowled Calhoun, threatening to involve "the country in countless woes."

There was no country, responded Garrison. This was why the craning overtures of the patriots were so mistaken, and the political road to emancipation apparently doomed. Webster's rallying cry of 1830—"Liberty and Union, now and forever, one and inseparable"—was a wedding vow without a bride. How could there be liberty where union meant "branding-irons and bloodhounds"? What kind of union entrusted freedom to men who despised it? Patriots were like Voltaire's hapless optimist Pangloss, greeting every disaster with a numbing catchphrase—everything is for the best in this best of all possible nations. "Thirty thousand escaped fugitive slaves in Canada and perhaps an equal number scattered all through the North," was the hard reality of a Faustian bargain masquerading as the light of the world. "While . . . the Union is preserved," feared Garrison, there was "no hope for peaceful deliverance of the millions who are clanking their chains on our blood-red soil."

Douglass was not convinced. The political process was broken, the Constitution gravely flawed, but neither was beyond redemption. If one story of the decade was the spread of the Slave Power in the federal government and judiciary, another was the infusion of abolitionist sentiment in a political game it had so long eschewed. In 1847, Douglass had looked forward to "the dissolution of the present unholy Union," which had been justly stigmatized as a covenant with death. He would, he said, "welcome the bolt, either from the North or the South, which shall shatter this Union." Two years later, he was beginning to think differently.

There was more than one way to read the Constitution, Douglass began to argue, as he grappled with a new antislavery constitutionalism, including Lysander Spooner's treatise *The Unconstitutionality of Slavery* (1845). The Constitution was a text in torment, a man of many parts. What was said to placate slave owners could not be taken for the whole. There was a preamble that spoke of justice, tranquility, and the blessings of liberty; there was a requirement that every state adopt "a republican form of government"; and there was a promise that "no person shall . . . be deprived of life, liberty, or property, without due process of law." Here was a theory to work with. The Constitution contained "principles and purposes, entirely hostile to the existence of slavery," Douglass now ventured. It was, after all, only the prose to the majestic poetry of the Declaration of Independence.

"Judge [a] people not by what they are, but by what they strive to become," urged the Russian novelist Fyodor Dostoevsky. There were "great and holy things . . . amidst the very villainy" to which men succumb. Such were Douglass's sentiments as he moved, with many of the abolitionists, from prophecy to politics, and from the force of eloquence to the logic of force. The future was with Douglass, not Garrison, as historical memory attests. Yet Garrison's challenge, at the root of his "profane" dream of disunion, remains unanswered: Can violence create freedom? Can a nation be forced to be a nation? Nowhere has history been more completely confused with myth than the American Civil War.

CHAPTER 3

The War That Never Ended

> It was then that untruth came down on our land. . . . The main misfortune, the root of all the evil to come, was the loss of confidence in the value of one's own opinion. People imagined that it was out of date to follow their own moral sense, that they must all sing in chorus, and live by other people's notions, notions that were being crammed down everybody's throat. And then there arose the power of the glittering phrase.
>
> —BORIS PASTERNAK, *DOCTOR ZHIVAGO*

Everybody knows what happened next. The nation plunged into a series of disasters, from guerrilla warfare in "Bleeding Kansas" to the execution of John Brown for a failed insurrection in Virginia to the final and long-threatened fracturing of the Union. And then "there was light." While zealots squabbled, one man kept his head, and he happened to be president. With iron will and preternatural dexterity, Abraham Lincoln steered the ship of state through its "fiery trial," saving democracy for the world. The story has every virtue except historical truth.

It is true that the Civil War ended the legal institution of slavery, but the practice remained, under different names, and the brutality of the conflict delivered a "freedom" that was crippled from the start. Rather than uniting the nation, the Civil War deepened the wounds of sectional division in ways that are yet to be resolved, and it created legacies of militarism and violence that continue to plague the nation. So argued the literary critic Edmund Wilson in *Patriotic Gore,* a blistering riposte to the eulogies brought forth by what he called the "absurd centennial" of 1961. A "day of mourning," he growled, "would be more appropriate." If we would understand the gigantic folly of a nuclear arms race, or the virulence with which the South resisted desegregation in the 1950s, he ventured, we have to think more bravely about this creation myth of modern America.

The Civil War did not save America: It scarred a fractured and febrile people. And the wounds are still weeping. "We have," Wilson said, "accepted the epic that Lincoln directed and lived and wrote," failing to see that the ignominies of the Reconstruction era were baked into Lincoln's formula—as were "the insufferable moral attitudes" that we have carried into all our subsequent wars. Americans can scoff at a Napoleon, ravaging a continent in the name of "Liberté, égalité, fraternité"; we can frown at the Soviets, pleading laws of historical necessity as their tanks roll into Budapest; but we are no different. "It is," Wilson urged, "very difficult for us to recognize that we, too, are devourers and that we, too, are talking cant." Wilson knew that no one would thank him for comparing Lincoln to Otto von Bismarck, the "Iron Chancellor" who forged the German state from a series of confected crises, but he embraced the opprobrium. If you want to defuse an atom bomb, you have to break the code. The Civil War was the war that never ended.

The power of *Patriotic Gore* was the method. Wilson neither asserted nor even argued his case. He presented it, through an anthology of forgotten voices. I appeal to a different cloud of witnesses, but my point is the same: Patriotism has obscured the reality of the Civil War, in academic and popular thought, and its spurring myth of redemptive violence continues to haunt our culture.

I

Lincoln's election in 1860 followed a rapid realignment of parties over the expansion of slavery in the Western territories. The Kansas-Nebraska Act of 1854 had shattered the compromise that had confined slavery to land south of the 36th parallel, heralding the nightmare of a slave empire engulfing the free states. The Dred Scott decision of 1857 confirmed the sense of conspiracy, as the Supreme Court found that a man living in a free state was still a slave, adding that people of African descent have "no rights which the white man was bound to respect." This, plus the forcible return of fugitives such as Anthony Burns, radicalized public opinion, drawing moderates like Lincoln into the moral firmament of antislavery.

Lincoln was no abolitionist. He accepted the fact of slavery in its ancestral homes of the South, and he felt few of the agonies that inspired Harriet Beecher Stowe to write *Uncle Tom's Cabin*. But he was horrified by the prospect of expansion, and he had the good fortune to live in the same state as Stephen Douglas, the architect of the Kansas-Nebraska Act, who paraded his indifference to slavery with goading defiance. Lincoln lost his battle with Douglas to represent Illinois in the U.S. Senate, but he made his name, and two years later earned the Republican nomination for president. It was a meteoric rise for a provincial lawyer with only two years of experience in national politics. Lincoln spoke with power and resolution, even if it was not entirely clear where he stood on the question dividing the country.

Sometimes his theme was equality, and the natural rights attendant to Black and white. Sometimes it was inequality, and the impossibility of the two races living in peace. Lincoln abhorred slavery, but he had none of the experience of the abolitionists, rubbing shoulders with free Blacks in the trenches of the antislavery movement. He remained a vigorous advocate of colonization, and much of his animus against slavery centered on its damage to America's reputation as the home of liberty. "Our republican robe is soiled, and trailed in the dust," he declared in a career-defining speech on the Kansas-Nebraska Act. Lincoln abhorred slavery for its injustice, but he resented it more for what it said about America. "I hate it because it deprives our republican example of its just influence in the world," he protested. It enabled "the enemies of free institutions . . . to taunt us as hypocrites." It was "the one retrograde institution in America . . . violating the noblest political system the world ever saw." This was nationalism, jostling with justice; shame, overriding guilt. Lincoln was hardly oblivious of the harm inherent in chattel slavery, but this notion of a blemish on an otherwise pure canvas condemned the question to secondary status. Much as he hated slavery, he said he would agree to its extension rather than see the Union dissolved, the latter being a much greater evil.

This tension between what slavery was and what it meant for the American project defined Lincoln's presidency and the secession crisis it precipitated. While he said enough to convince the Slave Power that he was another John Brown, ready to torch their barns, his priority was always to preserve the Union. When the slave states began to leave, Lincoln's concern was not whether slavery would finally crumble: it was how to force them back into the Union. This led to the paradox of an antislavery president waging war to force slaveholders back into a democratic republic. It was within this paradox, this confusion of aims, that the tragedy of the war lay.

Lincoln's patriotism led him to underestimate the scale of Southern antipathy and to overestimate his ability to crush what he euphemistically termed a "rebellion." In this taut and theoretical worldview, the United States was the guardian of democracy for the nations, and its survival in original form the test of whether such a mode of government could survive anywhere—regardless of its actual condition. The force of this conviction, the frisson of world responsibility, controlled all considerations of means. Lincoln said he would rather die than lose a single star from the Stars and Stripes, because the vessel—the ark of liberty—was as precious as the jewels. Indeed more so. With fierce and ponderous lucidity, Lincoln declared that he would "save the Union," with or without freeing a single slave. Lincoln cared about slavery. He cared more about preserving the Union, whatever that actually meant.

Lincoln was slow to grasp one of the foundations of political philosophy, stated by Edmund Burke as he implored Parliament to let the colonies go in 1775. Unity, advised Burke, can never be forced; land held against a people's will is never truly governed. With "force," he reasoned, "you impair the object by your very endeavors to preserve it. The thing you fought for is not the thing which you recover; but depreciated, sunk, wasted, and consumed in the contest." A version of this argument was pressed upon Lincoln many times between his election in November 1860 and the firing on Fort Sumter in April 1861, but the higher law prevailed. This was a patriotic war in which liberty and justice limped and straggled behind the majesty of the state.

Prior to the Civil War, America had a strong tradition of antimilitarism, drawing on the republican critique of standing armies and the pacific leanings of the founders, who held with Montesquieu that if war was the spirit of monarchy, peace was the soul of a republic. There is no such thing as a good war or a bad peace, wrote Franklin. One war is enough for one life, said Jefferson, on several occasions. The problem with war, he argued, is that the act of violence tends to strengthen the evil it aims to destroy. For man is the animal endowed with memory, and the injuries of war are not quickly forgotten. The United States, he proudly remarked in his first inaugural address, was a land mercifully separated from "the exterminating havoc" of Europe, and so it would continue. America would show the world that there are better ways of seeking justice than "appeals to arms."

Indeed, antimilitarism was a core component of early American patriotism. Standing armies had been "the scourge of the Old World," wrote Alexander Hamilton in Federalist No. 8. European history was a tale of bloated armies, petty conquests, and "battles that decide nothing," he said. "In this country the scene would be altogether reversed." A healthy distrust of military establishments would keep these "engines of despotism" at bay. Alexis de Tocqueville lauded the United States as "the least militaristic" country in the world in 1835, a quality essential to its democracy. "All those who seek to destroy the liberties of a democratic nation," he warned, "ought to know that war is the surest and the shortest means to accomplish it."

The secession crisis was not Shays's Rebellion, the farmers' revolt in western Massachusetts that provided one of the catalysts for the Constitutional Convention in 1787. It was the articulate, if democratically dubious, withdrawal of seven states from the voluntary compact of the Union. The Constitution authorized force against a rebellion or insurrection, but the convention rejected the notion of coercing "a delinquent state" into good behavior. As Madison reported his contribution to the discussion, "The more he reflected on the use of force, the more he doubted the practicability, the justice and the efficacy of it when applied to people collectively and not individually." Military coercion, he added, would be regarded "as a dissolution of all previous compacts by which [a state] might be bound." It would be a point of no return.

It was one thing to punish an individual, quite another to declare war against the established government of one of the states. Any notion of a right to use "force against the unconstitutional proceedings of the States," averred Madison in June 1787, was "visionary and fallacious." A government established on such terms would be more problematic than the cobbled confederation that the Constitution replaced. John Quincy Adams shared this view, asserting, in a speech marking George Washington's birthday in 1839, that "the people of each State in the Union [have] a right to secede from the confederated Union." Should the day come "when the affections of the people of these States shall be alienated from each other," he continued, "far better will it be for the people of the disunited States to part in friendship from each other, than to be held together by constraint." Adams was not advocating secession. He was appealing for unity based on the affections of "the heart," the only true foundation of a political community.

Clearly, then, there was no constitutional mandate for coercing an unhappy state back into the Union. Such a power, noted President James Buchanan in his State of the Union address in December 1860, "was expressly refused by the Convention which framed the Constitution." To compel union by physical force would fly in the face of "the whole spirit and intent of the Constitution." "Suppose such a war should result in the conquest of a State; how are we to govern it afterwards?" he wondered. Although the object would be to preserve the Union, the method "would banish all hope of its peaceable reconstruction." The vast amount of blood that would be shed in such a war would render "future reconciliation between the States impossible." "The fact is that our Union rests upon public opinion," he concluded, "and can never be cemented by the blood of its citizens shed in civil war. If it cannot live in the affections of the people, it must one day perish. Congress possesses many means of preserving it by conciliation, but the sword was not placed in their hand to preserve it by force."

On January 8, 1861, Buchanan explained why he had not sent reinforcements to Major Robert Anderson, who commanded the forts in Charleston Harbor, lest such an act furnish a "pretext" or "provocation" of war. Most Americans felt the same way. As Lincoln's rhetoric oscillated between conciliation and threats of coercion on his long journey to Washington in February, even friends wondered if reports of the latter were to be believed. In Indianapolis, Lincoln worked a crowd of twenty thousand into a frenzy by framing secession as the conceit of an impudent minority, threatening the survival of the whole nation. "By what principle of original right is it that one-fiftieth or one-ninetieth of a great nation, by calling themselves a State, have the right to break up and ruin that nation?" he wondered. Lincoln was a man of peace, but he was ready and willing to fight.

Newspapers said the message "breathed of war," and many of Lincoln's friends regretted the note of belligerence. William L. Hodge, whom Lincoln would later appoint to a Treasury post, called the speech "foolish" and "unfortunate," and one that was having a disastrous effect on a peace conference under way in Virginia. Friends of William H. Seward's sent a telegram asking if it was genuine. Lincoln was playing with fire, thought Cassius M. Clay. Any blow "to regain lost forts," he warned, "will unite the South." Others reported conversations in which Lincoln would not be steered from the path of confrontation.

Lincoln's first inaugural reveals how profoundly his patriotism framed his constitutionalism and his sense of the justice and efficacy of force. Characterizing the Union as a unique and perfect whole, Lincoln decried secession as something that would destroy the American experiment the way a crack destroys a vase. Yet his reasoning is strangely nebulous. "Perpetuity is implied, if not expressed, in the fundamental law of all national governments," Lincoln offered, as a general principle. "It is safe to assert that no government proper ever had a provision in its organic law for its own termination." Since "one of the declared objects for ordaining and establishing the Constitution was '*to form a more perfect Union,*'" any tear in that fabric constituted a fatal breach. To lose one or more of those original partners was to make the Union "*less* perfect" than it was before, annihilating this "vital element of perpetuity. It follows from these views that no State upon its own mere motion can lawfully get out of the Union," Lincoln concluded, with what can only be described as the force of an idea. The founders established a perfect union. A perfect union is one that lasts forever. Ergo, disunion is impossible. Our Southern brethren may *think* they have left the Union. But it's an illusion. Whether they like it or not, "the Union is unbroken." As such, he would execute the laws of the federal Union as his oath enjoined. It was "a simple duty."

Lincoln made a chain of deduction sound like the law of gravity, even though a more natural interpretation of "a perfect union" was that it was voluntary and that the words expressed the desire of the founders to live in peace. The preamble was, after all, an aspirational statement, a plea for domestic tranquility, not a template for action. But with the claim that God had commissioned "this favored land," Lincoln nailed his colors to an involuntary union. He added that secession was a doctrine of anarchy, and something that would revive the foreign slave trade. But these were speculative arguments, peripheral to his central theme of unity, as was the question of interfering with "the domestic institutions" of an unhappy South. Lincoln promised to enforce the Fugitive Slave Law to its original letter by way of appeasement, and he volunteered his support for a constitutional amendment that would protect slavery forever. "I understand a proposed amendment to the Constitution . . . has passed Congress, to the effect that the Federal Government shall never interfere with the domestic institutions of the States, including that of persons held to service," he noted. "Holding such a provision to now be implied constitutional law, I have no objection to its being made express and irrevocable." The Corwin Amendment did not receive the necessary approval of the states, and the attempt to ratify it was overtaken by events in Charleston, but Lincoln endorsed it in a spirit of masterly realism. The message of the inaugural was emphatic: Slavery may continue, but secession brings war.

To say that public opinion was opposed to military coercion would understate the dread and incredulity with which the idea was received in 1861. Can anything be "more atrocious" than this "steady roll" toward war? wondered *The New York Herald,* as the crisis at Fort Sumter inched toward consummation. "Nine out of ten of the people of the Northern and Central States repudiate the coercive policy which is hurrying the republic to destruction, and contemplate with terror and dismay the prospect before us." Oceans of blood were about to be expended to uphold "an impracticable theory, with no other conceivable end than to leave the country exhausted, impoverished and wretched." War would be anarchy and suicide, and the people "shrink aghast from the appeal that has been made to artillery and the bayonet."

Two weeks earlier, *The New York Times* spoke in similar terms: "It cannot be denied that there is a growing sentiment throughout the North in favor of letting the Gulf States go." Abolitionists had been in favor of dissolution from the beginning, and this was now "the sentiment and language of thousands who have no sympathy with the ultraists on either side," observed the *Times*. "Let us separate in peace," was the overwhelming consensus. The editor regretted the sentiment but agreed that war was not an option. "Force, as a means of restoring the Union, or of permanently preserving it, is out of the question," asserted the writer. "No war—no force can ever restore the Union." Cautious restraint, not suicidal zeal, was the order of the day.

These perspectives were widely echoed. After reading Lincoln's inaugural, the editor of Iowa's *Dubuque Herald* felt certain that Lincoln would try to "re-enforce Fort Sumter, and thus aggravate the already excited ire of the South, and provoke a conflict." Connecticut's *Hartford Daily Courant* reported that "public opinion in the North seems to be gradually settling down in favor of recognition of the New Confederacy." The prospect of "a bloody and protracted civil war," added the writer, "is abhorrent to all." In Pennsylvania, the notion that the founders intended "that the military and naval powers of the Federal Government should be called out to force *States,* against their will, to remain in the Union" was attacked with peculiar intensity. However egregious the doctrine of secession, warned one writer, war would be worse. It would create widows and orphans, but never a united people. "The idea of fighting for the preservation of the Union in its present circumstances is simply preposterous," declared a clergyman in Lancaster: "No victory in such a war could deserve to be considered a triumph." Military victory would be more detrimental to the nation than peaceable separation.

In a pained response to Lincoln's inaugural address, the journalist Thomas Low Nichols wondered why Lincoln had not made peace the priority of his administration. Ours is a government of consent: It could not be preserved by killing. Lincoln's determination to reclaim federal property along the coast was certain to provoke war and likely to drive the border states into the arms of the rebellion. Thus would commence "a long, bloody, fratricidal war." And then what? "When oceans of blood have been shed what will be the final result? Union? Harmony? Peace? Never!" In no sense could such a war be justified as self-defense, and the federal government would be responsible for all the consequences. As Nichols later defined Lincoln's philosophy, "War for the Union! Fraternity or death! Be my brother, or I will kill you!" It was an unparalleled madness. "Was it for this that Jefferson had laid the foundations of liberty in America?"

Horace Greeley, editor of the influential *New-York Tribune*, believed the principle of secession was legitimate, at least in theory, and that a government that suppressed it would be "clearly in the wrong." If "we hold with Jefferson" that communities have a right to alter or abolish their modes of government, "the Cotton states" had a right to leave the Union, and "we insist on letting them go in peace." While no state had a right "to remain in the Union and nullify or defy the laws thereof," advised Greeley, "to withdraw from the Union is quite another matter." And whatever legal sophistries might be gathered around the sword, military action was unthinkable. "We hope never to live in a republic whereof one section is pinned to the residue by bayonets," he wrote in November 1860. "If the cotton States unitedly and earnestly wish to withdraw peacefully from the Union," he repeated in a second editorial, "we think they should and would be allowed to do so. Any attempt to compel them by force to remain would be contrary to the principles enunciated in the immortal Declaration of Independence."

Greeley was careful enough to admit that the act of secession would require unmistakable popular support to be truly constitutional. But to many of the abolitionists, the legality of secession was moot. "Is it not self-evident that we are, and must be . . . two nations?" Garrison wrote to Sumner. As he'd argued for decades, slavery could not survive without the muscle and might of the federal government, and here was the great opportunity. "Would to God that the people of the North could see that the time has come for a separation from the South, in the spirit of peace," he wrote. Frederick Douglass agreed. If the Union could only be maintained with new concessions to the slaveholders, he declared, "let the Union perish." Disunion, urged an ecstatic Wendell Phillips, was the end of slavery.

Phillips had never let patriotism interfere with his passion for justice, as we have seen. Now he erupted. Slaveholders had ruled the nation for sixty years. "That cotton fibre was a rod of empire such as Caesar never wielded." For decades, the only peace America had known was a "bastard peace," earned in deference to slave lords. And now we breathe. At last, "we have *a people*." It was lunacy to put the poison back in the bottle. Phillips declared the bankruptcy of the patriotic creed, with its "opiate speeches" and scrambled priorities. "We were not sent into the world . . . to make Unions or save them," he said, but to do justice in the circumstances before us.

The Lincolns and the Sewards were prepared "to surrender anything to save the Union. . . . They think that, at the judgment-day, the blacker the sins they have committed to save the Union, the clearer will be their title to heaven." But a "Union is made up of willing States, not of conquered provinces," observed Phillips. It cannot be forced. The "Union of 1787" was "like an artificial waterfall or a Connecticut nutmeg," pretending to be something it was not. Bullets could no more redeem the fiction than save an unhappy marriage. "Is Abraham Lincoln capable of making fire and powder lie down together in peace?" he wondered. "In blood there is sure to be ruin."

Three days later, the war began.

The day after his inauguration, Lincoln had been alerted to the crisis at Fort Sumter, where supplies were running out and a feverish South Carolina was panting for war. General Winfield Scott, veteran of the Mexican War and Lincoln's most senior military officer, recommended evacuation. Scott had previously written to Seward suggesting that it would be unwise, if not impossible, to subdue the South by force of arms, and if he were in charge, his message to the Cotton States would be: "Wayward sisters, depart in peace!" The aged general pointed out that previous attempts to resupply the fort had drawn fire, and any effort to do so would surely provoke war. Scott felt so strongly he was prepared to circumvent his bellicose commander in chief. On March 11, he drafted an order instructing Anderson to evacuate the fort.

Lincoln was having none of it. The president counseled members of his cabinet on the wisdom of resupplying the fort. When all but one concurred with Scott on the imprudence of such a course of action, he went ahead anyway. Seward thought that it would instantly trigger war, and that it would drive the upper South and the border states into the Confederacy. Others advised Lincoln to defer to his generals, adding that the North would look like the aggressor in any war thus commenced. Salmon P. Chase, secretary of the Treasury and a future chief justice, said, "Let the South go." Only the postmaster general, Montgomery Blair, shared the president's appetite for war.

Irked by these reactions, Lincoln dispatched a secret envoy to Charleston, to test the mood on the ground. Was this a planters' conspiracy, or was there popular support for the impudent secession? The answer was plain. "There is no attachment to the Union," reported Lincoln's scout. Secession was an earnest reality. There were, he said, "hundreds of men delicately brought up, who never had done a day's work in their lives, yet who were out there on those islands throwing up entrenchments." The report seems to have destroyed Lincoln's last hope that "the Deep South would voluntarily return to the fold," notes Michael Burlingame, and his mood was not improved by the acquiescence of his party in the fait accompli of disunion. A leading Maine Republican told Lincoln that "the evacuation of Fort Sumpter will be fully approved by the entire body of Republicans in this State—and I doubt not in all the country." A wealthy Republican in New York advised him, "The public mind is fully prepared for the evacuation of Fort Sumpter." Similar counsel came from his home state of Illinois.

All of which makes the decision to send a supply boat to the imperiled fort remarkable for its audacity. By this point, Lincoln knew that such a move would provoke war, and it did. Lincoln told his old friend Orville Browning that it was his idea, and it had succeeded beyond expectation: "They attacked Sumter—it fell, and thus, did more service than it otherwise could." Having fallen to the Confederates, it provided a lightning rod for patriotic rage and the larger goal of reunion. Lincoln thanked the officer tasked with the aborted supply mission, noting that, on this occasion, failure was victory.

In the short term, he was right. Most Northerners, writes the historian David Williams, had opposed the war up to this point. Once it started, attitudes changed overnight, and only a handful of Americans saw that they had been played. Jersey City's *American Standard* castigated Lincoln for maneuvering the South into a war in which he was clearly the aggressor. His strategy of drawing the first fire from South Carolina was "a sham," "a mockery," and a transparent "pretext for letting loose the horrors of war." "With the facts before us," scolded the *Buffalo Daily Courier*, "we cannot believe that Mr. Lincoln intended that Sumter should be held. . . . War is inaugurated, and the design of the administration is accomplished." Or not. "I frankly say that my heart is not in the war which I see is to be thus commenced," confessed Major Anderson, the man at the center of the drama. Soldiers knew what zealots could not see: that no one wins a civil war.

II

Lincoln misread the enemy. Despite long conversations with Alexander Stephens, in which the Georgian begged him to understand that force would unite the slave states, Lincoln adhered to the "deluded masses" theory of Southern secession, which held that the people had been led astray by reckless demagogues and they could be wooed back into the Union. Perhaps so, but not by war. On April 4, a convention in Virginia had voted 89–45 against secession. When Lincoln demanded troops to suppress what was now officially a rebellion, the mood changed. A crowd in Richmond tore down the Stars and Stripes and hoisted a Confederate flag, and one more state joined the rebels.

In Baltimore, a mob attacked Union recruits passing through the city, and Maryland was prevented from voting for secession only by the arrest of pro-Confederate legislators. Lincoln's call for troops had a similar effect in Arkansas, Tennessee, and North Carolina, all of which cast their lot with Jefferson Davis. A rebellion of seven, headquartered in the obscurity of a hotel in Montgomery, Alabama, had grown to eleven, poised on the doorstep of the nation's capital. As Seward and countless journalists had predicted, instead of quashing the rebellion, Lincoln's threat of force turned friends into enemies. Robert E. Lee was a case in point. General Scott told Lincoln that Lee was the only man capable of leading his forces. Lee had opposed secession and said that there could be "no greater calamity . . . than the dissolution of the Union." But when the president came knocking, Lee refused to serve. He could not draw his sword against his people, or, as he sometimes put it, "my country." Lincoln had gambled on a patriotism that did not exist, and a version of Lee's dilemma played out across the South.

Robert Penn Warren's grandfather was a Union man from Kentucky who opposed slavery yet fought for the Confederacy nevertheless. Why? "You went with your people," he said. Blood was thicker than politics. Lincoln's aggression, argued Nathaniel Hawthorne in a scathing article in *The Atlantic Monthly,* had "converted crowds of honest people into traitors." There was, he said, no question that "thousands of warm-hearted, sympathetic, and impulsive persons have joined the Rebels, not from any zeal for the cause, but because, between two conflicting loyalties, they chose that which necessarily lay nearest the heart." Indeed, he suggested, "there never existed any other Government against which treason was so easy, and could defend itself by such plausible arguments as against that of the United States." Lincoln's error was to believe that men would rally to the abstraction of a nation, or "an airy mode of law," rather than the binding affections of "the altar and the hearth." It was the very scenario of which the antifederalists warned in 1787. Lincoln was asking people to sacrifice their families to a flag. Was it any surprise that these sullen rebels refused? "In the vast extent of our country—too vast by far to be taken into one small human heart—we inevitably limit to our own State, or, at farthest, to our own section, that sentiment of physical love for the soil," reasoned the novelist. This was the fallacy of the war.

Hawthorne was pilloried, but he was just saying what had been widely acknowledged before the fighting began, and what was evidently true of the South. "What do I care for patriotism?" said a woman in South Carolina, disdainful of Abraham Lincoln and Jefferson Davis alike. "My husband is my country. What is country to me, if he be killed?" Early in the war, a Union squad closed in on a ragged young Confederate, who obviously didn't own slaves and surely had no interest in the Constitution. "What are you fighting for anyhow?" they asked him. "I'm fighting because you're down here," he replied.

In Fredericksburg, Virginia, Jane Howison Beale was astonished by the attitude of Union soldiers who thrust their "unwelcome presence upon us" and then expressed surprise "not to find more Union feeling among us." What did they expect? "They must be most profoundly ignorant of the moral science of causes and effects to suppose that love for the 'Union' can be produced and cultivated by the persecutions to which we have been subjected," she wrote. "All history—all human experience teaches that those who suffer the tyranny of unjust warfare, learn to cling with a devotion to their principles that they would never have felt under milder influences." She did not think the Southern people would form an exception to the rule.

The point was sometimes made from the other side. The war, noted the Union soldier William Thompson Lusk in a letter to his mother, seemed to bring out "the most devilish propensities" in the men in blue. It might have been necessary "to use severe measures to bring deluded men to a sense of their errors," he granted. "Still I think, were low ignorant ruffians to visit my home while I was away fighting, burn my house, lay waste my property, insult mother and sisters, beggar the little children I might love, taunt the gray hairs I might respect, leave starvation in the place of plenty, I should feel singularly strengthened in my early delusion." Yet this was "a truthful picture" of what the administration meant "by a vigorous prosecution of the war." Lusk had little confidence in Lincoln or his advisers. "Abe has put down his big clumsy foot," he wrote, "and God help us!"

When General Benjamin Butler ordered the execution of William B. Mumford for tearing down a Union flag in New Orleans, and authorized his men to treat the women of the city as prostitutes, should their insults continue, he did not so much confirm a Confederate nationalism as create one. Winfield Scott had warned, "If the objective of the war is the reconstruction of the Union, if our enemies of today are to become our compatriots, it is impolitic to alienate them unduly." But war had its own proclivity. Defeat for the Union army at Bull Run in July 1861 had banished all hope of a short and cleansing triumph. From there, the war descended into a rhythm of industrial slaughter. New weapons, old tactics, and a seemingly limitless supply of manpower. These were not soldiers; they were boys. Their guns belonged to the nineteenth century, but their generals were living in the age of the saber and the bayonet charge. Before the new, rifled muskets, men melted like snow. In two days of fighting at Shiloh, the United States sustained more casualties than in all previous wars combined; Grant had to plan his operations under a tree to escape the shrieks of his men as limbs were amputated in the tents.

Ambrose Bierce recalled men choking on their own blood; men left with brains oozing from shattered skulls. He described soldiers turning in panic as they disembarked from the steamboats and surveyed the terror to which they had been summoned. But as Bierce grimly reported, "The death which they would not meet at the hands of the enemy they will meet at the hands of their officers." Deserters were shot with the same demented fury that greeted the rebels. "Humanity . . . is not made for this," he wrote. Even the trees seemed to shudder in disbelief, their leaves curling in the heat of a premature summer. The casualties at Shiloh rivaled the deadliest battles of the Napoleonic Wars, but this was just the beginning. Twenty such battles would be fought before the war's end. As the field nurse Clara Barton remarked on the vastness of the suffering, "It has come that man has no longer an individual existence but is counted in thousands and measured in miles."

It was after Shiloh that the administration moved from a "limited" to a "total-war philosophy," in which boundaries between soldiers and noncombatants dissolved and destruction occurred "on a massive scale." "I gave up all idea of saving the Union except by complete conquest," said Ulysses S. Grant after the battle, and Lincoln embraced the paradox. In the contorted parlance of the administration, the Confederates were at once a mortal enemy and the unsevered members of an unbroken union. Which would it be?

"I shall not surrender this game leaving any available card unplayed," declared Lincoln, as he approved a new set of measures designed to "maul" the rebels. Lincoln replaced dithering traditionalists, squeamishly beholden to the West Point Code, with ruthless warriors, unmoved by blood. General George B. McClellan had a well-earned reputation for arrogance and indecision, but there was a reason the soldiers loved him: He hated to see them killed. "I'm tired of the sickening sight of the battlefield with its mangled corpses and poor suffering wounded," he wrote. "Victory has no charms for me when purchased at such cost." Lincoln quickly saw that he would win nothing with men like McClellan. In Philip Sheridan, William Tecumseh Sherman, and Grant, he had the marbled antithesis. Grant's distinguishing quality as a general, thought Mary Todd Lincoln, was that he had "no regard for life." "He is a butcher," she said. "He loses two men to the enemy's one." And that, said his friend and admirer Sherman, was the nature of the beast. "War is cruelty and you cannot refine it," he advised, as he prepared to make Georgia howl. "We are not only fighting hostile armies, but a hostile people," he reasoned, "and we must make old and young, rich and poor, feel the hard hand of war."

The effects were instant. "Our men now believe they have a perfect right to rob, tyrannize, threaten & maltreat any one they please," said a Union general, after Lincoln authorized new penalties for those found guilty of "aiding, countenancing, or abetting" the enemy—which could be anyone. A European observer said that the new Northern war policy had "cast mankind two centuries back toward barbarism." Hard war meant the plundering of homes, the annihilation of crops, and the violation of bodies. While "hard war tactics did not sanction the rape of white women," notes the historian Elizabeth Varon, Black women were the constant targets of sexual assault, and the taboo surrounding whites was often broken. "Instances are reported of deeds of violence perpetrated upon respectable ladies . . . which are without a parallel save in the annals of the infamous Yankee race," raged one indignant Southerner. In Selina, Tennessee, the Union major Thomas J. Jordan told a group of local women that "they had better sew up the bottoms of their petticoats," if they were going to persist in their truculence. Such events would not be forgotten.

Everyone had "a tale of horror," reported one woman. And these, she seethed, "are the people we have been led to believe were so much in advance, and so much better, than us poor ignorant Southern people in morals, and manners, education, piety, sobriety, and every Christian virtue. I can only say deliver me from such." A Tennessee infantryman issued the same protest: "Submission has been made impossible by the conduct of our insolent foe, and the only tolerable alternative left us is resistance to the bitter end. We must fight, we can do nothing else, if necessary forever." You can kill us, said a woman in South Carolina, but we will never be subdued.

Yet Lincoln had one more card to play.

III

Although ending slavery was no part of Lincoln's agenda in 1861, the outbreak of war delivered a surge of hope to the abolitionists. The prospect of crushing slavery, and the release of emotions uneasily contained over a generation, turned pacifists into warriors, and skeptics into patriots. To support a war for union, wrote Wendell Phillips shortly before it began, he would have to "start anew with a new set of political principles, and admit that my life has been a mistake." But this he did. Within a week of the bombardment of Fort Sumter, the famed orator was standing on a platform in Boston, "profusely decorated with the Stars and Stripes," preaching the gospel of war. "I rejoice," he said, "that now, for the first time in my antislavery life, I speak under the stars and stripes, and welcome the tread of Massachusetts men marshalled for war." At last, he proclaimed, "abolitionist is merged in citizen, in American." The struggle was between barbarism and civilization, and such could only be settled by guns. What words had begun, "the muskets of Illinois and Massachusetts can finish up."

It was a stunning reversal, but he was destined for disappointment. Like Douglass, Greeley, and Sumner, Phillips implored Lincoln to include a plan to end slavery within his war measures. When Greeley challenged the president to take a more definite position, in August 1862, Lincoln replied to a rival newspaper with words that chilled abolitionist hearts. His paramount object was to save the Union, and he would do it with or without freeing slaves. Lincoln did not merely state the point: He drove it home in a way that made the abolition of slavery sound like an adolescent preoccupation, next to the hard and eternal work of saving the Union. He made the slaves sound like pawns in a much larger game. "If I could save the Union without freeing any slave I would do it, and if I could save it by freeing all the slaves I would do that," he wrote with imperious nonchalance. "What I do about slavery, and the colored race, I do because I believe it helps to save the Union," he added, without a single reference to Congress, the cabinet, or the will of the people. In two short paragraphs, Lincoln used the word "I" thirty-five times. But it was the message that enraged Phillips. He called it "the most disgraceful document that ever came from the head of a free people."

Lincoln was, of course, speaking to a larger audience, priming them to believe that any subsequent moves on behalf of the enslaved were soundly patriotic and military decisions. This was not a time to lose the support of slaveholders in the still-loyal border states. Yet Phillips and Douglass were right to perceive a tragic dissonance in this rhetoric of union. There was truth, as well as strategy, in Lincoln's grinding insistence that the real issue was to put down the rebellion. However eloquent he could be on the subject, the slave question remained a means to an end. Servants in freedom, as well as bondage.

Emancipation was a self-driven affair; something seized, not granted. It began when enslaved people took advantage of the dislocation of war to elude their captors, fleeing in hundreds to Union lines. The problem was significant enough for Jefferson Davis to alter the terms of the Confederacy's conscription laws, to relieve anyone who owned more than twenty slaves from military service. Welcomed by the more enterprising of Lincoln's generals as "contraband of war," fugitive slaves quickly became the magic ingredient of the Northern war effort—knowledge, manpower, and finally soldiers themselves. Robert Small's decision to steer a Confederate warship into Union waters, without a shot fired in anger, was one of many instances of African American valor.

Inspired by such events, and harried by the abolitionists, Lincoln decided to make a statement, throwing the weight of his administration behind this initially subversive process of self-emancipation. Ridiculed in the foreign press for applying *only* to territories where Lincoln held no executive power, the Emancipation Proclamation nevertheless marked a turning point in a desperate and failing war. "I never saw joy before," said Douglass, as he recalled the moment on January 1, 1863, when news rippled through a meeting in Boston that Lincoln had signed the proclamation. "These are the times foretold by the Prophets," declared a Freedmen's Convention in Wilmington, North Carolina, "when a Nation shall be born in a day."

Suddenly the war had meaning, and the prospect of success. It was in this context that Lincoln spoke of nobly saving "the last best hope of earth"—even if the sentiment was blunted by his continuing advocacy of colonization. Douglass had always resented the cant and cajolery of providence, openly deriding Lincoln's announcement of a national fast in October 1861, to petition "Divine Aid" for Union victory. A national day of prayer, without a word on the national crime of slavery, was "an abomination," he said. Now that Lincoln had spoken, Douglass swallowed his doubts. He had once smiled at phrases like "manifest destiny," he confessed, but he could now say with confidence that it was "the manifest destiny of this war to unify and reorganize the institutions of the country." Such was "the sacred significance" of the struggle: "national regeneration." "The Negro had passed along from a loyal spade and pickax to a Springfield rifle," and pro-slavery generals were forced to eat their words. The war was a revolution, and one that would complete "our glory as a nation."

Charles Sumner, who thought that Lincoln had acted unconstitutionally in starting the war, now spoke in a different key. The skies were brighter and the air purer, now that slavery had been "handed over to judgment." Today, he said, "the glorious flag of the Union . . .

becomes the flag of Freedom." And Sumner, who had lacerated the doctrine of manifest destiny and the absurdity of trying to "conquer a peace," now adopted the same expression as he clamored for total subjugation. "If blood must be shed, better for a year than for an age," he asserted. "With victory will come conciliation, clemency, amnesty. But first victory." "We conquer for liberty everywhere," he said. "In saving the Republic we shall save civilization," declared the once-pacifist Sumner. "All who die for country now, die also for humanity. Wherever they lie, in bloody fields, they will be remembered as the heroes through whom the Republic was saved and civilization established forever."

Lincoln's Gettysburg Address was the supreme expression of this theological, world-saving account of the war, a statement glistening with images of life, healing, and salvation. Lincoln framed the war as the completion of the nation's mission of liberty, and the soldiers as its glorious martyrs. The war, he said, was the test of whether this nation, "or any nation so conceived," could endure. And the men who "gave their lives" for America died for all nations. Lincoln placed the war on a global footing, and hailed the victory as a giant step toward a democratic future: "We here highly resolve that these dead shall not have died in vain—that this nation, under God, shall have a new birth of freedom—and that government of the people, by the people, for the people, shall not perish from the earth." In two hundred words, Lincoln turned the blood and gore of the battlefield into something sacred and profound, marveled Garry Wills in a prizewinning homage. The Gettysburg Address "complete[d] the work of the guns" and "remade the nation."

Such was the myth—the "Lincoln legend," as H. L. Mencken termed it. Mencken felt that he was committing sacrilege as he parsed its meaning, fifty years later. He offered the usual tribute to Lincoln's poetry, which made "all the whoopings of the Websters [and] Sumners" sound positively silly. But he could not accept Lincoln's "doctrine" that this scene of slaughter was a moment of salvation. "Am I the first American to note the fundamental nonsensicality of the Gettysburg address?" he wondered. "Think of the argument in it!" The claim was that the soldiers "sacrificed their lives to the cause of self-determination" so that democracy would not "perish from the earth." This was more than poetic falsification, he countered: "It is difficult to imagine anything more untrue." The battle was fought to assert the power of the federal state over an unwilling people, and its practical effect was coercion and enduring hatred. Lincoln had a gift for making elegant phrases, ruminated Mencken. That did not mean they were true.

Mencken's critique recalls Benjamin Rush's point that it is easy to confuse the prestige of the state with the sovereignty of the people. "The humble but true origin of power in the people is often forgotten in the splendor and pride of governments," noted Rush. Lincoln frames the battle as an act of "devotion"—a willing sacrifice of young lives for the democratic principle—when the true agent, the real decision-maker, was Lincoln as commander in chief. He conflates victory in battle—whatever that meant on this occasion—with the triumph of freedom. This, argued Randolph Bourne during another war for democracy, was a category error and a blunder. "War is the health of the state," he famously contended. It strengthens the government and the structures of power. Everything else is blown into oblivion. In a sermon delivered a week after the Gettysburg Address, a preacher in Maryland struck a more skeptical note: "When victories mean nothing but wholesale slaughter . . . the victory mainly ascertained by measurement of blood and calculation of corpses, I fail to see in it the occasion of thanksgiving to God."

Most of the "men" who fought at Gettysburg were there under some degree of coercion, both sides having resorted to conscription to replace enormous losses and to stem the flow of desertions. By 1863, 25 percent of the Union army consisted of immigrants, many of whom did not speak English and could hardly have subscribed to the president's narrative of redemption. After the battle, several thousand rifles were recovered with unfired cartridges, rounds loaded backward, and other deliberate or accidental blunders sufficient to put the weapon out of action. It was quite common, note the historians David Goldfield and David Williams, for soldiers to shoot off a finger or perform other acts of self-mutilation to spare themselves the terror of combat. These men did not give their lives for the Union; they were given. "Rarely," writes Williams, "has any nation so widely and willfully slaughtered its own youth."

Meanwhile, those who contested the administration's war policy faced arrest and martial law. In a speech delivered to the House of Representatives in January 1863, the Ohio congressman Clement Vallandigham disputed the logic of union by conquest. "Union is consent, and good-will, and fraternal affection. War is force, hate, revenge," he said. It was a "monstrous delusion" to think that the South could be "whipped back into love and fellowship at the point of the bayonet." "Causeless it may have been; wicked it may have been," secession was a fact, and one that deserved "to be dealt with by statesmen as a fact." Instead, Lincoln was spilling blood like water and sending his critics to jail. "There has been nothing like it since the Crusades."

Four months later, the war came for Vallandigham. He was arrested for a speech deemed to express treasonable sympathy with "the enemy," tried and convicted by a military commission, and banished from the country. Vallandigham wound up in Canada, where he ran for governor of Ohio in absentia. "Must I shoot a simple-minded soldier boy who deserts, while I must not touch a hair of a wily agitator who induces him to desert?" pleaded Lincoln, in defense of his severity. But Vallandigham was a congressman, not an agitator, and he said nothing that could be construed as an inducement to desert. His crime was to challenge an administration sliding into despotism under a messianic creed of patriotism.

What about the Thirteenth Amendment, the abolition of slavery? Surely this was the redemption of which Douglass spoke. In his second inaugural address, delivered in March 1865, Lincoln interpreted the war's violence as divine punishment for 250 years of slavery, suggesting that it was God's will that "every drop of blood drawn with the lash shall be paid by another drawn with the sword." With the balance now even, the nation could move on to a just and lasting peace—"with malice toward none, [and] charity for all." Apart from the presumption of ascribing his own actions to a supernatural power, this notion that peace was going to spring like a flower over the graves of "these honored dead" was a fantasy.

Like Douglass, Lincoln sometimes proposed that the very act of fighting would generate respect for African Americans, that war itself was the crucible of freedom. "There will," he promised, "be some black men who can remember that, with silent tongue, and clenched teeth, and steady eye, and well-poised bayonet, they have helped mankind on to this great consummation." He did not consider the more prosaic possibility that war might inflame, not assuage, racial animosities and that freedom won by gunpowder may last only as long as that transient commodity.

"Whoever may be benefitted by the results of this war," warned Hawthorne, in his caustic *Atlantic Monthly* article, "it will not be the present generation of negroes"—a position he still held seven months after the Emancipation Proclamation. "You cannot possibly conceive . . . how little the North really cares for the negro-question," he wrote to Elizabeth Peabody, in July 1863. Indeed, the sense that Black people were somehow the cause of the war exposed them to outrages hitherto unknown outside the Cotton Kingdom. Lincoln's conscription act, which exempted wealthy whites capable of paying the three-hundred-dollar fee, triggered riots in several cities, including three days of atrocities in New York, where white mobs hanged and burned Black people with frenzied brutality. In Philadelphia, *The Christian Recorder* observed a rapid deterioration of racial relations since the coming of the war. It was, mourned the editor, "almost impossible for a respectable colored person to walk the streets without being insulted."

Reflecting on such events many years later, Douglass had no doubt that some of the responsibility lay with the president. "'The Negroes were the cause of the war,' said Mr. Lincoln, and straightway the loyal soldiers of the Republic began to kick and beat the poor Negroes on the banks of the Potomac," he alleged. "It is dangerous even to a dog to be given a bad name."

The occasion to which Douglass referred was an "audience" with colored men at the White House, in August 1862, where Lincoln canvassed their support for the colonization of Americans "of African descent" in Liberia and Central America. In an unbroken monologue, reported in excruciating detail in the *New-York Tribune,* Lincoln urged that "we are different races. We have between us a broader difference than exists between almost any other two races," and whether this was strictly fair, both races paid a price. While the Negro race had been wronged, "ours suffer from your presence," he explained. And "even when you cease to be slaves, you are yet far removed from being placed on an equality with the white race," he said, as if this were an immutable reality. There was "an unwillingness on the part of our people, harsh as it may be, for you free colored people to remain with us." So he asked them to leave. "But for your race among us there could not be war," he said, "although many men engaged on either side do not care for you one way or the other." It was a stunning analysis, and Lincoln did not ask so much as tell: "For the sake of your race you should sacrifice something of your present comfort for the purpose of being as grand in that respect as the white people," meaning that grandeur would be gained in emigration.

Lincoln's admission that neither side "care[s] for you one way or the other," and his solicitude for the nation over the chimera of equality, was the sum and substance of the war. Lincoln sold emancipation as a war measure, with a guile that historians continue to applaud. Yet that is what it was. Changing perceptions of the war's meaning did not change the reality: a struggle for union in which Black Americans were the means, not the end. The conduct of the Union army toward fugitives who could not shoulder a musket spoke more loudly than the rhetoric of redemption. When Sherman's army swept through Georgia, hundreds of slaves fled their plantations, hoping to find refuge with the conquering army. As Sherman's men crossed Ebenezer Creek near Savannah, on December 9, 1864, with Confederate cavalry in hot pursuit, they pulled up their pontoon bridges, leaving more than five hundred terrified refugees stranded on the opposite bank. Some were shot down by Confederate soldiers; others jumped into the swollen river, with children on their backs, and drowned. Survivors were rounded up and sent back to their owners. "Where," wondered an appalled Union soldier, "can you find in all the annals of plantation cruelty anything more completely inhuman and fiendish than this?"

Such expressions of sympathy, notes David Williams, were rare among white Union soldiers, who blamed not just slavery but slaves themselves for the war. The historian William Gilmore Simms called the soldiers who sacked Columbia "monsters of virtuous pretension," waving their "banner of streaks and spangles" as they set fire to the city. He also cited "outrages of [an] unmentionable character" practiced upon women in the suburbs. Two "young negresses" were drowned in a puddle after one such assault. It was a cycle of violence from which nobody was spared. Two months after the burning of Columbia, Lincoln was assassinated by a dashing agent of Southern vengeance, a famous actor whom he had once invited to the White House. On April 9, 1865, Lee surrendered to Grant at Appomattox, in scenes of stoic gentility. But the war was not over. It had decades to run its course.

IV

"The real war will never get into the books," mused Walt Whitman, in one of many moments of abject despondency. He could not have known how faithfully the books would honor the prophecy. In the morality play of conventional history, the "Copperheads"—Northern Democrats who opposed the war—are villains and traitors; Lincoln, an unflappable sage. But the Copperheads knew something that Lincoln had forgotten: that the means must be consistent with the end. The claim that the loss of seven Southern states would signal the destruction of our government, argued Alexander Long, in April 1864, was unsustainable, and hardly grounds for war, when so much of the country opposed it.

What was true was that three years of brutal warfare had decimated the democratic principles that the president claimed to defend. Lincoln had governed "by dictatorial power," closing newspapers and arresting opponents, and he had destroyed whatever Union sentiment might have remained among the Southern people, creating "eight million bitter enemies upon the American continent." The words "Shiloh, Antietam, Gettysburg, Murfreesboro,

Richmond, Vicksburg, and Fort Donelson," said the congressman, "are words of division and disunion, and will serve to bring emotions of eternal hate." The nature of war was to "cut and cleave asunder, but never to unite." Oaths of allegiance could mean nothing under such circumstances. Like Galileo humoring the papacy with a strategic retraction, the Confederate leaders will renounce their heresies but hold other ideas in their hearts.

James A. Garfield, who had served as a major general in the Union army and was now representing Ohio in the House of Representatives, rose to accuse Long of treason. Yet all of these charges were fair. By the war's end, fourteen thousand Americans had been jailed for opposing the administration, denied legal redress after Lincoln suspended the writ of habeas corpus. Historians have praised Lincoln for holding a free and fair election in the maelstrom of a civil war. But it was hardly a fair fight when so many critics had been removed from the fray. Long's basic point was precisely the one made by Thomas Hobbes when he asserted the difference between military and political power. "He that is slain is overcome, but not conquered," Hobbes famously remarked, "for he is still an enemy." For Hobbes, and the whole tradition of the social contract, power rests on consent, and the degree to which it is forced is the degree to which it is lost. The sword of the state hovers in the background, but it is a bluff that is rarely called. "All governments rest on opinion," wrote James Madison, and "it is the reason of the public alone that ought to control and regulate the government."

Lincoln's declaration of war outside that framework, in advance of congressional approval, averred Lysander Spooner, was a catastrophic error. Lincoln's claim to have done it all in the service of democracy was akin to a champion of religious liberty embracing the methods of the Spanish Inquisition. "If the successors of Roger Williams . . . had taken to burning heretics with a fury never before seen," protested the abolitionist, the inconsistency would not have been greater than "this astonishing absurdity" of waging war "to establish, 'a government of consent' "—that is, "one to which everybody must consent, or be shot." Lincoln's principle was that "men may rightfully be compelled to submit to, and support, a government that they do not want; and that resistance, on their part, makes them traitors and criminals." It was all so glib, reductive, and unnatural.

Treason implied deceit. A traitor was someone who professes friendship while secretly betraying that trust. Secession was no such thing. Men of the North brayed that "they have 'Saved the Country!' That they have 'Preserved our Glorious Union!' " They failed to see that there could be no "Union, glorious or inglorious, that was not voluntary." A government that could shoot and hang men as traitors for "refusing to surrender . . . to its arbitrary will" was a despotism, not a democracy, and its boasted "peace" was a mirage. The claim that the war was fought for the abolition of slavery, added Spooner, was a pious fraud. The government freed the Black man because it wanted him to fight; then it dropped him like a stone. If the object had been to destroy slavery, the North could have put its own house in order by offering freedom to anyone who entered its gates. Slavery would "have been abolished at once," and perhaps "a million" lives would have been spared. But the motive was power, not freedom, and in the end neither was gained.

This was harsh but fair. The war claimed one in four men of fighting age in the South, leaving countless others wounded, maimed, and scarred. Less than 10 percent of these men owned slaves. Figures released in 2012 indicate an overall death toll of 752,000, equivalent to 10 million, as a proportion of today's population. "It is very difficult for us to appreciate the fact that we have suddenly become not only a military, but a warlike people," lamented a clergyman in Baltimore. The war had made Americans "indifferent to the value of life."

After Union victory at Vicksburg, Mississippi, on July 4, 1863, the Stars and Stripes waved triumphantly over the town square, and Lincoln rejoiced that "the father of waters again goes unvexed to the sea." The Fourth of July would not be celebrated in Vicksburg again for eighty-one years. "They first cut our throats, then send us an adhesive plaster," raged William Gilmore Simms, from the ashes of Columbia. The war, wrote David Goldfield, was like a ghost that roamed the land seeking vindication and retribution: "an event without temporal boundaries, an interminable struggle that has generated perhaps as many casualties since its alleged end in 1865 as during the four preceding years when armies clashed on the battlefield." The target of that retribution was the freedman. "As the war for the Union recedes into the past, and the negro is no longer needed to assault forts and stop rebel bullets, he is in some sense of less importance," mourned Douglass. "Peace with the old master class has been war for the negro," he said. "As the one has risen, the other has fallen. The reaction has been sudden, marked, and violent."

It does not belittle the magnitude of the Thirteenth Amendment to say that without political rights or physical protection from white terror the abolition of slavery was a Pyrrhic victory. If the "cornerstone" of the Confederacy was, as Alexander Stephens put it, "the great truth that the negro is not equal to the white man," the war left the foundation intact, and possibly renewed. The doctrine of Lincoln's second inaugural, that punishment would bring penitence and peace, was essentially theological: a mysticism of redemption in which division is swallowed in sacrifice. It was the old Puritan belief that God will not let his anointed come to shame. God had never forsaken "his almost chosen people," declared Lincoln shortly before the fighting began. The American Revolution, he said in a phrase almost lifted from George Bancroft, "held out a great promise to all the people of the world to all time to come."

Yet faith was no substitute for reason. Lincoln's patriotism seems to have blinded him to the scale of the division and the poverty of his chosen instrument of war. The antebellum South, writes the historian Edward Baptist, was a world of unexampled brutality, where "white people inflicted torture far more often than in almost any human society that ever existed." The idea that such a society could be healed by more violence was fanciful. Lincoln hailed Louisiana's new constitution as providing better conditions for Black citizens than Illinois, and one of his generals rejoiced that slavery was now more likely to appear in Rhode Island than the Bayou State. This was the delusion, the myth of redemptive violence. "The problem after a war is with the victor," wrote the twentieth-century pacifist A. J. Muste. "He thinks he has just proved that war and violence pay." He soon finds that hearts are harder to win than battles.

"There is little difference between the Antebellum South and the New South," wrote Ida B. Wells, almost thirty years after the Confederate defeat. In the course of a decade, Nathan Bedford Forrest went from slave trader to Confederate general to the first grand wizard of the Ku Klux Klan. Forrest claimed to have killed more men, in hand-to-hand combat, than any other soldier in the war, and he presided over the Fort Pillow Massacre, in which hundreds of Black Union soldiers were stabbed and clubbed to death after they had surrendered. A state park still bears his name. Every time a white Southerner encountered a freedman, writes Goldfield, he saw his defeat. Every time a freedman saw a statue of Nathan Bedford Forrest, he saw his own.

Lynching was a communal crime, an exemplary terror, encouraged by the "leading citizens" of the South, noted Wells. Even slavery returned under such names as the convict lease system, in Georgia, where floggings were frequent and sometimes fatal. The harsh truth, averred Douglass in a speech marking the twenty-sixth anniversary of emancipation in the District of Columbia, was that the Negro "is worse off, in many respects, than when he was a slave." "Though he is nominally free he is actually a slave." As Joseph C. Price, a young Black educator, put it, in words redolent of Hobbes, "The South was more conquered than convinced" by the Civil War; "it was overpowered rather than fully persuaded." The Confederacy conceded the war at Appomattox, not "its convictions." Robert Penn Warren expressed the point more sharply. The Civil War was "a crime of monstrous inhumanity"—a reckless endeavor that created "a South more southern than before," and one that duly abandoned those it claimed to have liberated. The Gettysburg doctrine, about a war that saved the Union, was "the biggest lie any nation ever told itself."

Yet minds were always changing, even in those sanctuaries of New England virtue. Julia Ward Howe, who penned the words of the "Battle Hymn of the Republic," began to wonder if the whole thing had been a ghastly mistake. After the war, she became a pacifist and the leading spirit behind the establishment of Mother's Day as an international day of peace. She would take nothing away from the brave men who died, but the Civil War was conducted by men seduced by "the military method" and blind to its inherent flaws. War was "mutual murder," she now believed, and no basis for a just and peaceful world. In this, she was not alone. Howe became a symbol of a new patriotism, which would flourish in the twentieth century: a patriotism of peace. It would not defeat the old, martial variety. But it would offer new ways to be an American.

CHAPTER 4

A Nation of Nations: The Patriotism of Peace

How can patriotism be a virtue in our time, when it demands . . . not the recognition of the equality and brotherhood of all men, but the recognition of one state and nationality as predominating over all the others?

—TOLSTOY, *CHRISTIANITY AND PATRIOTISM*

We must perpetrate the paradox that our American cultural tradition lies in the future.

—RANDOLPH BOURNE, "TRANS-NATIONAL AMERICA"

William Lloyd Garrison was in no mood for fireworks. Reconstruction was on the brink of collapse, the federal government was mired in scandal, and both parties were ready to abandon the freedmen of the South. Garrison had just turned seventy, he had recently lost his wife to pneumonia, and now, on July 4, 1876, he was expected to celebrate the nation's hundredth birthday. While neighbors frolicked, Garrison secreted himself in his study, in

Roxbury, Massachusetts, where he assembled the only kind of explosive he knew.

Garrison's "Centennial Reflections" appeared two days later, in the *Independent*—a progress report on the American experiment. It seemed churlish to disdain the festivities, he confessed, but this urge "to burn incense to the memories of the famous dead" was unhealthy and demoralizing. Breathless tributes to "our Revolutionary fathers" were at once tedious and debilitating, holding Americans in a perpetual childhood. The Declaration of Independence was a radical document, destroying all hereditary and dynastic pretensions at a stroke, but its seed was blighted by the "shameless inconsistencies" of the Constitution and the men who drafted it. The founders were heirs of a revolutionary tradition but cold and recusant to their creed. Jefferson owned slaves all his life, making no provision to free them after he died. Washington did slightly better on that score, but he too was an unrepentant slaveholder who preached liberty with a forked tongue. "On what ground is he to be exempted from the application of the moral law?" wondered Garrison. The answer was patriotism. Washington's status as the "father" of the nation shielded him from scrutiny and burdened the country with an ugly paradox, and "the nation has never repented of its great transgression."

Even now, after the "slaughter of hundreds of thousands" in a bloody civil war, the inconsistency remained. Slavery had been abolished as a military necessity, not a moral principle, and the South was still brutal to the race it once held in chains. The freedmen had a majority in South Carolina, Mississippi, and Louisiana, noted Garrison, but their advantages would be annihilated in the coming election "by the bludgeon, bowie-knife, and pistol." If that were not enough, at this very hour of jubilee, "our troops are eager in slaughtering as many 'red skins' as possible" on the Western plains, "and their extermination is regarded as only a question of time."

Yet it was still an article of faith among educated Americans that the United States was a uniquely virtuous nation, and that all peoples were being drawn to its example. "What throne has yet been shaken in consequence of our example?" inquired Garrison. None—because we are yet to honor "those fundamental principles and self-evident truths." If there were a miracle to embrace on this noisy anniversary, it was that the Almighty had not "utterly consumed" so arrogant and guilty a people.

At least one reader thought the editorial was in poor taste. A gentle rebuke arrived in the mail from his son Wendell Phillips Garrison, who thought this was not the time to throw stones. Whatever their failings, men like Jefferson and Washington were models of decency, whose example could lift "the country from the curse of political corruption [and] public dishonesty."

The patriarch was unmoved. He was sickened by all the "gush" and "glorification," and he wished people could see how the praise conduced to complacency. Decent or otherwise, the founders were "too cowardly" to adhere to their principles, and "they entailed upon their posterity as great a curse as could be inflicted upon any people."

Both Garrisons had a point. The abolitionist was right to interrogate the authorized version of the Civil War and to expose the way patriotism continued to oil the wheels of oppression. But Wendell was surely entitled to his exasperation with the prophetic idiom and his inclination to retrieve rather than condemn. In that, he was more typical of the practical instincts of the Progressive Era, when reformers and social radicals, such as William Jennings Bryan, Jane Addams, and Randolph Bourne, would seek to reclaim rather than reject the patriotic spirit for a more just and peaceable world. For them, the American heritage was wider and richer than the canonical utterances of the founders, and it included people like William Lloyd Garrison himself. Theirs was an attitude at once internationalist and proud of America as an alternative to the war machines of Europe, in theory if not always in practice. Although their struggles to prevent the United States from entering on a career of empire were unsuccessful, they developed profound ways of thinking about America and its place in the world: a patriotism of the future, not the bloodstained past.

I

In the short term, Garrison's gripe that patriotism is the disposition to overlook criminality seemed to be justified. In the West, the Indian Wars raged unabated as Lincoln's triumvirate of generals drove the Plains Indians off their lands with appeals to manifest destiny and the newly hallowed methods of total war. As Sheridan rationalized the policy in a letter to Sherman in 1873, "If a village is attacked and women and children killed, the responsibility is not with the soldiers but with the people whose crimes necessitated the attack. During the war did any one hesitate to attack a village or town occupied by the enemy because women or children were within its limits? Did we cease to throw shells into Vicksburg or Atlanta because women and children were there?" Sherman was in total agreement: "We must act with vindictive earnestness against the Sioux, even to their extermination, men, women, and children."

In the South, white supremacy was expertly reengineered under a discourse of providence and national reconciliation. In *The Souls of Black Folk,* W. E. B. Du Bois described the "practical reenslavement" of the freedmen in the decades after the war. "The former slaves were intimidated, beaten, raped, and butchered by angry and revengeful men," and the courts used every method of ingenuity to reduce them "to serfdom." There was scarcely a white man in the South who did not regard emancipation as a mistake and its nullification as a duty, he wrote. "For this much all men know: despite compromise, war, and struggle, the Negro is not free. In the backwoods of the Gulf States, for miles and miles, he may not leave the plantation of his birth; in well-nigh the whole rural South the black farmers are peons, bound by law and custom to an economic slavery, from which the only escape is death or the penitentiary."

Should anyone have been surprised? This was as much the continuation as the betrayal of a war fought for union, not equality. With the exception of Radical Republicans, like Charles Sumner, and an army of New England schoolmarms, who descended in "calico dresses" to bring "the rhythm of the alphabet" to a gun-blasted terrain, Northern opinion was indifferent to the freedmen. After the war, there were three people in the South, "the Conqueror, the Conquered, and the Negro," and the last of these was forgotten before the guns fell silent. The speed with which the North washed its hands of the freedmen gave the lie to the heroic, liberationist account of the Civil War immortalized in the Gettysburg Address. Lincoln's earlier pledge, to save the Union with or without touching slavery, was the more faithful omen.

Southern leaders knew this, shrewdly appealing to Northern patriotism as they wove a fresh fabric of oppression. Southern intellectuals such as Henry W. Grady mounted a public relations campaign to end federal oversight of Dixie. Send us your money and your sons, he pleaded the power brokers of Boston and New York, but leave the "race problem" to us. Grady was a young, ebullient newspaper editor from Atlanta who became the face of the "New South" and a symbol of sectional reconciliation. In a series of deftly crafted speeches, he urged peace between North and South, on the basis of a shared commitment to the nation's providential destiny. "I always bet on sunshine in America," he told an audience in Virginia in 1889. God had "surely lodged the ark of His covenant" with the United States. Whatever our differences, the republic would endure. As Emerson had so wisely remarked, "Our whole history looks like the last effort by Divine Providence in behalf of the human race." Yet all of this was strategic. This happy future would be marked by "the clear and unmistakable domination of the white race."

At a banquet in Boston, where he shared a platform with Grover Cleveland and the industrial titan Andrew Carnegie, Grady turned on the charm before turning the screw. He spoke of a higher loyalty, breathed by God; a love that "trusts Georgia alike with Massachusetts—that knows no South, no North, no East, no West; but endears with equal and patriotic love every foot of our soil, every State of our Union." For "we, sir, are Americans," he announced, "and we fight for human liberty." Our history "has been a constant and expanding miracle from Plymouth Rock and Jamestown," and so it continues as "the wounds of war [are] healed in every heart." One nation—"compact, united, indissoluble in the bonds of love."

That is—all except "an ignorant and inferior race," which must never again be allowed to terrorize the good people of the South. "We wrested our State government from negro supremacy," reported Grady, while defending "the right of the whites to unite against this tremendous menace." Having established his patriotic credentials, Grady had the temerity to defend the work of vigilantes before the great and good of Boston. "If there is any human force that cannot be withstood, it is the power of the banded intelligence and responsibility of a free community," he said. "It is the inalienable right of every free community—and the just and righteous safeguard against an ignorant or corrupt suffrage." America had a glorious future, a divine calling. But votes for Negroes would squander the commission. Grady had just defended the Klan and ridiculed the Fifteenth Amendment, which guaranteed the right to vote, regardless of race. And he got away with it—by clothing himself in the flag.

"Never did oratory cover up the weak points of a repulsive cause more splendidly," scolded the Boston *Pilot*. "When all is said about it, the burden of Mr. Grady's eloquence meant the re-enslavement socially, if not legally, and forever, of the millions of black Americans in the South." This was a fair comment. None of these pieties prevented Southern journalists from blaming Black enfranchisement on the meddling of "white aliens from the North." Unity was a mirage. Nationalism was again the pale apology of a nation.

Grady's logic was precisely that of Thomas Dixon Jr. in his bestselling novel *The Clansman* and its cinematic incarnation, *The Birth of a Nation,* which took America by storm in 1915. In the book and the film, North and South are reconciled over the bleeding bodies of impudent Blacks, in a dismal version of what anthropologists have called "the scapegoat mechanism." Following a tawdry account of Reconstruction as Black aggression, viewers were treated to an orgy of vengeance, complete with plunging daggers set to the sound of Beethoven's Pastoral Symphony. Why had he called the movie *The Birth of a Nation* rather than *The Clansman*? someone asked the director, D. W. Griffith. "Because it is," he coolly replied. "The Civil War was fought fifty years ago. But the real nation has only existed in the last fifteen or twenty years. . . . The birth of a nation began . . . with the Ku Klux Klans, and we have shown that." The fact that the movie was greeted with such enthusiasm in cities like New York, where it ran for forty-four weeks at the unprecedented asking price of $2.20, showed how effortlessly North and South could bond around a myth of racial purity.

The Birth of a Nation is a racist epic, as most commentators agree. It is also an essay in the exclusionary potential of patriotism: "saving the nation" as a rationale for white supremacy, and white supremacy as the natural condition of a great nation. Framing Black power as a threat to the providential order, Griffith offered lynching as a national prerogative. The hideous practice had spread, noted Ida B. Wells, "till men in New York State, Pennsylvania and on the free Western plains feel they can take the law in their own hands with impunity."

If lynching was condoned under an "unwritten law" of personal honor, patriotism was part of the unwriting. In the closing decades of the nineteenth century, a surprising number of American thinkers were prepared to extol the virtues of lynch law, from the historian Frederick Jackson Turner to the aspiring statesman Theodore Roosevelt. The metaphysics had shifted from Calvinism to a crude and clumsy social Darwinism, but the idea was the same. Violence isn't violence when it is building a nation. As Garrison explained his "special abhorrence" for a resurgent doctrine of manifest destiny in 1871, no one is more dangerous than the man who knows history. But if providence was back and on the march, so was a calmer, humbler patriotism that wanted to be something before it marched anywhere.

II

The closing of the frontier in 1890 and the lightning pace of urbanization posed difficult questions for American character and identity. What is an American, when a single precinct in Chicago contains thirty-six nationalities? What is a man, when work means a desk and there are no more Indians to fight? Theodore Roosevelt had a solution: Build an empire. As assistant secretary of the navy in 1898, Roosevelt was instrumental in the prosecution of the Spanish-American War, which started with the liberation of Cuba and ended with the capture of the Philippines in 1902. In one of his most famous speeches, "The Strenuous Life," Roosevelt extolled war as adventure and imperialism as the rescue of a faded and enervated people—meaning his own. Expansion was America's duty and destiny. Opponents were cowards, prattlers, and weaklings. He had little patience for those who shrank from the task of governing the Philippines out of fear. He had "even scanter patience with those who make a pretense of humanitarianism to hide and cover their timidity, and who cant about 'liberty' and the 'consent of the governed,' in order to excuse themselves for their unwillingness to play the part of men." To condemn expansion was to condemn the *Mayflower* and the whole history of American settlement.

For Roosevelt, war was romance and nostalgia, though recent history loomed larger than the nation's founding. "Thank God for the iron in the blood of our fathers, the men who upheld the wisdom of Lincoln, and bore sword or rifle in the armies of Grant!" The nation owed much to its commercial giants, but "our debt is yet greater to the men whose highest type is to be found in a statesman like Lincoln, a soldier like Grant," he asserted. These were men of action and Roosevelt's models as he urged a policy of decision and will. Albert Beveridge, a senator from Indiana, offered a more theological case for empire, but he too drew on the memory of the Civil War. "Wonderfully has God guided us," he exulted. "Abraham Lincoln was His minister and His was the altar of freedom the Nation's soldiers set up on a hundred battlefields." For Beveridge, the flag was the argument; victory, its own defense. He who would oppose it was "an infidel to American power."

The Philippine War precipitated what the historian Jonathan Hansen has called a crisis of patriotism, in which the term was either rejected or reclaimed on terms more faithful to the nation's founding ideals. Was patriotism a martial sentiment, as the great Russian writer Leo Tolstoy argued: violent from the beginning? Or could patriotism be distinguished from nationalism—a love of country from a love of war?

In just over a year, America drove the Spanish from Cuba and the Philippines, acquired Puerto Rico and Guam, and then—to howls of astonishment—decided to hold on to the Philippine archipelago, beginning a three-year war to defeat the native independence movement led by Emilio Aguinaldo. This, in addition to the annexation of Hawaii in 1898, following the overthrow of Queen Lili'uokalani's government five years earlier. For a new band of anti-imperialists, such events represented a regression and a betrayal. "Is our national character so weak that we cannot withstand the temptation to appropriate the first piece of land that comes within our reach?" protested William Jennings Bryan in June 1898. "Our guns destroyed a Spanish fleet," he told a crowd in Omaha, Nebraska, "but can they destroy that self-evident truth that Governments derive their just powers, not from superior force, but from the consent of the governed?" In the same month, the Anti-Imperialist League was founded in Boston, and the question of imperialism dominated the presidential election of 1900. A fight for American identity was under way.

Bryan was the rare public figure whose popularity transcended that of his party: a mesmerizing orator who could speak in the language of the ordinary man. Bryan acquired the nickname the Great Commoner when he declined the offer of a private rail carriage on one of his campaigns, and he earned the Democratic presidential nomination in 1896 and 1900. The first of his campaigns will always be remembered for his image of the American farmer "crucified" on the dogmas of Wall Street. The second was a quest to save America from "the swaggering, bullying, brutal doctrine of imperialism."

Bryan invoked the founders against Roosevelt and democracy against empire. The Republicans pleaded commerce and the necessity of new markets, but it is "not necessary to own people in order to trade with them," responded Bryan. He placed "the philosophy of Franklin against the sordid doctrine" of those who would justify a war of conquest on the grounds that it would pay. If the Republicans would censure all opponents of conquest, "let them censure Jefferson," urged Bryan: Jefferson, who said that "if there be one principle more deeply rooted than any other in the mind of every American, it is that we should have nothing to do with conquest." Jefferson, who declared that conquest "is inconsistent with our government."

The forcible annexation of territory differed as sharply from the Louisiana Purchase, Bryan argued, "as a monarchy differs from a democracy." Indeed one of the reasons the founders disavowed conquest was the fear of standing armies: a symbol of monarchy and "the personification of force." A culture of "militarism will inevitably change the ideals of the people," he said, counting Washington among his witnesses. "In what respect does the position of the Republican party differ from the position taken by the English Government in 1776?" he wondered. "The Republican party has accepted the European idea and planted itself upon the ground taken by George III." The policy of expansion was "the doctrine of thrones."

Bryan's argument was patriotic in its appeal to the founders, but it rejected the Calvinist conceit that Americans stood on higher ground than foreign peoples. The Declaration of Independence said "all," not "some." It was inherently internationalist. He was "not willing to believe that an all-wise and an all-loving God created the Filipinos and then left them thousands of years helpless until the islands attracted the attention of European nations." Bryan cited a poet who described the terror that overcame a soldier who found that he had slayed his brother in battle. All nations needed to feel that terror, that horror of shedding blood. Some said it was our duty to hold the Philippine Islands. "It is our duty to avoid killing a human being," thundered the Commoner, "no matter where the human being lives or to what race or class he belongs." Bryan was taking on the master narrative of the chosen nation, in the name of liberty and equality. "When our opponents are unable to defend their position by argument," he observed, "they fall back upon the assertion that is destiny." This was twaddle and sacrilege to the deeply religious Bryan. "Destiny," he growled, "is the subterfuge of the invertebrate."

For the anti-imperialists, the idea that one had to support the government, whatever the government happened to do, was an absurdity. Before you agree to die for your country, William Everett advised the graduating class at Harvard in 1900, you need to know what your country is. Was it the soil? Was it the state, or the government of the day? No. The country is the nation, the people who choose the government, explained the philosopher. Militarism reversed the chain of command. It identified the country with the state rather than the people, and it turned citizens into subjects. General Grant confessed in his memoirs that he believed the Mexican War unjust from the beginning, yet he went and fought anyway, out of duty to his country. "I call this sentimental nonsense," responded Everett. When our government embarks on a reckless and unjust war, "it is our duty as patriots to say so."

William James, the preeminent American philosopher of his time, felt even more strongly. "I've lost my country," he wrote to a friend, on news of an American assault in the Philippines. This war against a weak and unoffending people brought James to his John Adams moment. "God damn the U.S. for its vile conduct in the Philippines!" he vented to the British philosopher F. C. S. Schiller in 1902. " 'Duty and Destiny' have rolled over us like a Juggernaut car," he told the New England Anti-Imperialist League, "and our outcries and attempts to scotch the wheels with our persons haven't acted in the least degree as a brake." James was astonished how quickly the war spirit had trounced democratic sentiment, leaving the anti-imperialist like an old man brandishing the Declaration of Independence in the face of a steam train. "Phrases repeated have a way of turning into facts," James observed, and the mantras of demagogues had become the truth of a nation. Lies had been excused, tortures whitewashed, massacres condoned. For James, this was the closing of an adolescence:

> We used to believe . . . that we were of a different clay from other nations, that there was something deep in the American heart that answered to our happy birth, free from that hereditary burden which the nations of Europe bear, and which obliges them to grow by preying on their neighbors. Idle dream! pure Fourth of July fancy, scattered in five minutes by the first temptation. In every national soul there lie potentialities of the most barefaced piracy, and our own American soul is no exception to the rule. Angelic impulses and predatory lusts divide our heart exactly as they divide the hearts of other countries. It is good to rid ourselves of cant and humbug, and to know the truth about ourselves.

The lesson, beyond the catharsis of disillusionment, was that political virtue does not follow geographical divisions. The division between right and wrong runs not between nations but *within* them—between those who would govern by force and brute possession and those who would move the world by reason and conscience. As resolute anti-imperialists, they were only the "American section" of an international movement, James reflected, "playing our part in the long, long campaign for truth and fair dealing which must go on in all the countries of the world until the end of time." It was the same struggle everywhere—"light against darkness, right against might, love against hate."

James was not rejecting patriotism: He was redefining it as a quest to save the country from delusions of grandeur. In a famous essay titled "The Moral Equivalent of War," James attempted to demilitarize American identity, blaming the catastrophe of the Philippines on the corruption of the national idea. For the swashbuckling imperialist, readiness for war is "the essence of nationality, and ability in it the supreme measure of the health of nations." This was a disastrous development and one that had to be fought on its own imaginative ground. The issue had reached far beyond moral reasoning or political calculation into the realm of the aesthetic, and it was here that it had to be contested. For it was the writer as much as the statesman who casts the spell, fattening the popular imagination on thoughts of war. "Dead men tell no tales," James somberly reflected. So the living must fill the void, meeting the romance of war with a poetry of peace. Reason can take us only so far in such a struggle, urged the philosopher. We need a different kind of patriot: someone who can say no to the crowd.

Who better than Jane Addams? Where most of the anti-imperialists looked back, with an indignant sense of "what would Jefferson do?" Addams looked forward to a day when nationalism would evolve into internationalism and patriotism would denote something larger than a willingness to fight. Hers was the most creative response to the imperial moment, and one that would define the struggle against American involvement in World War I. "Some of us," she told a meeting of anti-imperialists in April 1899, "were beginning to hope that we were getting away from the ideals set by the civil war, that we had made all the presidents we could from men who had distinguished themselves in that war, and were coming to seek another type of man." She wanted Americans "to be proud of our title as a peace nation; to recognize that the man who cleans a city is greater than he who bombards it, and the man who irrigates a plain greater than he who lays it waste."

Addams was the founder of the Hull House settlement in Chicago, and her commitment to peace grew out of her passion for justice. Armed with a Quaker ancestry and a deep affection for the teeming nationalities of her adopted Chicago, Addams proposed a new patriotism, based on cooperation and mutual esteem. The curse of nationalism and the cult of individualism were two sides of the same coin, she argued in *Newer Ideals of Peace,* and contact with the foreigner could cure Americans of both. "We are driven to the rather absurd phrase of 'cosmic patriotism,'" she wrote: an attempt to move "men out of their narrow national considerations and cautions into new reaches of human effort and affection."

A key figure for Addams was the Italian statesman Giuseppe Mazzini, who saw the necessity for "unity with all human beings," even as he guided the unification of Italy in the mid-nineteenth century, and the need to cultivate a "universal affection" strong enough "to devour the flimsy stuff called national honor, glory, and prestige, which incite to war." Addams recalled her father's grief on hearing news of Mazzini's death, and this idea that one could feel genuine kinship over the barriers of geography and nationality struck her as something profound. Another was Leo Tolstoy, who exposed the artifice of nationalism with thrilling clarity. Tolstoy showed how governments "hypnotize" their subjects into fighting pointless and sterile wars, while revealing the humanity that shines through the lives of ordinary people. Tolstoy's austerity, and his total estrangement from the tendrils of government, made him a prophet, rather than a guide. But the eloquence with which he elevated the human above the military state electrified Addams—even if a visit to the great man dissolved into embarrassment when he remarked on the extravagance of her clothes.

More than Mazzini or Tolstoy, however, Addams extolled the diversity of the modern city as the "active and tangible" model of a new internationalism, turning a century of swagger on its head. In *Fortune of the Republic,* Ralph Waldo Emerson had offered the hoary commonplace that America is "the new nation, guide and lawgiver of all nations." "When I see the emigrants landing at New York, I say, There they go—to school," he wrote—the school being America. In another piece, Emerson disparaged "the superstition of Travelling"—in which the tourist bows in childish wonder before the crumbling "idols" of Italy, England, or Egypt—as an insult to fair Columbia. "The man who loves other countries as much as he does his own," scoffed Theodore Roosevelt, in a similar vein, "is quite as noxious a member of society as a man who loves other women as much as his wife." We are a nation, he sneered, "not a polyglot boarding house."

Addams could not have disagreed more. She found color and nobility in foreign tongues—a medley of rebukes to a stout and serious nation. Before we attempt "to naturalize the bewildered immigrant," she suggested, we should consider what we might learn from her. There was no more "striking reproach" to the oppressive materialism of modern life than the sight of men and women "on a solemn Jewish holiday," standing on a bridge amid the din and bustle of Chicago and "casting their sins upon the waters." Outsiders could see the flaws in the American worship of mammon, and they were often among the most vigorous advocates of child labor laws and compulsory education. The "cosmopolitan humanitarianism" of a community like Hull House, where working people of many complexions engaged in cultural and educational projects, was ripe for emulation on a larger stage. This was her vision for America and her remedy for war: "When this newer patriotism becomes large enough, it will overcome arbitrary boundaries and soak up the notion of nationalism. We may then give up war, because we shall find it as difficult to make war upon a nation at the other side of the globe as upon our next-door neighbor."

It was a brave ambition, and it faced the greatest of tests.

III

The struggle to keep America out of World War I was an epic of failed eloquence and thwarted idealism. In April 1917, Woodrow Wilson took the nation to war, in the hope of making the world "safe for democracy," and critics, such as Eugene Debs, found themselves in jail for daring to dissent. But if the war brought disaster to Europe and a crisis of democracy at home, it also summoned some of the most creative reflections on American identity ever submitted for consideration.

The drift toward catastrophe began with an arms race and a web of treaties that, far from protecting any of the signatories, exposed everyone to retaliation. The assassination of Archduke Franz Ferdinand, heir to the Austro-Hungarian throne, in June 1914 triggered the bloodiest conflict the world had ever known in a cause that no one could quite understand. The opening months brought devastating losses, with more than five million casualties by the end of the year. Rarely had Americans been more grateful for the separation of an ocean. But when a German U-boat sank a British liner carrying American citizens on its way from New York to Liverpool, in May 1915, Wilson's official stance of neutrality came under strain. Unofficially, the United States was already a belligerent, supplying arms in vast quantities to its British ally, including the several million rounds of rifle ammunition on board the doomed *Lusitania*. Thus began a two-year debate over American involvement and its identity as a voice of reason in a world gone mad.

For militarists, such as Henry Cabot Lodge and the war-hungry Theodore Roosevelt, by then a private citizen, the *Lusitania* incident underlined the necessity of military preparedness and a willingness to retaliate. For Roosevelt the issues were simple: Wilson was a coward; the military was scandalously underequipped; and pacifists were traitors. But if this was a war created by militarism, countered the peaceniks, why would America enter the morass? For them, the real war was within, not between, nations: between militarism and internationalism; between war and respect for human life. *Four Lights* magazine juxtaposed breathless demands for war from "Colonel" Roosevelt with similar statements by the kaiser. A cartoon published in *The Masses* showed a "Preparedness Advocate" pointing toward a continent in flames. "If we don't prepare as they did," he says, "it'll happen to us!"

For feminists, such as the lawyer and journalist Crystal Eastman, the war was a man-made catastrophe, in the plainest sense of the term. There was no stronger argument for women in public life than the persistence of militarism and the worship of force. Inspired by Addams's *Newer Ideals of Peace,* Eastman described herself as a radical internationalist, and she enlisted Addams to chair the Woman's Peace Party, formed in January 1915 and working in tandem with the American Union Against Militarism. Eastman wanted to puncture stubborn mythologies about the grandeur of war, organizing antiwar exhibits with her English husband, which tried to show the other side of the great romance. The comic prelude was a seventeen-foot dinosaur called Jingo, bearing the words "All armor plate—no brains. This animal believed in 'Preparedness' and is now extinct." Against the war god, Eastman preached concert and collaboration: "a new kind of world understanding" based on "a warm, real knowledge of other races and their contribution to the world's values—a delight in the culture of other nations as well as our own."

The embodiment of the principle was the International Congress of Women held in the Netherlands in April 1915. At the head of the U.S. delegation was the indomitable Addams, who also toured seven capital cities, meeting foreign ministers and soldiers from several warring nations. Addams was thrilled and horrified by her encounters. She met the mother of a young professor of chemistry who had discovered, just before he died, that his research on asphyxiating gases had been employed by his own government for "the brutal use of killing men." It was, he wrote, "as if science herself in this mad world had also become cruel and malignant." Part of the tragedy was that while the mother no longer believed in the cause, his young wife was still "filled with a solemn patriotism which never questions any aspect of the situation." But for her, the grieving mother, the state had become "an alien and hostile thing."

This, noted Addams, was the essence of war—the nearest thing to "human sacrifice" in a modern age. Under current conceptions of patriotic duty, fighting was not merely tolerated: It was exalted. Yet citizens of every nation, she was glad to report, were beginning to desert the idol. Among the women of the Old World, Addams found signs of a "humble internationalism . . . interlacing nation to nation with a thousand kindly deeds." And there were glimmers of hope in the corridors of power. After they had made their pitch for ceasefire and negotiation to the Austrian prime minister, Karl von Stürgkh, with a softening remark that such words probably sound terribly foolish, he banged his fist on the table and said, "Foolish? These are the first sensible words that have been uttered in this room for ten months!"

Alas for Addams, little such warmth awaited her back home. Just days after her return in July, she reported her findings in a blistering speech at Carnegie Hall, titled "The Revolt Against War." Straying far beyond her script, Addams set the wisdom of the terrified soldiers against the crashing pieties of the ruling classes, who spoke in tedious abstractions, using the same "theological or nationalistic words" in every country. "Everywhere one heard the same phrases, the identical phrases, given as the causes and as the reasons for the war," she related, with the fatuous admonition that "a nation at war cannot make negotiations." Here, in the drab circularity of expression, was the poverty of militarism. After a few of these meetings, she said, "I almost knew what to expect, what phrases were coming next." None of them could see that the more desperately they clung "to their armies for their salvation," the more elusive this goal of negotiation was going to be. Most of the passions driving the war seemed to be generated by the war itself: "Germany has done this, the Allies have done that, somebody else tried to do this . . . and what awful people they are, and they must therefore be crushed." Addams ridiculed the dogmas of the warring patriots as exhausted clichés, and she noted the absurdity of having to avoid mentioning "peace" in their overtures to the various governments. "Isn't it hideous that whole nations find the word peace intolerable," she gasped. Yet worse was to come.

Building her case that the war was contrived and had been forced upon the young, Addams reported disdain for patriotic shibboleths among many of the soldiers, and the widespread use of alcohol to get them to fight. A young German in Switzerland told Addams that he had never "once shot his gun in a way that could possibly hit another man," and that "nothing in the world could make him kill." His brother was an officer, in similar revolt, and he knew "dozens and dozens" of men who also refused to kill. Others preferred to commit suicide than return to the trenches. No wonder the authorities fell back on stimulants to drive the men into battle. The English used rum; the French, absinthe; and the Germans had their own regular formula. "Think of that," shuddered Addams. War is so foreign, so offensive to the human spirit, it can proceed only by intoxication. "But in the end human nature must reassert itself," she insisted. Or a generation will be lost.

Few could have imagined the reaction such words would generate in a still-neutral United States. Addams had spoken with sympathy for the soldiers, but her breezy demolition of national honor and the gleeful disclosure of the uses of liquor in the trenches triggered fury and outrage. *The New York Times* congratulated her for revealing "the weakness and silliness of those who clamor for an ending of the war on any terms. . . . For months we have seen her flitting from capital to capital, asking the nations to lay down their arms," scoffed the writer, but this was theater, and likely only to perpetuate the war. It was sad to see anyone flushed with self-importance, but deeply regrettable to see "JANE ADDAMS" stoop so low. Letters denounced her insults to the brave men on the front. Richard Harding Davis, a veteran war correspondent, castigated her for showing contempt for the dead and denying the Allied soldier the "credit of his sacrifice." "She strips him of honor and courage," he complained. No speech since the war began had "been so unworthy or so untrue."

Not to be outdone, Theodore Roosevelt derided "poor foolish Jane Addams" as just another member of "the shrieking sisterhood."

He told a British correspondent (who happened to be Winston Churchill) that neither she nor "her noxious mission abroad" should be taken seriously. Seldom had patriotism appeared more patriarchal. Each of these men seemed personally offended that Addams had stepped on their terrain, even though, as the historian James Cracraft notes, scholars have since confirmed her observations about drink and martial courage. Her sin was to have attacked "the sacred nationalist myth that modern, well-disciplined soldiers gladly fought and died for their country out of their love for it, bravery, and sense of duty." Addams called the fallout from the Carnegie Hall speech an instance of "mass psychology," yet she was wounded by the episode and briefly hospitalized under the stress. The "pacifist in wartime," she later wrote, is "in the keeping of those who control the sources of publicity and consider it a patriotic duty to make all types of peace propaganda obnoxious." They succeeded.

Patriotism might have made the war, but the war was remaking patriotism in its own implacable image. "War," observed the journalist Randolph Bourne, "becomes almost a sport between the hunters and the hunted. The pursuit of enemies within outweighs in psychic attractiveness the assault on the enemy without." Pacifists were not the only ones who felt the chill. "The only man who is a good American is the man who is an American and nothing else," asserted Roosevelt, as he demanded a "hundred percent Americanism" in every community. "There are citizens of the United States," declared Wilson, "born under other flags but welcomed under our generous naturalization laws . . . who have poured the poison of disloyalty into the very arteries of our national life."

One part of Wilson was an eloquent internationalist who frowned on militarism and yearned for "peace without victory." Another was the proud Presbyterian who believed that "we are chosen and prominently chosen to show the way to the nations of the world how they shall walk in the paths of liberty," even if that meant war. "If I did not believe in Providence," he said in the year he was elected president, "I would feel like a man going blindfolded through a haphazard world." That is exactly how some people saw him. His mind, observed the economist John Maynard Keynes, was "essentially theological." He could have preached a sermon on any of his fabled Fourteen Points, but he had no idea how to put "the flesh of life" on his Olympian utterances. Like Lincoln, whose phrases saturate his speeches, Wilson could speak about war without mentioning the violence; he could arraign the fallacy of militarism while exempting his own nation from the charge. Wilson had warned, with a clarity that thrilled the pacifists, that a decisive victory for either side would lead to another war for revenge. But as the Germans resumed their submarine attacks, Wilson refused all negotiation or compromise on transatlantic commerce, adopting a rhetoric of honor and redress that brought him in line with the nationalists. The infamous Zimmermann telegram, which revealed the Germans courting an alliance with Mexico, was the final straw—not to mention the fact that the United States was bankrolling the Allies to the tune of several billion dollars, all of which would be lost should the Germans win.

Wilson's speech to Congress in April 1917, seeking approval for military intervention, is the Magna Carta of American innocence. "It is a fearful thing to lead this great peaceful people into war," he said. There would be "many months of fiery trial and sacrifice ahead," he warned, drawing on Lincoln. But "the world must be made safe for democracy." Victory would "bring peace and safety to all nations and make the world itself at last free." As if to address the contradiction with his "peace without victory" speech, Wilson anchored his case to the unique virtue of the American people. For "we act without animus," he insisted. "We fight without rancor and without selfish object." As such we will conduct ourselves "as belligerents without passion," observing "with proud punctilio the principles of right and of fair play." It sounded like a game of cricket. America was privileged "to spend her blood and her might for the principles that gave her birth," he concluded. "God helping her, she can do no other."

Senators "not only cheered, but yelled," reported *The New York Times*. The applause was "so deep and so intense" it sounded like a storm. Chief Justice Edward Douglass White pounded the arm of his chair like a boy at a football match, reported another journalist. Wilson's phrase about making the world safe for democracy almost passed without notice, observed the *Times,* until the meaning began to register and the chamber erupted into a roar of satisfaction. Only Wisconsin's senator Robert La Follette stood icy and grim, with his arms folded tightly across his chest, so that nobody could possibly mistake him for a disciple of war.

In a Flag Day speech delivered two months later, Wilson defined the war as a crusade "for the salvation of the nations"—including the German people, beguiled by the sophistries of their imperial government. If we fail, he warned, with another echo of Lincoln, "political freedom must wither and perish" from the world. History would vindicate American courage, and "a new glory shall shine in the face of our people," prophesied Wilson, with an allusion to Moses descending from Mount Sinai. But in the same breath came a threat: "Woe be to the man or group of men that seeks to stand in our way in this day of high resolution."

The nation rallied. It should never be forgotten, observed Bourne, "that nations do not declare war on each other, nor in the strictest sense is it nations that fight each other." There was, he thought, no case in modern times of a people being consulted in the initiation of a war. But the moment it begins, "the mass of the people, through some spiritual alchemy, become convinced that they have willed and executed the deed themselves." Then, with the exception of a few malcontents, they "allow themselves to be regimented, coerced, deranged in all the environments of their lives, and turned into a solid manufactory of destruction." Patriotism becomes the dominant feeling, and "luxuriant releases of explosive hatred" fill the air. For this "herd-feeling," this newly awakened consciousness, "demands universality"—"a one hundred percent Americanism, among one hundred percent of the population."

Liberals who cleaved to Wilson when he promised a "democratic and antiseptic war" should not have been surprised by the ugliness that followed. The pacifists opposed the war because they knew that this notion of a clean and ennobling struggle was "an illusion, and because of the myriad hurts they knew war would do the promise of democracy at home. For once the babes and sucklings seem to have been wiser than the children of light."

Max Eastman—Crystal's brother and editor of *The Masses*—cringed before the cyclone. "Nothing could be more calamitous than for patriotism to become the established religion of this country," he wrote in July 1917, shortly before his journal was forced out of circulation. "The patriotic religion," wrote this agnostic son of liberal Protestant preachers, "has a hold here that God never had. God wanted people to be humble." But patriotism lets us brag without knowing that is what we are doing. Eastman had always found the sentiment distasteful, but the "sudden and copious flow of malice" that followed the declaration of war brought him to the brink of despair. "You will see how everything that was erect in this country bows down to that sentiment. The love of liberty, the assertion of the rights of man, what little of the ethics of Jesus we had—these things must obviously yield." Not only morality but intelligence, perception, and the very capacity of "truthful seeing" were being sacrificed to "this facile religion of the fatherland," this "orgy of nation-worship," this "peculiar hypnotizing force."

The watchword of the patriot was "Liberty and Union, One and Inseparable, Now and Forever"—the words that adorn the statue of Daniel Webster in New York City's Central Park. But if the phrase had any meaning, the war had shown it to be false. Far from preserving or nurturing liberty, patriotism was a spirit of intolerance, which forced the constituents of freedom, "like justice and proportion and mercy and truth," to run for their lives. Eastman was especially provoked by a speech at a Red Cross memorial in which Wilson predicted that the outcome of the struggle would be that "every element of difference amongst us will be obliterated," promising that when "suffering and sacrifice have completed this union, men will no longer speak of any lines either of race or [class] association cutting athwart the great body of this nation." If so, countered Eastman, we are off to a slow start.

At an establishment called Rector's on Broadway, three "heretics" of the national religion had recently refused to stand during the national anthem. Within moments, "chairs, tables and salad bowls were employed by the orthodox to enforce the tenets of their creed," and "a policeman was summoned in the name of the fatherland." The men were arrested and severely reprimanded by a judge—that is, the men who refused to stand, not the ones who assaulted them. Eastman felt a strange solitude as he watched the nation unravel. "To argue against these tribal and egoistic instincts," he wrote, "is like arguing against gravitation." The following month's cover of *The Masses* showed a haunting image of the face of Liberty, turned upside down.

Soon afterward, Eugene Debs was arrested for an antiwar speech delivered in Canton, Ohio. "They have always taught you that it is your patriotic duty to go to war and slaughter yourselves at their command," he told the crowd. "You have never had a voice in the war." Although he was careful not to call for draft resistance, the government argued that such had been his intention. His sentence, later confirmed by the Supreme Court, was ten years in jail. Another socialist, Charles Schenck, was arrested for distributing leaflets denouncing Wilson's draft law as a form of "involuntary servitude." The Supreme Court upheld his conviction unanimously under the Espionage Act, and it was here that Oliver Wendell Holmes Jr. delivered his famous judgment that "the most stringent protection of free speech would not protect a man in falsely shouting fire in a theatre and causing a panic." Strong words, but a terrible analogy. There *was* a fire, and Schenck was trying to stop people walking into it. His crime was to dispute the state's power to send men to die without their consent, and to prison he went. Emma Goldman suffered a similar fate, and was later deported as an "undesirable alien."

From the lynch mob to the Supreme Court, justice quailed before the flag. In April 1918, a German-born immigrant called Robert Prager was seized from his home in Collinsville, Illinois, stripped to his underwear, and forced to walk down a street draped in an American flag. After a policeman rescued him and held him in jail, a crowd stormed the building and hanged him from a tree. As the historian Adam Hochschild observes, in a chilling account of the episode, the murder drew little outrage, and the eleven men put on trial posed proudly outside the courthouse holding American flags. Their defense lawyer claimed that the lynching was justified by "an unwritten law allowing patriotic murder in time of danger," and the jury clearly agreed. All of them were acquitted. As the economist Thorstein Veblen dryly remarked of the reborn vigilante code, "He is an indifferent patriot who will let 'life, liberty and the pursuit of happiness' cloud the issue and get in the way of the main business in hand."

This was what Bourne meant by the madness of war: the "derangement of values" under the jealous gaze of national honor. When public opinion accepts the justice of prison sentences for mere utterances, it was clear that the nation was suffering some sort of neurosis. These draconian punishments had no relationship to national security or the tangible depletion of the armed forces. The real crime was "sacrilege." Throughout the war, dissident opinion and affronts to the flag had been punished more ferociously than "actual pragmatic crimes," he thought. If only people could see that they were trampling on their country when they crouched before the flag. Bourne remained patriotic, deeply committed to what he called the "American promise." But he wanted to save the nation from war, and to rescue patriotism from slavish devotion to the state.

Everyone is part of a country, wrote Bourne, for better or for worse. We are molded and formed by its customs, and they are part of us. By a certain age, we have the stamp of that civilization, and we could hardly be mistaken for the child of any other country. The nation is the body of people who share those habits and affections, though not in a spirit of exclusion. Indeed "this feeling for country is essentially non-competitive," ventured the journalist. "We think of our own people merely as living on the earth's surface along with other groups, pleasant or objectionable as they may be, but fundamentally as sharing the earth with them. In our simple conception of country there is no more feeling of rivalry with other peoples than there is in our feeling for our family."

We are also born into a state, which is often confused with the country, and that is where the seeds of nationalism are sown.

"Country is a concept of peace, of tolerance, of living and letting live," he wrote. "But State is essentially a concept of power, of competition; it signifies a group in its aggressive aspects." The history of America as a country was quite different from that of America as a state. These histories needed to be disentangled, if not pulled apart.

In war, the state stages a coup against the country, claiming to speak for the people while striding imperiously through their needs and imaginations. "Men are told simultaneously that they will enter the military establishment of their own volition, as their splendid sacrifice for their country's welfare, and that if they do not enter they will be hunted down and punished with the most horrid penalties." The state asserts a perfect kinship with the nation, which is in fact perfect control—an illusion sustained by romantic patriotism. The patriot thinks he is saving a country when he is actually serving the state, which rises fitter and stronger from the battlefield, while men are left to bleed.

The symbol of the confusion was the flag: an inanimate object that excited strange and unworthy emotions. The flag was a banner of war: a clarion of discipline and uniformity, incapable of representing the nation in its real and organic life. A healthy patriotism required something more dynamic than flags, anthems, and national holidays. Bourne found it in the diversity that professional patriots loved to hate.

Bourne's appeal for a "trans-national America," published in *The Atlantic Monthly* in July 1916, is among the most creative responses to the war, and a fitting answer to Crystal Eastman's demand for something more than "negation" in these days of trial. One of the most unfortunate effects of the war had been the resurgence of nativism, with angry demands for assimilation, and the rage of books like *The Passing of the Great Race*, which warned of "race suicide," should the aliens win. Bourne turned the tables, asserting the bankruptcy of the "melting pot" ideal and calling for internationalism as the only way to save "this Western world of ours from suicide." The Americanism demanded by the likes of Roosevelt was only a replica of the tight and jealous nationalism tearing Europe apart. "To seek no other goal than the weary old nationalism, belligerent, exclusive, inbreeding, the poison of which we are witnessing now in Europe," he challenged, "is to make patriotism a hollow sham, and to declare that, in spite of our boastings, America must ever be a follower and not a leader of nations."

The irony was that "Americanizing" meant "Anglo-Saxonizing," when stripped to essentials. The priests of Americanism were still pining for a colonial past. They scolded the immigrant for not being melted in a pot that they too had refused to enter. In this brilliant rhetorical maneuver, Bourne outed the persecutors as relics of the Old World, and hailed the outsider as the key to American renewal. Indeed, "we must perpetrate the paradox," he contended, "that our American cultural tradition lies in the future." Bourne was not advocating the defiant pluralism outlined by the Jewish intellectual Horace Kallen, where nations remain *in* but not *of* the wider culture. In his vision, the "threads of living and potent cultures" would be woven into a "novel international nation, the first the world has seen." And this future was already in the making.

In a city like Chicago or New York, or a "vivid American university," Bourne reflected, one feels oneself a "citizen of a larger world." Here, internationalism is a reality, not a creed; "the sting of devastating competition has been removed." "In a world which has dreamed of internationalism," he marveled, "we find that we have all unawares been building up the first international nation." America was coming to be "not a nationality but a transnationality"—a "Beloved Community" in which every citizen may have a hand in its destiny. Bourne's essay offers a striking parallel to Frederick

Douglass's lecture on America as a "composite nation," refreshed and renewed by the oxygen of exchange. As Bourne buoyantly concludes, "The failure of the melting-pot, far from closing the great American democratic experiment, means that it has only just begun."

IV

Bourne died in the flu pandemic of 1918, at the tender age of thirty-two—one of the "myriad hurts" of a war he said would bring only suffering. In a Memorial Day address delivered at Suresnes Cemetery in France, five months later, Woodrow Wilson likened the recent dead to those who fought for the preservation of the Union in the Civil War: "As those men gave their lives in order that America might be united, these men have given their lives in order that the world might be united." In another speech, he told of the Frenchwomen who had adopted American graves, in boundless gratitude to the United States. "France was free and the world was free because America had come!"

Only it wasn't. Wilson had conducted the war in a spirit of imperious idealism, issuing lavish promises about the nature and consequences of American power. Not even his allies, the French prime minister, Georges Clemenceau, and his British counterpart, David Lloyd George, had the slightest intention of falling into line. Ruthlessly maneuvering for their Carthaginian peace, they left Wilson and his Fourteen Points fluttering in the wind. Wilson, "this blind and deaf Don Quixote," as Keynes described him at the Paris Peace Conference, came away with almost nothing. He could not even persuade his own country to join the League of Nations. This, mourned an editorial in Max Eastman's new journal, *The Liberator,* was "a peace with wars already in its womb." As Keynes coldly prophesied, before the ink on the Treaty of Versailles had dried, "There are few episodes in history which posterity will have less reason to condone."

The problem was deeper than the bungled negotiations in Paris. Wilson joined a long line of patriots who confused theology with policy, thinking the world could be forced into agreement with a proud and parochial providence. Yet the voices of dissent were never silenced. Jane Addams, Randolph Bourne, and Max and Crystal Eastman—to name only four—spoke for a different America and a larger patriotism. Addams won the Nobel Peace Prize in 1931, and Bourne, unknown for two generations, was rediscovered during the Vietnam War as an almost prophetic observer of the military mind. "Malcontentedness may be the beginning of promise," he once wrote, and the sentiment was not forgotten. Nor was Eugene Debs, who finally emerged from the Atlanta federal penitentiary on Christmas Day 1921 after President Harding commuted his sentence. When a journalist asked him if he was sorry not to have received a pardon, which would have restored his full rights as a U.S. citizen, Debs summoned a smile. "Now," he answered, "I am only a citizen of the world."

CHAPTER 5

Playing God: The Cold War and Its Discontents

It has been our fate as a nation not to have ideologies but to be one.

—RICHARD HOFSTADTER

In the days ahead, we must not consider it unpatriotic to raise certain questions about our national character.

—MARTIN LUTHER KING JR., *WHERE DO WE GO FROM HERE: CHAOS OR COMMUNITY?*

The Big Country is the greatest movie you have never seen—a sweeping Western that broke every rule of the game. Starring Gregory Peck, Jean Simmons, and Charlton Heston, under the restless gaze of director William Wyler, it is a film of unparalleled visual beauty with a new kind of hero: the man who refuses to kill. President Dwight D. Eisenhower enjoyed it so much he showed it on four consecutive nights in the White House.

While he was thrilling to Peck's insouciant heroism, Eisenhower might not have appreciated the larger message of *The Big Country*:

a penetrating critique of Cold War ideology, with its blind patriotism and suicidal doctrines of retaliation. A retired sea captain (Peck's Jim McKay) is traveling west to meet the family of his fiancée, Pat Terrill, when he is rudely accosted by local hoodlums, who toss his hat in the air and attempt to shoot holes in it, though missing every time. Laughing off the incident as a case of high spirits, McKay quickly discovers that his future in-laws, the Terrills, have other ideas. The boys were members of the Hannassey clan, a rougher, poorer family of cattle ranchers—longtime enemies of the Terrills who must be punished for the good of the community. As McKay pleads the innocence of the affair against the avenging moralism of his future father-in-law, "Major" Henry Terrill, a lecture on self-defense descends into a tirade. The Hannasseys are "animals," raves the Major. "They're a pest, a plague. Like Sodom and Gomorrah. It'd be a blessing for this country if a flood would wipe them off the face of the earth." The appearance of Pat, in flowing silk, interrupts the diatribe, but McKay has seen enough. There are deep and implacable hatreds under this veneer of civility, and the family's horror over his brush with the Hannasseys is only a pretext for shedding blood. McKay tries to persuade the Major to call off his "war party," but reason is powerless before honor. This is "a big country," he is told. "You have to be your own law."

The feud deepens. The violence escalates, and McKay's refusal to have any part in it brings charges of cowardice and betrayal. Sympathizing with the underdog, McKay attempts to mediate a solution, and it is then that he grasps the malignancy of the quarrel. Presented with a way out, neither side will take the offer, because after soaring speeches about the welfare of the people, these men prefer to be at war. Exposing the egotism beneath the valor, McKay drives a wedge between the patriarchs and the people, preventing a bloodbath in the canyon. The "men" who emerge from behind rocks to lay down their arms are boys, spared an almost certain death, while the feuding chiefs fight it out alone. War is yesterday's idea. In a stunning denouement, these giants in their own imagination are reduced to dots on a cosmic landscape: small men, inching toward destruction. The glamour has faded, the grandeur of a cause stripped to the petulance of a grudge.

Peck, who co-produced the movie, confirmed that Wyler conceived *The Big Country* as an allegory on the Cold War. They both believed the United States should have retained good relations with the Soviet Union and China, and the movie probes the dark underbelly of self-defense: the security that is really self-harm. The Terrills are the Americans. The Hannasseys are the Soviets. The film's running joke that this "is a big country" is a gentle dig at national pride. Both sides are trapped in their narratives, drunk on their injuries, though the weight of the critique falls on the all-American Terrills, who look down on their swarthy neighbors and deny their very humanity. *The Big Country* condemns patriotism as patriarchy: nationalism as arrested development.

It is easy to see why Eisenhower would have enjoyed this film. He might have seen himself in Peck's cool and urbane protagonist. Raised by pacifists, Eisenhower was an unlikely general who opposed the dropping of the atomic bombs in 1945. In his "Chance for Peace" speech of April 1953, Eisenhower channeled William Jennings Bryan as he decried the folly of an arms race, which placed the whole world "under the cloud of threatening war." More famously, Eisenhower used his farewell address of January 1961 to cry foul on the growth of a "military-industrial complex," and its danger to our liberties and democratic processes. Only "an alert and knowledgeable citizenry," he counseled, could stem the tide of militarization and preserve "our peaceful methods and goals."

Yet Eisenhower *was* the military-industrial complex. His presidency heralded the largest peacetime expansion of military force in history and a propensity for covert aggression that would leave a trail of destruction around the globe. At the start of his presidency, America possessed a thousand nuclear bombs, enough to destroy life on planet earth. At the end of his term, there were twenty-two thousand, including intercontinental ballistic missiles capable of annihilating a nine-hundred-square-mile "target" at the touch of a button. While Eisenhower was right to demand an alert and educated citizenry as the only antidote to the military malaise, the patriotism he promoted as president was of the kind that could only lull those citizens to sleep.

This was the golden age of the civil religion: a vast renewal of the American covenant and the myth of the chosen nation—the birth of the presidential prayer breakfast, a pledge of allegiance emboldened with the words "under God," and a currency whispering and preaching "In God We Trust." There was no "almost" in this formulation. But under the canopy of providence reigned a politics of destruction. If World War I and the Great Depression had left a nation chastened and introspective, triumph over fascism in World War II signaled a return to self-confidence and prestige. In 1941, Henry Luce had announced "the American Century" in *Life* magazine, and our duty, as the "most powerful and vital nation," to shape the world "for such purposes as we see fit and by such means as we see fit."

The hard truth was that such language brought America closer to, not further from, the fascist ideologies that were carving up the world at the time, and closer to the European imperialism so thoroughly humbled by the conflagration. America entered the war promising to defend the "Four Freedoms" of Western civilization, as Franklin D. Roosevelt defined them in January 1941. It ended the war by dropping nuclear bombs on civilians and beginning an arms race that threatened human life as never before. America helped to found the United Nations, with the aim of protecting future generations from the devastation of war; then it chafed at the enterprise and bristled at regulation. The "good war" became the Cold War, in which a democracy assumed the mantle of a superpower, and a puzzling blend of triumphalism and paranoia filled the air. Resurgent nationalism led America into a disastrous foreign policy and an age of intolerance, in which constitutional principles melted before the eyes. Who will save freedom from "freedom"? wondered the conservative philosopher Peter Viereck. Who could save America from Americanism? The best answers, as always, came from the margins.

I

The real problem with nationalism, wrote George Orwell in 1945, is intellectual. The nationalist not only tolerates atrocities committed by his people; he doesn't even notice them. "One prod to the nerve of nationalism, and the intellectual decencies can vanish, the past can be altered, and the plainest facts can be denied." For the nationalist, it is not merely pity or compassion that ceases to function; it is perception: the ability to see and observe things as they are—which helped to explain "the astonishing failure of military prediction in the present war." Nationalism was now a religion, in the least attractive sense of the term. Breaking its spell was the challenge of the twentieth century.

Albert Einstein felt the same way, calling nationalism "an infantile disease" and "the measles of mankind." During World War I, Einstein had bravely denounced the nationalist passions behind this "fratricidal" conflict, and his distaste only grew in the years that followed. "I am by heritage a Jew, by citizenship a Swiss, and by makeup a human being, and *only* a human being, without any special attachment to any state or national entity whatsoever," he wrote to a friend in June 1918. Einstein happened to be in the United States when Hitler came to power in 1933, and he decided to stay, praising "a country where civil liberty, tolerance, and equality of all citizens before the law are the rule." Seven years later, the preeminent scientist of his era became a naturalized U.S. citizen, though never a patriot. It wasn't long before he saw the disease at work in his new home, and by lending his support to the development of the atomic bomb, he played a critical role in its incubation.

"The world was promised freedom from fear," observed Einstein in a Nobel anniversary speech of December 1945, "but in fact fear has increased tremendously since the termination of the war." Had Roosevelt retained the peaceable and internationalist Henry Wallace as his running mate in 1944, history might have looked different. Under the narrow and belligerent Truman, a binary worldview became a way of life, and "the survival of the free world" was premised on the ability to destroy it. Since the Puritans, a determination to read conflict in terms of "types" and analogies had frustrated diplomacy and understanding. So it continued. In the Cold War, a recent ally who performed the lion's share of Hitler's defeat was recast as the new Hitler. The Cold War, writes the political scientist Mary Kaldor, was "the imaginary war," an essentially "theatrical" conflict. David needed his Goliath.

The Soviets had lost a staggering twenty-seven million lives during the war, including nearly nine million military deaths. They were in no mood for another war. But in February 1946, a "Long Telegram" written by an American diplomat in Moscow, George F. Kennan, framed the Russians as "unceasing" and pathological belligerents, wired by tradition and ideology for aggression. Kennan came to regret its contribution to Truman's joyless strategy of containment, likening himself to "one who has inadvertently loosened a large boulder from the top of a cliff and now helplessly witnesses its path of destruction in the valley below." But as the military historian Andrew Bacevich has suggested, the scribblings of diplomats would have counted for nothing without a prior disposition to interpret the drama in religious terms. The hubris of a nuclear arsenal was better attributed to "the original sin of American exceptionalism" than anything Kennan had to say about the Russians. If Satan didn't exist, we would have to invent him.

"How do American actions since V-J Day appear to other nations?" wondered Henry Wallace, as the Truman administration established air bases across the globe and tested newer, larger bombs in the Pacific Ocean. "How would it look to us if Russia had the atomic bomb and we did not, if Russia had 10,000-mile bombers and air bases within a thousand miles of our coastlines, and we did not?" he challenged Truman in an open letter. To say that communism and democracy cannot coexist in the same world, and that one must inevitably defeat the other, was, "from a historical point of view, pure propaganda." What can and will bring disaster, on the other hand, was this psychology of denigration and distrust. The glib and easy familiarity with which self-styled "realists" spoke of atomic weapons betrayed the poverty of their thinking. "We know that America will never start a war," they said. So "what's wrong with trying to build up a predominance of force"? Everything, thought Wallace. The weapons are the war. The Soviets duly unveiled their own bomb in August 1949, with expertise gleaned from the Manhattan Project, and the arms race was born.

What could be America's objective in testing a hydrogen bomb in the crystal waters of the Bikini Islands? wondered the Indian prime minister, Jawaharlal Nehru, in April 1954. "Surely to announce to the world . . . this might of the United States of America and their readiness to blow up any people or country who came in the way of their policy." These ghastly displays sowed fear and terror, leaving the unavoidable impression that "the great men who control our destinies are dangerous self-centred lunatics," prepared "to rain death and destruction all over the world." The Americans had learned how to split an atom, but their minds were stuck in the old ruts of Western arrogance, making peace a distant dream. "We have heard much of the four freedoms and of the brave new world to come," wrote Nehru, but the only freedom augured by this latest advance of civilization was "the freedom to die."

Soon, squinting specialists were muttering about a "missile gap" in which a naïve and benevolent America lagged behind the diabolical sophistication of the Soviets. It was fantasy. In 1961, the United States had 170 intercontinental ballistic missiles; the Soviets had 4, and would not have had any had they not been goaded and beckoned into the game. The real gap, submitted the philosopher Hannah Arendt, was between the monstrous accumulation of killing power and the patriotic twaddle that gilded the madness. "To sound off with a cheerful 'give me liberty or give me death' sort of argument in the face of the unprecedented and inconceivable potential of destruction in nuclear warfare," she wrote, "is not even hollow; it is downright ridiculous."

Many Americans felt the same way. In Stanley Kubrick's black comedy, *Dr. Strangelove, or: How I Learned to Stop Worrying and Love the Bomb,* five-star generals rave about "degenerate atheist commies," while the Russians scramble to close the "doomsday gap" opened up by the Americans. The ingenious Soviets have also conspired to put fluoride in American drinking water, contaminating our "precious bodily fluids," and for this reason Brigadier General Jack D. Ripper, commander of Burpelson Air Force Base, orders an attack: "There's no other choice. God willing, we will prevail in peace and freedom from fear and in true health through the purity and essence of our natural fluids. God bless you all."

The satire is unending. As deliberations in the Pentagon descend into a brawl, the president primly admonishes, "Gentlemen, you can't fight in here, this is the War Room!" Nobody can work out how to override the attack code, and as Dr. Strangelove—the evil genius behind the bomb—is wheeled out to advise, he accidentally addresses the president as "Mein Führer," involuntarily raising his arm in the Nazi salute. Powerless to halt Armageddon, he suggests that "a nucleus of human specimens" be hurried to safety in underground mines, signaling further worries that the Soviets are ahead of the game. "Mr. President, we must not allow a mine shaft gap!" splutters an anxious General Turgidson. No dogma is left unscathed. *Dr. Strangelove* is patriotism pushed to paranoia: national security as licensed insanity. As General Ripper orders the boys to drop "fourteen hundred megatons" on the Russians, just enough to prevent "red retaliation," a sign above his head beams with the motto of the U.S. Strategic Air Command: "Peace Is Our Profession."

Like *The Big Country,* a parody on the scale of *Dr. Strangelove* indicates that there were Americans who shared the international community's revulsion at the bombs. Yet these were outliers. More typical of the Cold War consensus was *Shane,* a gun-blazing Western that charmed the nation in 1953 with its flawless, soft-spoken, and ruthlessly efficient protagonist. This, notes the historian Stephen Kinzer, was how Americans preferred to see their country acting in the world—perhaps because the truth was so brutal, so brutally inept, it could never have functioned as a screenplay. The sordid tale of coups and assassinations conducted by the United States under the leadership of John Foster Dulles as secretary of state, and his brother Allen, at the newly established Central Intelligence Agency, has been brought to light by a number of outstanding scholars. Less well known is the degree to which this litany of violence was ordered and orchestrated under the old rubric of providence.

John Foster Dulles was a diplomat who didn't believe in diplomacy. Allen was a spymaster who preferred destroying governments to spying on them. Both were true believers in American destiny. Like Woodrow Wilson, John Foster Dulles was a Presbyterian elder—a "priestly nationalist," fully convinced of America's divine credentials, not to mention his own. He needed communism the way Puritans needed sin, remarked the British spy and double agent Kim Philby, and he "always seemed to be on the brink of foreclosing on all human hope and happiness." Feeling that containment reeked of compromise, Foster outlined a new "policy of boldness" in *Life* magazine in May 1952. Writing in a tone of pious exasperation, he said that there was "one solution and only one" for the menace of Soviet aggression. It was for the "free world" to develop massive and irresistible "punishing power" so that we who honor freedom and human dignity can "strike back where it hurts." Dulles never saw a contradiction between his sermons on moral law and his constant advocacy of military force. A fervent belief in American exceptionalism reconciled the paradox. "We were from the beginning a vigorous, confident people, born with a sense of destiny and of mission," he wrote. Such people don't go begging to communists.

Before a conference in Geneva convened to resolve the crisis in Indochina, Dulles issued a memorandum that captured his imperious outlook. The Soviets' goal, he told staff, would be to create the "appearance that the West concedes the Soviet a moral and social equality," and they should do everything in their power not to give that impression. Dulles humiliated Chinese officials by refusing to shake hands for a photograph, and when a reporter asked if he had any plans to meet his Chinese counterpart, Zhou Enlai, he smugly retorted, "Not unless our automobiles collide." He told Eisenhower not to smile during a meeting with Nikita Khrushchev, lest warmth be taken for weakness. For Dulles, there was no difference between Stalin and Khrushchev, whatever the latter's attempts to move on. These charm offensives were simply examples of "the classic Communist maneuver known as 'zigzag,'" he coldly advised, and they could be dismissed out of hand. No ground was too low for "God's Cold Warrior." In 1958, Dulles refused to allow an American zoo to import a giant panda called Chi Chi. As Walter Lippmann admonished, after Eisenhower pulled the Sugar Kings baseball team out of Havana over the boyish pleas of a sports-mad Castro, there was a danger of driving our neighbors "behind an iron curtain raised by ourselves."

In January 1956, Dulles provoked an outcry when he gave an interview to *Life* in which he defined diplomacy as "the art" of bringing your opponent "to the brink of war," claiming that "the Reds" (China) had been forced to negotiate over Korea in 1953 only by the palpable threat (delivered via Nehru of all people) of nuclear assault. "I'm not bloodthirsty," he once boasted, "but I hope the Soviets never stop thinking I am." Winston Churchill thought he was a fanatic. "Foster Dulles," he growled, "is the only case I know of a bull who carries his own china shop around with him."

American aggression brought decades of misery and blowback, not least in Vietnam. In the Cold War, the ideology was the strategy. And it was fatally flawed. A recent study, by the political scientist Lindsey A. O'Rourke, found that the United States conducted sixty-four covert regime change operations during the Cold War, in addition to the better known "overt" operations in countries such as Chile and Iran. Of these, thirty-nine failed outright, while the ones that appeared to succeed invariably triggered violent outcomes, including coups, assassinations, and civil wars. As O'Rourke soberly reports, more than 50 percent of the leaders installed by the United States were later violently removed from power. Typically, these interventions "decrease the likelihood of democratization" in the target states and "increase the likelihood of government-sponsored mass killings" in the years that follow. Yet the policy persisted. Regime change was an addiction to which no amount of failure could supply a cure.

In *The Quiet American,* Graham Greene painted an unforgettable portrait of an ingenuous idealist working for the CIA, oblivious of all the harm he caused: "When he saw a dead body he couldn't even see the wounds." But nothing is really seen when it is seen from a great height. Among the indictments leveled at the Dulles brothers, one of the most telling is that they tended to replace experts with ideologues, preferring men who shared their worldview to those who knew and understood the targets of their zeal. The result was what the sociologist C. Wright Mills called "crackpot realism," in which "a high-flying moral rhetoric is joined with an opportunist crawling among a great scatter of unfocused fears and demands."

Mills was talking about foreign policy, but he might have been describing J. Edgar Hoover's FBI. "We have warned repeatedly that atomic diplomacy could lead only to atomic terror," advised a left-wing periodical in March 1946. And so it did. The Cold War came home.

II

Some called it security. Others called it a witch hunt. Joseph McCarthy called it "Americanism with its sleeves rolled up." Parallels between McCarthyism and the hunt for communists abroad were unmistakable: A legitimate concern fanned into an apocalyptic struggle. The success of the strategy of containment, noted the authors of NSC-68, the top-secret document that outlined the case in 1950, "hangs ultimately on recognition by this Government, the American people, and all free peoples, that the cold war is in fact a real war in which the survival of the free world is at stake." This was almost an admission that the enemy would have to be created. Fed on a theory of irrepressible Soviet aggression, the American public was groomed to hate. Even the scholarly term "totalitarianism" tended to fuel the mythology, implying a devil's kinship between the rampant Nazi expansionism that caused the war and the wounded bear that helped to end it. The Soviet Union was grim and gray. It was not controlling America's water supply.

It was communist resistance to fascism in Germany and Spain that had endeared many intellectuals to the movement in the 1930s, when Stalin's crimes were largely unknown, and the near ruin of capitalism after the Wall Street crash of 1929 gave luster to Marxist prophecy. Serious thinkers such as Richard Wright were persuaded. But in the fierce air of the 1950s, when one after another ex-communist came forward to confess their sins to the House Un-American Activities Committee, it was hard to think that anyone could harbor Marxist sympathies without working for the Soviets.

In August 1948, the former communist Whittaker Chambers sent shudders through the establishment when he accused Alger Hiss, a high-ranking State Department official, of being a Soviet spy, in a case replete with betrayal, fuming defiance, and evidence retrieved from a pumpkin. The tragicomedy of the Hiss trial was followed by the horror and anguish of an atomic espionage scandal, in which Julius and Ethel Rosenberg were found guilty of leaking classified information and executed by electrocution, leaving two orphaned children.

"I feel that we're looking at developments that are all too familiar," wrote Hannah Arendt to her friend and mentor Karl Jaspers, in May 1953. She did not think the Red Scare was fundamentally anti-Semitic, but she did see parallels between the scapegoating that brought Hitler to power and the hysteria of McCarthyism. Arendt's most controversial insight, developed during her coverage of the trial of Adolf Eichmann for *The New Yorker,* was the concept of "the banality of evil"—the idea, or observation, that the worst crimes are committed by the most ordinary people. The truth of "the human condition," she wrote in a book of that name, was that men are unreliable: They can give no "guarantee today who they will be tomorrow." This was an insight that endeared John Adams and the authors of *The Federalist Papers* to her, and one that was being lost in these days of purity and recrimination.

Arendt had seen her own professor and idol at the University of Marburg, Martin Heidegger, fall under Hitler's spell, a phenomenon that weakened her respect for intellectuals and strengthened her belief in the importance of an active and articulate political life. This was what thrilled her when she arrived in America as a Jewish refugee from Germany, and the reason she saw McCarthyism as a "clear and present" danger to the republic.

"There is so much I could say about America," she had written to Jaspers in 1946. "There really is such a thing as freedom here and a strong feeling among many people that one cannot live without freedom," she reported. "The republic is not a vapid illusion. . . . people here feel themselves responsible for public life to an extent I have never seen in any European country." Arendt had been placed with a family in Massachusetts, to give her an opportunity to learn English. She found them impossibly provincial, with their spartan diet and abhorrence of a cigarette, but she was amazed by their political engagement and the vigor with which they responded to news that Japanese Americans were being taken from their homes on the West Coast and held in camps. These earnest New Englanders immediately wrote to their congressman, demanding a change of policy. They had never seen or met a Japanese American, yet they felt a compulsion to act. This, marveled Arendt, was the real thing: a public liberty, anxious for the stranger.

When Arendt became a naturalized citizen in 1951, she called her new passport that "beautiful book." She immersed herself in the works of the American founders, in search of the "lost treasure" of political liberty. The Cold War, she quickly perceived, had distorted this vital principle of participation, preaching the "monstrous falsehood" that freedom consists in a free market and little more. The pursuit of loyalty and ideological conformity was devouring the freedom it professed to defend. In her letter to Jaspers on McCarthyism, Arendt reported the "breathtaking speed" with which anticommunism had gripped the nation, paralyzing the entertainment industry, casting fear over the universities, and crippling the machinery of government. "Everything melts away like butter in the sun," she wrote. People were afraid to talk, afraid to laugh, and driven to forms of self-censorship more exacting than any court of law. Anticommunism had created a rogue constitutionalism, which turned ancient protections against self-incrimination on their head. Anyone who refused to say whether they had ever been a communist, pleading a right to silence under the Fifth Amendment, was guilty in the eyes of society and likely to lose their job. The administration, with a vacuous, "golf-playing president," was oblivious of the crisis. A proud democracy was unraveling.

Arendt's own brush with the jealous god of "Americanism" was the intense irritation of being called "un-American" for quoting Plato at a public event in 1953. The charge, blithely affirmed by the philosopher Sidney Hook, was issued by the president of Brooklyn College, who explained that he didn't need pagan philosophers to know right from wrong, because he was born and raised in Iowa. It was especially galling to see an intellectual like Hook join the inquisition—Hook, who once defined the history of thought as the history of heresy, piously lamenting that "we suffer from a dearth of heretics" in this country. This very author was now frowning at Plato and advocating the removal of suspected communists from the universities. The whole thing was an absurdity, "but the power of public opinion is so great in this country that nobody does anything," she complained. As Arendt would state the problem in one of her later works: "Public opinion is the death of opinions." When prisoners of war were due to return from Korea, the army issued a statement saying that those who had been "infected" with communism would be placed in psychiatric clinics. This might not have been done, she noted, "but the thinking is typically American." Arendt had no desire to join the chorus of European anti-Americanism, but she could no longer "stand up for America" without reservation.

Einstein was no less appalled by the persecutions, fearing that "the German calamity" of the Weimar period was repeating itself. Einstein appealed for clemency for the Rosenbergs, and he rallied round educators caught in the squall. William Frauenglass, a high school English teacher in New York, was fingered for a series of lectures he had given six years earlier titled "Techniques of Intercultural Teaching"—a primer on how to "ease intercultural or interracial tensions" in the classroom. This was enough to invite accusations of un-Americanism, and Frauenglass was summoned before the Senate Internal Security Subcommittee to explain his communist connections, where he refused to testify. Facing suspension from his job, Frauenglass wrote to the great scientist, asking for advice.

Einstein received him at his home in Princeton and penned a public letter of support, published in *The New York Times*.

Frauenglass had been right to refuse to incriminate himself, agreed Einstein, but it was equally clear that in the atmosphere fomented by "reactionary politicians," refusal amounted to incrimination. Like Arendt, Einstein felt that the law had been emasculated by the unwritten law of Americanism. Framing his advice as a series of questions, he threw the dilemma back at Frauenglass: "What ought the minority of intellectuals to do against this evil? Frankly, I can see only the revolutionary way of non-cooperation in the sense of Gandhi's. Every intellectual who is called before one of the committees ought to refuse to testify, i.e., he must be prepared for jail and economic ruin, in short, for the sacrifice of his personal welfare in the interest of the cultural welfare of his country."

This was not Thoreau's advice to hearken to the voice of conscience, and let the nation be damned. It was an appeal for civil disobedience to restore "the spirit of the Constitution." As such, it was a patriotic argument, though one that provoked a fierce rebuke from *The New York Times,* as an invitation to break the law. Frauenglass lost his job, along with five similarly accused colleagues, at a meeting "punctuated with high emotions," after twenty-three years of service. McCarthy denounced Einstein as an "enemy of America," and letters arrived at Princeton, demanding his removal. "The man needs lessons in Americanism," asserted a woman from Los Angeles. Eminence as someone who "discovered something" was no excuse for disloyalty to the United States. "I suggest he move to Russia—and soon!" urged a letter from New York City. Robert Oppenheimer, Einstein's boss at the Institute for Advanced Study, protected him, just as Einstein supported Oppenheimer when he too came under the searchlights.

But no one felt the chill like Paul Robeson, in a case where Americanism confronted the Constitution and won.

Robeson was a college football star with an exceptional mind: a two-time All-American who graduated from Rutgers as valedictorian in 1919. He was only the third African American to attend the college. Spurning a career as a professional athlete, he earned a law degree at Columbia University, before finding his voice as an actor and singer when legal work became impossible. Robeson played Shakespeare's Othello to critical acclaim on Broadway but was best known for his soul-rendering performance of "Ol' Man River" in the musical *Show Boat*. Robeson's father had been a slave who escaped via the Underground Railroad at the age of fifteen, achieving a degree of renown as a preacher and evangelist for social justice in Princeton. His mother was a Quaker from a family of ardent abolitionists. Robeson never lost that pedigree, describing the Princeton of his youth as a university town with the feel of "a Southern plantation." As he traveled the world "singing the songs of many lands in the languages of those peoples," he developed a profound "belief in the oneness of humankind," and a deep respect for the socialist republics standing up to fascism. He saw music as one of the purest expressions of this basic human kinship, and he used it to glide defiantly above the jaded compulsions of the Cold War.

Robeson sang for Republicans fighting Franco in Spain. He championed the cause of Welsh miners in Britain. And in June 1949, he went to Moscow and sang African American spirituals and the "Song of the Warsaw Ghetto" before an "adoring, almost worshipful" audience in the Bolshoi Theatre. It was the most audacious act of cultural diplomacy of the Cold War. Members of an American opera group said they had "never heard such applause in their lives." Later that month, Robeson spoke at a peace conference in

Paris, rejecting the "hysterical raving" that breathed war from every platform. "We shall support peace and friendship among all nations," he said, "with Soviet Russia and the People's Republics." The Soviets named a mountain after him. America disowned him.

Among Robeson's crimes was to say that he had walked "in complete human dignity" in the Soviet Union, "a dignity denied everywhere in my native land, despite all the protestations about freedom, equality, constitutional rights, and the sanctity of the individual." He was also reported to have said it would be "unthinkable" for American Negroes to go to war against a Soviet Union far ahead of America on racial equality, though he disputed the phrasing.

Not since Voltaire published his *Letters on the English* in 1733 had praise for another country so savored of betrayal. The baseball legend Jackie Robinson was enlisted to denounce Robeson's sentiments before the House Un-American Activities Committee, which he duly dismissed as "very silly," and even friends were confused by the display of affection for a hated rival. Robeson told how he'd been stopped and greeted by a fan in Harlem who stunned him by whispering, "Paul, were you born in Russia?" He laughed and tried to convince the well-wisher that both he and his politics were authentically American. Somehow, it seemed, "the masters of the press and radio" had convinced us all "that a person who fights for peace, for admission of People's China to the UN, for friendship with the Soviet Union, for labor's rights and for full equality for Negros now, cannot be a 'real' American, must be 'born in Russia.'" This was the lie eating into the American mind. "Today," Robeson declared in the article describing the incident, "I defy any part of an insolent, dominating America, however powerful . . . to challenge my Americanism."

But the nation was not in a forgiving mood. A concert in Peekskill, New York, devolved into a riot when hundreds of locals, including members of the American Legion and the Ku Klux Klan, pelted the audience with rocks. More than eighty scheduled concerts were canceled in the next few months. Robeson would arrive to find venues almost empty and FBI agents taking down the license plates of anyone brave enough to attend. Robeson's status as America's "No. 1 entertainer" was over. "Because of my beliefs, my fight for peace, my fight for friendship between nations, my fight for the complete liberation of my people," he lamented, people said that "I'm not an American and that I should be cut off from the very people from whom I was born." In 1950, the State Department canceled his passport, signaling an eight-year struggle for its return. These were brutal years for Robeson, and the strain was apparent when he was finally summoned to appear before the House Un-American Activities Committee in 1956:

> Are you now a member of the Communist Party?
> *Oh please, please, please.*
> Are you now a member of the Communist Party?
> *Would you like to come to the ballot box when I vote and take out the ballot and see?*
> You are directed to answer the question.
> *I stand upon the fifth amendment.*

So it continued. Robeson had never been a member of the Communist Party, but he refused to be bullied into any kind of disclosure. Had he visited the Soviet Union in 1949? Yes, "and I also sang for the Soviet people, one of the finest musical audiences in the world," he proudly confessed. The Russians had produced great composers, "and Tolstoy," he added, before the chairman cut him off. "They have helped our culture and we can learn a lot [from them]," he insisted, as the tone of the hearing moved from hostility to contempt. If you admire Russia so much, why don't you stay there? asked a member of the committee. Robeson began to lose his cool:

> Because my father was a slave, and my people died to build this country, and I am going to stay here and have a part of it just like you. And no Fascist-minded people will drive me from it. Is that clear?

"The reason you are here is because you are promoting the Communist cause in this country," responded the congressman. "*I am here because I am opposing the neo-Fascist cause which I see arising in these committees,*" Robeson shot back, adding, "*Jefferson could be sitting here, and Frederick Douglass could be sitting here and Eugene Debs could be here.*" Finally, as the committee derided the notion that the New York councilman Ben Davis could be both a communist and a patriot, Robeson erupted:

> I say that he is as patriotic an American as there can be, and you gentlemen belong with the Alien and Sedition Acts, and you are the nonpatriots, and you are the un-Americans and you ought to be ashamed of yourselves.

The hearing was adjourned amid shouts of indignation, and Robeson was denied the chance to read his prepared statement. "It is a sad and bitter commentary on the state of civil liberties in America," he wrote, that the forces of reaction, typified by this "committee of inquisition," had robbed him of the freedom to work or travel or speak his mind. It would be more fitting "for me to question [them]," he said, "than for them to question me." That would include John Foster Dulles, who had denied Robeson's passport appeal on account of his support for anticolonial movements in Africa. When, demanded Robeson, did it become a crime for an American to advocate freedom from colonial oppression? To these men, "the Constitution is a scrap of paper" to be invoked or ignored as the occasion may demand.

Robeson had shown that McCarthyism was bigger than McCarthy, and that John Foster Dulles and J. Edgar Hoover were partners in crime—nationalists at war with their own political traditions. Robeson was one of thousands of activists stalked and hounded by Hoover's FBI, whose empire of surveillance was fed and watered by fears of communist takeover. From 1946 to 1957, not one American teacher was found to have foisted communist ideas on their students, and the membership of the Communist Party was not only minuscule but sustained by the prying state. In 1962, a former agent, who had blown the whistle on Hoover's "autocratic" management of the bureau, estimated that FBI informants accounted for fifteen hundred of the Communist Party's eighty-five hundred members, a considerable drain on the bureau's budget. To compound the absurdity, this "dues-paying F.B.I. contingent" had made the bureau "the largest single contributor to the coffers of the Communist party." Other sources, reported *The New York Times,* had complained of the "authoritarian" culture established by Hoover and of "the anti-liberal, anti-Negro and anti-Semitic attitudes of bureau officials and agents."

If, as Arendt observed, rotation in public office was one of the founders' most "highly valued [and] carefully elaborated" protections against tyranny, J. Edgar Hoover's fifty-year tenure at the head of an organization devoted to spying on American citizens would have been their living nightmare. If the CIA created poisons and hallucinogens to induce witnesses to spill secrets, the FBI's use of moles, wiretaps, and blackmail was not far behind. Coretta Scott

King was certain that the bureau was trying to goad her husband to commit suicide in 1964. It was a reign of lawlessness in the name of law and order. From the Palmer Raids of 1919 to the assassination of the Black Panther Fred Hampton in 1969, Hoover ran a licensed vigilante operation in which racism and anticommunism combined with an astonishing capacity to hold a grudge. Hoover had files on everyone. He once ordered an investigation of a new translation of the Bible, sensing communist influence in the rendering of the word "virgin" as "young woman." He was fond of quoting a verse from the prophet Micah about loving mercy and walking humbly with your God. His actual philosophy, according to the FBI agent G. Gordon Liddy, later convicted for his role in the Watergate scandal, was "Nobody fucks with J. Edgar."

When the scale of Hoover's criminality was revealed to a Senate committee, chaired by Frank Church in 1975, Walter Mondale delivered an incredulous summary of the FBI playbook. "Yesterday," he said, "this committee heard some of the most disturbing testimony that can be imagined in a free society. We heard evidence that for decades the institutions designed to enforce the laws and Constitution of our country have been engaging in conduct that violates the law and the Constitution." For decades, the FBI had taken "justice into its own hands by seeking to punish those with unpopular ideas," deciding that it didn't need authorization before proceeding "to investigate and suppress the peaceful and constitutional activities of those whom it disapproved." In order to protect the country from those it believed to have totalitarian views, the bureau had, in fact, "employed the tactics of totalitarian societies against American citizens." No meeting was too small, no group too obscure, to escape the bureau's attentions. The FBI had created indexes, or "enemy lists," targeting thousands of innocent Americans for "special harassment," and it had even tried to destroy "one of our greatest leaders in the field of civil rights." All of this was done in secret, without the approval of Congress or the American people, under the unsmiling caprice of a single man. How was it possible?

One answer was that Hoover was a nationalist who sharpened his axe on the rock of American exceptionalism. For Hoover, like many patriots, national pride and personal dignity were almost synonymous. When Hoover decided that someone was un-American, their rights and liberties ceased to be. A young recruit recalled being laughed at when he queried some of the bureau's methods during a training session. "You're still in law school—which means you're still an idealist," joshed the special agent conducting the class. "When it's for the right reasons, the end does justify the means," he insisted. And what were the right reasons? "These moral ends," writes the historian Lerone A. Martin, "were determined by the Bureau's Christian nationalism, not the US Constitution."

As early as 1946, Hoover was lecturing the American Legion in Oakland on the need for urgent steps to stem the tide of "red fascism" in the United States, warning them not to be beguiled by the "sly propaganda" of the leftists and their "false preachments on civil liberty." It was the very language that had condemned the likes of Emma Goldman in 1919. And providence, once again, was the permission slip. "This Nation, carved from the virgin resources of a new continent, was founded as a God-respecting land of justice and opportunity." It was a "bastion of hope" to millions of people around the world. But godless communists were trying to destroy it. Hoover summoned those who had defeated fascism with bullets to fight with vigilance against this malignant "foreign 'ism' which has crept into our national life." For these wars were evidently continuous. As Hoover summarized his speech for a huddle of reporters outside, "There is room only for Americanism in the United States."

Fifteen years later, the pistons were still firing: an assault on liberty in the name of freedom. "We are at war with the Communists and the sooner every red-blooded American realizes this the safer we will be," declared Hoover in a speech titled "The Faith to Be Free." We face "a cunning, defiant, and lawless" enemy, and there was "little basic difference between the fascism of Adolf Hitler and the atheistic tyranny practiced behind the Iron Curtain." The Soviet Union was "a godless dictatorship ruled by warped and twisted minds," and the depth of their malevolence vindicated every caution that he, as bureau chief, might consider necessary. Those who would follow the "road of appeasement" did not understand the challenge. "America does not have to apologize to anyone," he insisted. "Certainly not to the arrogant, shoe-pounding Khrushchev and his puppets." Then Hoover sealed his credentials with a burst of patriotic zeal: "America's emblem is the soaring eagle, not the blind and timid mole. Fear, apologies, defeatism and cowardice are alien to the thinking of true Americans. As for me, I would sooner be dead than Red."

These are the words of a demagogue. Yet Hoover was the director of the government's top law enforcement agency, and his speech entered the *Congressional Record*. The subject was domestic security; the theme was nationalism. "Ours is the greatest republic in the history of mankind," he declared. "Our Nation holds in trust the last hope of a free civilization." Compromise was not an option. And Hoover felt that the greatest of all Americans was on his side. "At another hour of grim challenge a full century ago," he perorated, "Abraham Lincoln urged the American people, 'Let us have faith that right makes might, and in that faith let us . . . dare to do our duty as we understand it.'"

As *we* understand it. Nationalism was at once fiercely conformist and rampantly subjective. To the man of faith, the rules are as the morning mist. Mondale might have been stunned by the "totalitarian" habits disclosed by the Church Committee, but presidents and attorneys general knew what Hoover was up to. And if the public was innocent of the details, they broadly supported the cause as Hoover preached it from myriad pulpits, including columns in Billy Graham's magazine, *Christianity Today*. Hoover was no anomaly. He was the Cold War incarnate. But liberty lived in some of the people he tried to destroy, including that charismatic civil rights leader whose personal life exposed him to such terror.

III

"It can be plausibly argued—it is even possibly true—that patriotism is an inoculation against nationalism," suggested Orwell, in his classic essay—just as a humane and rational religion can be a guard against superstition. George Kennan, who lived with a permanent sense of guilt for his part in starting the Cold War, made a similar distinction: "Real love of country, implying as it does the sense of a people's tragedy as well as of its virtues and accomplishments, is one thing; romantic nationalism and illusions of superiority are another." Was Martin Luther King that difference? Was the civil rights movement patriotism in action, or was it a total rejection of the conceit of exceptionalism and the myth of preeminence?

I suggest that it was both, and that King's ability to debunk the myth was integral to his quest to fulfill the American promise. "King's America was less a redeemer nation than a nation in need of redemption," writes one scholar. Yet he never gave up on the idea, the sacred vision of the Declaration of Independence, offering his philosophy of nonviolence as a "militant middle ground" between the ambient cruelties of white America and the despairing rage of

Malcolm X. America was "the prodigal son," he said, "but it's not too late to return home."

King shared much of Malcolm X's historical analysis, even if it took him longer to reach the latter's withering conclusion that "Mississippi is anywhere south of the Canadian border." After a brutal reception in the Windy City in 1966, King offered a rare glimpse of anger: "I think the people from Mississippi ought to come to Chicago to learn how to hate." Both he and Malcolm X had the ability to lace thunder with humor, and both understood the race question in structural or historical terms. People wondered what Harlem had to do with the South, noted Malcolm, as he shared a platform with the voting rights activist Fannie Lou Hamer in 1964. Everything, he insisted. Because the problem "isn't actually Mississippi—it's America." "There's no such thing as a Mason-Dixon Line—it's America. There's no such thing as the South—it's America." Thinking of racism as a Southern problem was the nation's way of avoiding it. So Malcolm attacked the narrative with an intensity redolent of Frederick Douglass.

"We didn't land on Plymouth Rock; the rock landed on us," he once remarked. The difference was important. "We see America through the eyes of someone who has been the victim of Americanism," he said in his signature speech "The Ballot or the Bullet." "I'm not a Republican nor a Democrat nor an American," he declared. He was just one of the 22 million Black victims of a creed. But now those victims were waking up, recognizing that "Uncle Sam" had blood on his hands and no inclination to change. So "our next move is to take the entire civil rights struggle . . . into the United Nations and let the world see that Uncle Sam is guilty of violating the human rights of 22 million Afro-Americans."

Malcolm X is often known as an advocate of violence, but he

was, at heart, an internationalist who wanted to bring America's race problem before the eyes of the world. He found inspiration in the anticolonial movements sweeping Africa and Asia. As the European powers experienced what the postcolonial writer Aimé Césaire called the "boomerang effect" of empire, Malcolm saw Black power as the long payback for slavery. We are "witnessing how the enslavement of millions of black people in this country is now bringing White America to her hour of judgment, to her downfall as a respected nation," he announced in 1963. "And even those Americans who are blinded by childlike patriotism can see that it is only a matter of time before White America too will be utterly destroyed by her own sins, and all traces of her former glory will be removed from this planet forever."

This was an octave too high for most ears—although the gospel singer Mahalia Jackson recalled the same attitude filtering through her fan base in the 1960s. After performing to a jubilant crowd at Constitution Hall in 1961, Jackson was confronted by a girl who could not have been older than sixteen. "Miss Jackson," she protested, "how can you sing 'My country, 'tis of thee, sweet land of liberty' as if you believed it when you know the white people in America don't want us here? It's not our country." "It *is* our country," she responded. And there are "better days ahead." But she was stunned by the sentiment. It was Mahalia Jackson who nudged King to depart from his text as he labored through his prepared remarks at the March on Washington in 1963, thus precipitating one of the greatest rhetorical performances of modern times. "Tell them about the dream, Martin!" she gently demanded. He did, and this one was "deeply rooted in the American dream."

Ever since he was thrust into the leadership of the Montgomery bus boycott, King had demanded racial justice as an American prerogative. In his hastily assembled speech to the Montgomery Improvement Association, following Rosa Parks's arrest in December 1955, King fused his philosophy of nonviolence to the letter and logic of the Constitution. "The only weapon that we have in our hands this evening is the weapon of protest," he declared, to deafening applause at the Holt Street Baptist Church. "And certainly, this is the glory of America, with all of its faults. This is the glory of our democracy. If we were incarcerated behind the iron curtains of a Communistic nation we couldn't do this. If we were dropped in the dungeon of a totalitarian regime we couldn't do this. But the great glory of American democracy is the right to protest for right." This was more than a rhetorical strategy. King saw a perfect alignment between the cause of justice and the promise of America. "If we are wrong, the Supreme Court of this nation is wrong. If we are wrong, the Constitution of the United States is wrong. If we are wrong, God Almighty is wrong." Yet this was patriotism without exceptionalism: a freedom to be earned, not invoked. And "when the history books are written in the future, somebody will have to say, 'There lived a race of people, a *black* people . . . who had the moral courage to stand up for their rights. And thereby they injected a new meaning into the veins of history and of civilization.' And we're gonna do that."

Poised between the promise and the fulfillment, King affirmed the sanctity of the American creed while reserving his highest praise for the people who would bring it to life. He was thankful to America, for the privilege to protest, but he knew that the car would not drive itself. The old providence was static, fixed, and complacent. King's is dynamic, urgent, and hopeful. When King and his co-warriors formed the Southern Christian Leadership Conference in 1957, they chose as their motto "To save the soul of America," fired by the words of Langston Hughes:

O, yes,
I say it plain,
America never was America to me,
And yet I swear this oath—
America will be!

This was the spirit in which he addressed that ocean of faces, stretching from the Lincoln Memorial almost as far as the Washington Monument, in 1963. America's greatness was again conditional: its glory, an open question. The dream was that the nation would "rise up and live out the true meaning of its creed: 'We hold these truths to be self-evident, that all men are created equal.'" But all of this was in the future; "the Negro [was] still sadly crippled by the manacles of segregation and the chains of discrimination." Slavery was still a reality that loomed over American life, and the Constitution was like "a bad check," thrown back in the face of Black Americans. King imagined a better time, when "the sons of former slaves and the sons of former slave owners will be able to sit down together at the table of brotherhood." He painted the future that he wanted to see, and he subjected all patriotism and national greatness to this new test of racial harmony. "If America is to be a great nation, this must become true," he demanded. Then, in a final rhetorical sweep, he gathered the discordant elements into his symphony of brotherhood:

And so let freedom ring from the prodigious hilltops of
New Hampshire.
Let freedom ring from the mighty mountains of New York.
Let freedom ring from the heightening Alleghenies of
Pennsylvania.

Let freedom ring from the snowcapped Rockies of
Colorado.
Let freedom ring from the curvaceous slopes of California.

He continued, summoning the heartlands of white supremacy, and the very birthplace of the Ku Klux Klan, into his new and capacious nation:

Let freedom ring from Stone Mountain of Georgia.
Let freedom ring from Lookout Mountain of Tennessee.
Let freedom ring from every hill and molehill of
Mississippi.
From every mountainside, let freedom ring.

"He's good. He's damn good," said President Kennedy, having watched it all from the White House. King was performing the America he wanted to see: realizing an idea by the force of his eloquence. As Jonathan Eig wrote in his prizewinning biography, he made the radical seem reasonable and, finally, inevitable.

At least part of that energy and power of persuasion was patriotic. Defending his tactics against the scorn of the white moderate, in the "Letter from Birmingham Jail," King noted that "the Boston Tea Party represented a massive act of civil disobedience." Those who kept telling him to "slow down" did not know their history. The demand for racial justice was nothing less than the attempt "to make real the promise of democracy and transform our pending national elegy into a creative psalm of brotherhood." Groups like Elijah Muhammad's Nation of Islam had "lost faith in America," but King's message was ultimately affirmative. "We will reach the goal of freedom in Birmingham and all over the nation," he said, "because the goal of America is freedom." And one day, even "the South will know that when these disinherited children of God sat down at lunch counters, they were in reality standing up for what is best in the American dream . . . bringing our nation back to those great wells of democracy which were dug deep by the founding fathers."

Eig suggests that King himself became "one of America's founding fathers" when he took his fight against Jim Crow into the fortresses of white supremacy, and won. The homage is worthy, but it understates King's radicalism and the degree to which he felt the need to puncture the mystique of the founders to reach his promised land. Something changed after the bombing of a church in Alabama and the murder of several civil rights activists, forcing King into a more vigorous analysis of the American project. Jim Crow and the war in Vietnam were not the anomalies that he wanted them to be. Having roused "the liberal elephant to stomp the racist lion," as one scholar put it, King started to wonder whether the elephant had ever been committed to the task.

In *Where Do We Go from Here: Chaos or Community?*, King describes the Constitution as a compromise that allowed for the enlargement of slavery and the spread of Southern racism, which explained why the United States, despite its superior wealth, was "still far behind European nations in all forms of social legislation." We have to go forward, not backward. We cannot measure freedom against the example of the founders. "Virtually all of the Founding Fathers of our nation, even those who rose to the heights of the presidency," he notes, "were so enmeshed in the ethos of slavery and white supremacy that not one ever emerged with a clear, unambiguous stand on Negro rights." Not one of them "had a strong, unequivocal belief in the equality of the black man."

George Washington was a fourth-generation slaveholder who had moments of guilt but never made a public statement condemning slavery. "Here, in the life of the father of our nation," writes King, "we can see the developing dilemma of white America"—a "haunting ambivalence" resolved into desperate compromise. Jefferson personified it, and even Lincoln, the Great Emancipator, labored under "this strange duality," always believing that whites were superior to Blacks, and uncertain whether the two races could live together. Then came emancipation—an abstract freedom, denuded of substance. King has moved beyond the metaphor of the promissory note. He is not here to color anyone's canvas. "Humanity is waiting for something other than blind imitation of the past," he urges. "We must be hammers shaping a new society rather than anvils molded by the old."

King's critique of the revolutionary violence preached by Frantz Fanon in *The Wretched of the Earth,* the "bible" of the Black Power movement, was that it was still essentially European. He agreed with everything Fanon or Malcolm X had to say about the poison of colonialism, but he saw violence as more of the same. "Let us not pay tribute to Europe by creating states, institutions and societies which draw their inspiration from her," demanded Fanon. But what could be more European than a gun? responded King. Inspired by Gandhi, King saw nonviolence as the answer to the "deadly Western arrogance" that believed it had everything to teach foreign peoples and nothing to learn. It was his answer to a national mythology that led Americans to believe they had arrived before they had gotten out of bed. These anodyne tales of ascent were "the psychological cataracts that blind us to our individual and collective sins."

King's most challenging contention is that nationalism and racism are twins—the national story and the national sin are two sides of the same coin. Racism is the "arrogant assertion that one race is the center of value and object of devotion before which other races must kneel in submission. It is the absurd dogma that one race is responsible for all the progress of history and alone can assure the progress of the future." Nationalism is the mirror image: the conceit that we were born to lead and called to act as "God's military agent on earth." Both of these ideas preceded the Lockean philosophy of equality and natural rights, enshrined in the Constitution, and they have lived to menace the dream.

"Our nation was born in genocide when it embraced the doctrine that the original American, the Indian, was an inferior race," King wrote in *Why We Can't Wait.* "We are perhaps the only nation which tried as a matter of national policy to wipe out its indigenous population." Not only that, but we have "elevated that tragic experience into a noble crusade." Even today, "we have not permitted ourselves to reject or to feel remorse for this shameful episode. Our literature, our films, our drama, our folklore all exalt it. Our children are still taught to respect the violence which reduced a red-skinned people of an earlier culture into a few fragmented groups herded into impoverished reservations." As he sighed from the security of his Ebenezer pulpit, "Now a nation that got started like that has a lot of repenting to do."

In his famous sermon "The Drum Major Instinct," King asserted a painful, sometimes hilarious, equivalence between class snobbery, racism, and the spurious "divinity" of national pride. We all like to come first. We all like to see our names in the newspaper. If we went to a posh university, we like other people to know. But personality is distorted, and ultimately disfigured, when the lust for recognition is unchecked. We all know those people who just talk about themselves, and the talking is boasting. And we all know those nations. "I would submit to you this morning that what is wrong in the world today is that the nations of the world are engaged in a bitter, colossal contest for supremacy," he ventured, and "I am sad to say that the nation in which we live is the supreme culprit. And I'm going to continue to say it to America, because I love this country too much to see the drift it has taken. God didn't call America to do what she's doing in the world now. God didn't call America to engage in a senseless, unjust war . . . in Vietnam. And we are the criminals in that war." Deep down, most people knew this, including our leaders in Washington. But "we won't stop it because of our pride and our arrogance as a nation." Every now and again, he said, "I go back and read Gibbon's *Decline and Fall of the Roman Empire,*" to see what happens to nations that fancy themselves gods. "The parallels are frightening."

King was still a patriot, preaching through "tears of love," but he disdained all illusions of preeminence. It is the belief that we are better than other nations that makes us worse; it is the belief that we are above the laws of nature that brings us crashing down to earth. This was an age of "guided missiles and misguided men," and we have to recover our humanity. "Ultimately, a great nation is a compassionate nation," he urged in his Nobel Prize lecture of 1964. It is one that grasps "the interrelated structure of reality." King called for a "peace race" to replace the arms race, grounding his plea in a metaphysics of unity. As the poet John Donne had written, "No man is an Island, entire of itself." The death of one diminishes us all. For we are all "tied in a single garment of destiny."

For centuries, nations had acted on the principle that "self-preservation is the first law of life," King noted in an essay drawing on the Nobel lecture. But this was a false assumption. "I would say that other-preservation is the first law of life," he countered. A nation secure in its own wisdom was like a stagnant pool, gloomy and stale. Life required curiosity and grace. We are not really nations, in the final analysis, but co-residents of a single "World House." "Every nation is an heir of a vast treasury of ideas and labor to which both the living and the dead of all nations have contributed. Whether we realize it or not, each of us lives eternally 'in the red.' We are everlasting debtors to known and unknown men and women" of many lands, he wrote, with shades of Jane Addams and Randolph Bourne. We get our clothes from one country, our coffee from another, our tea and cocoa from still more exotic lands. "Before we leave for our jobs we are already beholden to more than half of the world." And it was time to stop insulting communists. "Communism is a judgment on our failure to make democracy real," he averred, just as atheism is born of disappointment in the church. Our only defense against a hostile ideology is to be what we proclaim.

These ideas came together with spectacular ferocity at the Riverside Church in New York City, in April 1967, a year to the day before his assassination. In a withering analysis of the Vietnam campaign, King argued that nationalism had turned the United States into a brutal and counterrevolutionary force on the global stage—even "the greatest purveyor of violence in the world today." But King was not alone in breaking his silence. Backed by the prosaic-sounding Clergy and Laymen Concerned About Vietnam, he thought this might be "the first time in our nation's history that a significant number of its religious leaders have chosen to move beyond the prophesying of smooth patriotism to the high grounds of a firm dissent." Why? Because we "deem ourselves bound by allegiances and loyalties which are broader and deeper than nationalism." He wanted to speak for the victims of American power and for those called the enemy. For no government or ideology could make these people "any less our brothers."

True compassion was the ability to see the enemy's point of view and to know his assessment of us. This was where nationalism failed. We are floundering in Vietnam because we haven't even tried "to understand the arguments of those who are called enemy," he contended, in studious disdain for the vocabulary of war. When the Vietnamese people proclaimed their independence in 1945, after a combined French and Japanese occupation, they quoted the American Declaration of Independence. Instead of supporting them, in keeping with its commitment to self-determination, the United States threw its weight behind France in the reconquest of its former colony. We harped on freedom as we poisoned their water, destroyed their crops, and killed their children. It was a strange liberation. "What do they think as we test our latest weapons on them," he wondered, "just as the Germans tested out new medicine and new tortures in the concentration camps of Europe?" Perhaps only a "sense of humor and of irony" could save Ho Chi Minh from despair "when he hears the most powerful nation of the world speaking of aggression as it drops thousands of bombs on a poor weak nation more than eight thousand miles away from its shores."

King spoke as an American to leaders of his own nation. He also spoke "as a citizen of the world, for the world as it stands aghast at the path we have taken." The world was demanding "a maturity of America that we may not be able to achieve." Advising ministers of draft age to seek status as conscientious objectors, he said that "our lives must be placed on the line if our nation is to survive its own folly." For the bombs were exploding at home. A nation spending more on weapons than welfare was on the precipice. "If America's soul becomes totally poisoned, part of the autopsy must read Vietnam."

King's "Beyond Vietnam" speech was an act of courage, exciting fury in the White House and charges of treason from both sides of the aisle. "What is that goddamned nigger preacher doing to me?" raged Lyndon Johnson in the Oval Office. *The New York Times* thought the speech "facile" and melodramatic, bristling at the comparison with Nazi Germany, while the editor of the *Saturday Review* said he would no longer publish King's work, dubbing the peace movement a "Hate America" movement. *Life* magazine, where Luce had announced the American Century and Dulles had unveiled the "policy of boldness" behind the doomed campaign, called the speech a "demagogic slander that sounded like a script for Radio Hanoi." All of which was to prove the speaker's point that nationalism is where reason goes to die. If it was reckless to speculate that the war might already have taken a million lives, the number would be more than twice that by the time those helicopters lurched out of Saigon in 1975—eight years after King had the temerity to demand a cease-fire.

King was the only icon of the American civil religion who had the nerve to attack it—probing its theocratic pretensions with unswerving audacity. He loved his country and saw criticism as an expression of that love. As James Baldwin remarked in an elegiac essay, King believed in the idea of America more than his nation did.

"The whole future of America will depend on the impact and influence of Dr. King," said the Hebrew scholar Rabbi Abraham Joshua Heschel shortly before his assassination. He would probably say the same thing today.

CHAPTER 6

The Flag and the Constitution

> It is hard to defy the wisdom of the tribe: the wisdom that values the lives of members of the tribe above all others. It will always be unpopular—it will always be deemed unpatriotic—to say that the lives of the members of the other tribe are as valuable as one's own.
>
> —SUSAN SONTAG

> I really love America. I just don't know how to get there anymore.
>
> —JOHN PRINE

One of the great intellectual tussles of the twentieth century was between Rabindranath Tagore, poet and Nobel Prize winner, and Mahatma Gandhi, on the wisdom of patriotism. In late 1920, Gandhi had launched a nationwide campaign of noncooperation with the British, involving the boycott of British-run schools, colleges, and law courts, and the burning of foreign cloth. Tagore, who had been lecturing around the world on the "bondage of nationalism" and the coming age of international brotherhood, was horrified by the spectacle, challenging the Mahatma in person and print. Gandhi, as you would expect, stood his ground with an eloquent defense of nationalism as self-respect, but Tagore might have got the better of an argument that concerned more than the fate of India. The taming of nationalism was the challenge of the modern age.

Tagore had been wrestling with the problem for years. "To worship my country as a god," he came to believe, "is to bring a curse upon it." He told his son in 1916 that the task of his remaining years would be to "rid the world of the suffocating coils of national pride." If nationalism was ruling India under the British flag, why would we replicate the pathology under our own? One did not have to succumb to "the colourless vagueness of cosmopolitanism" to see that this cult of nation worship was ruining the world. Nationalism was one of the "most powerful anesthetics that man has invented." It produced "callousness of feeling in men who are not naturally bad." And while it puffed people into visions of omnipotence, it reduced them to slaves. How else could men be persuaded to die for a flag? Under this strange fascination, "the individual willingly allows the Nation to take donkey-rides upon his back."

Great things had come out of the West, Tagore acknowledged, such as freedom of conscience and the sacredness of law, which protects society from "individual caprice." But this was precisely what was lost when "the spirit of the Western nationalism prevails." He saw it in Britain, and he felt it in the United States. To imbue a people with a sense of superiority, to flatter them that they are "the salt of the earth, the flower of humanity," was to shatter all genuine virtue. For pride always breeds blindness in the end. None of these hymns and "blasphemous prayers in the churches" could "hide the fact that the Nation is the greatest evil for the Nation." Nationalism was a hunger that will turn on its own. "The whole world is suffering today from the cult of a selfish and short-sighted nationalism," he told Gandhi. Tagore enjoyed none of Gandhi's confidence that pride in India would not turn into "hatred of Indians different from oneself."

Gandhi's response was masterful, if ultimately ambiguous. "I hope I am as great a believer in free air as the great Poet," he said. "I do not want my house to be walled in on all sides and my windows to be stuffed. I want the cultures of all the lands to be blown about my house as freely as possible. But I refuse to be blown off my feet by any." It was one thing to respect the British. It was quite another to live in their house as "a beggar or a slave." And such was the effect of English clothing and language. Their tendency was "to dwarf the Indian body, mind and soul." When we follow these ostensibly innocent customs, "we surrender our reason into somebody's keeping."

Gandhi could not have agreed more on the folly of nationalism as preeminence. The beauty of nonviolence was the chance to achieve power without striving for mastery. We are, he said, "altering the meaning of [the] old terms, nationalism and patriotism, and extending their scope." There would be "room for the least among God's creation" in this new and gracious temple. No pride of race, religion, or color. The goal was inclusion: "Patriotism spelt humanity." The secret was to ensure that patriotism and freedom move in concert. If India could not heal the Hindu-Muslim divide, or offer dignity to the "untouchables," at the bottom of the caste system, swaraj would be an empty name. As Gandhi told the American writer Katherine Mayo in 1926, "Untouchability for me is more insufferable than British rule."

This conversation, conducted with consummate respect on both sides, is pregnant with insight for America. Tagore's account of nationalism as an "interminable parody of providence" was aimed at the United States as surely as Britain, and he toured the country preaching the message and raising money for his international school, in 1916. But it was Gandhi's intuition that patriotism is essential to freedom, yet something that must be consistent with that precious commodity, that captures the American dilemma. The British had forced Indians to crawl along streets on their hands and knees. They had tied insurgents to the mouths of cannon, before blowing them into pieces. Gandhi knew as well as any revolutionary that freedom meant standing up. Self-rule, by definition, implied a new political community. But Gandhi was no less certain that freedom bought at the expense of an entire caste of his fellow countrymen would melt at the first touch.

This was America's problem: a liberal polity superimposed on a riot of complexity; a democracy grafted onto a slave power. From the moment the clause "reprobating" the slave trade was omitted from the Declaration of Independence, in nervous "complaisance to South Carolina and Georgia," patriotism has haunted the cause of liberty. From the moment Madison brushed aside the antifederalists with airy tributes to the exceptional character of the American people, patriotism has been papering over the cracks. The doctrine of the chosen nation declared victory before the work had begun. It was a glorious evasion, and one that came loaded with theocratic entitlement.

In Martin Luther King, America found a leader prepared to dismantle the myth in the name of the promise—the "last founding father," as some have called him. But with every action came a reaction, and we inhabit that storm.

Collecting his Nobel Peace Prize in December 1964, King cited the defeat of Barry Goldwater as a signal of progress in America. In rejecting a presidential candidate "identified with extremism, racism, and retrogression," he reported, "the voters of our nation rendered a telling blow to the radical right. They defeated those elements in our society which seek to pit white against Negro and lead the nation down a dangerous Fascist path." To elect a candidate who opposed civil rights for African Americans, and offered nothing but bombs and belligerence to a broken world, would have threatened the "survival of our nation," King had warned earlier in the year. Like many commentators, he saw the humbling of the abrasive senator as a watershed in American politics and a sign of a nation coming of age. They had no idea what was coming.

I

Few words are more misleading in modern life than "conservative." The movement that assumed the name in the 1960s channeled free-market economics, ferocious anticommunism, and variously disguised racial resentment into a philosophy of combat in which the battle made the rules. Modern conservatism, argues Rick Perlstein in a series of outstanding histories, was an insurgency, no less hostile to the mottled certitudes of the political establishment than to Joan Baez or Jimi Hendrix. Finding, in FDR's New Deal, the root of all evil, and in Eisenhower, a fatal spirit of compromise, the new conservative convinced himself that the nation had been founded by pious libertarians with a taste for war, and that most of what followed was a mistake. So began a culture war in which vital elements of the constitutional tradition were anathematized as un-American.

Barry Goldwater's manifesto, *The Conscience of a Conservative*, exemplified the problem—pouring scorn on the United Nations, as a quasi-communist organization, and defending force and free markets as American prerogatives. The word "conscience" was a misnomer, for this is a catechism in which the reader is told what to love and what to hate in a grinding and joyless monotone. Even more than communism, Goldwater and his ghostwriters hate all trace of egalitarianism, wincing at the Jeffersonian ideal of equality as the fruit of a godless Enlightenment. "We are all equal in the eyes of God," he concedes, "but we are equal *in no other respect*." America was built on talent. Taxing the rich to inflate the prospects of the poor was an offense to "the American concept of justice." Goldwater has Americanized the free market and damned the social contract. The only part of the state that meets his approval is the military, and Goldwater is itching to use it. There is a waft of nihilism in these hasty brushstrokes: a mind fully adjusted to destruction. It is no accident that the message found its most receptive audience in the Deep South.

As a traditional conservative, excommunicated for sins of moderation, Peter Viereck was in a better position than most to diagnose a malady that would soon be America's. The prophets of this new conservatism, he lamented, are fundamentally intolerant. Born in the toiling seas of McCarthyism, their response to communism was a counter-crusade in which liberal economists and agnostic professors would be purged from public life. Men like William F. Buckley, founder of the conservative weekly *National Review*, cannot abide the pluralist quality of modern life, observed Viereck. Their notions of liberty are narrow and harsh, and far from what he considered the true conservative ideal of humility and respect for the past. "Which is it," he wondered, "triumph or bankruptcy, when the empty shell of a name gets acclaim while serving as a chrysalis for its opposite?"

The warning signs were gleeful acquiescence in the persecutions of the 1950s, followed by book-length apologies for Joseph McCarthy as a misunderstood patriot. Buckley and Goldwater knew how to marginalize extremists, such as the archconspiracist John Birch Society founder, Robert Welch, while harnessing their rage. The result was "a bigger and better Welchism." At best, conservatism had come to mean a ruthless free-market philosophy, divorced from social obligation. At worst, it signified an ugly "thought-controlling nationalism, uprooting the traditional liberties . . . planted by America's founders." Slowly, these ideas permeated a Republican Party reeling from the turbulence of the 1960s. "This country is going so far right you are not even going to recognize it," crowed Nixon's attorney general, John N. Mitchell, in 1970. And it did.

Nixon was more of a pragmatist than a zealot, but he personified the descent of politics into a state of war. In 1968, the Kerner Commission, appointed by Lyndon B. Johnson to examine the causes of the civil disorders widely understood as race riots, delivered its solemn verdict: "Our Nation is moving toward two societies, one black, one white—separate and unequal." In language unusually candid for a government report, the authors blamed the white majority for the miseries of the urban ghetto. "What white Americans have never fully understood—but what the Negro can never forget—is that white society is deeply implicated in the ghetto. White institutions created it, white institutions maintain it, and white society condones it." The commission recommended a raft of initiatives to break the cycle of failure that haunted the cities and weakened American society as a whole. "It is time now to turn with all the purpose at our command to the major unfinished business of this Nation," urged the authors. "It is time to make good the promises of American democracy to all citizens—urban and rural, white and black, Spanish-surname, American Indian, and every minority group."

It was a stirring injunction, but Nixon saw a different kind of opportunity. The government was blaming the victims. The report seemed to blame everyone for the riots except the perpetrators. The answer was not welfare but "law and order" and a government prepared to stand up for the "decent, law-abiding citizens" so slandered by radicals and elites. Such language became the foundation of Nixon's fabled Southern strategy, in which filibustering "Dixiecrats" migrated from the party of civil rights to the party of coded defiance. Patriotism, once again, supplied the code. In his dexterous play for the "great silent majority," Nixon invoked providence as conservatism and destiny as law. "I know it may not be fashionable to speak of patriotism or national destiny these days," he said in a speech on Vietnam in November 1969, but America remained "the hope of millions in the world." Those who opposed the war violated that calling. "North Vietnam cannot defeat or humiliate the United States," he maintained. "Only Americans can do that." This was unity as division, patriotism as power. Patriotism meant trusting Richard Nixon to do whatever he deemed necessary to win a misconceived war, and it was permission to call the antiwar brigade traitors. Such was the hubris that destroyed a presidency.

Watergate and Vietnam, observed Hannah Arendt in a bicentennial address of 1975, were birds of a feather—crimes of innocence, chaperoned by myth. The Watergate scandal was the classic instance of "the boomerang effect, the unexpected and ruinous backfiring of evil deeds on the doer." It was the war, crashing home through the kitchen window. The infamous burglary was masterminded by the CIA agent responsible for the Bay of Pigs fiasco of 1961, and Nixon's team of "plumbers" had previously broken into the office of a psychiatrist, hoping to find dirt on Daniel Ellsberg, the defense analyst who had exposed the web of deceit behind the Vietnam War in what came to be known as the Pentagon Papers. All was fair in love and war. G. Gordon Liddy built a career out of his role in the scandal, publishing a defiant autobiography and launching a popular right-wing talk show. He drove a car with a personalized license plate that read "H20GATE," and he appeared on TV shows such as *Miami Vice*. "I played only villains," he joked. That way, "I don't have to act."

The joke was on America. Arendt thought the speed with which the pardons and book deals were handed out after Watergate was a bad omen for the nation at two hundred. The urgency to rehabilitate the criminals was not confined to their political allies. It reflected a "market" and its demand for "positive images" of the nation, regardless of the truth. Indeed one of the reasons politicians can and do lie, she contended, was the people's "addiction" to an image of their nation as "the mightiest power on earth"—an old idea now wafted into American homes by the wizardry of television and advertising. Forgiveness was one thing; "amnesia" was quite another. Amnesia cannot heal "our wounds."

Arendt might have been describing Ronald Reagan.

If Jimmy Carter, despite a surprisingly hawkish foreign policy, pressed pause on the rhetoric of innocence, Reagan was the great restorer. America was the shining city on a hill, the last best hope of man on earth, the chosen. The Soviet Union was the evil empire, "the most dangerous enemy that has ever faced mankind in his long climb from the swamp to the stars." The Manichaean worldview underwrote a frenzy of military spending, as might be expected, and a politics of violence at home. Interpreting crime under the same rubric of light against darkness, Reagan encouraged patriots to arm themselves against the enemy within. Having survived an assassination attempt of his own, he disdained the option of regulation. "I don't know of any place where it is not against the law to carry a concealed weapon," he told journalists. More laws would not help. Instead, Reagan began to dismantle the regulatory framework, signaling a revolution in gun rights. At the time, only Vermont allowed residents to carry a handgun in public without a permit. Forty years on, no state is *allowed* to prohibit the practice, and shootings punctuate the news cycle with a frequency unknown to earlier generations. As the Maryland attorney general, Joseph Curran, described the revolution in an urgent report of 1999, "The market has changed fundamentally from guns designed for killing animals to guns designed to kill people," a national tragedy. Ten years later, there were more firearms than people, and both parties began to speak of gun ownership as a constitutional right. All of this was new. Under the seductive mandate of patriotism and a mythologized history, America's long tradition of regulating firearms was taken apart.

In a brilliant analysis of the cultural legacy of the Cold War, the historian E. P. Thompson observed a nation locked in fear and distrust. "I have crossed the Atlantic a good many times in the past 15 years," he remarked in 1982, "and I can testify that, while the flight-time is getting less, the Atlantic Ocean is getting wider." The United States had many virtues, including a more open and less stuffy society than Britain's, but its political culture was now at an immense distance from that of western Europe, he said, "brutalised" by long addiction to anticommunism. "Patriotism is love of one's own country," he wrote, "but it is also hatred or fear or suspicion of others." Only patriotism could "explain the ease by which one populist rascal after another has been able to float to power—and even to the White House—on nothing but a flood of sensational Cold War propaganda."

Since communism meant controlled economies, the free market became holy by default—a cruel mistress that one had to love. The American dream had always implied grit and self-reliance, but rarely such hostility to government per se. The journalist Molly Ivins wondered if it had been a good idea to appoint a president who had been going round for years saying "government was the problem"—like hiring a chef who didn't believe in cooking. This was a rampage disguised as a restoration: an assault on American institutions and what remained of a welfare state. Reagan managed to spend two trillion dollars to protect Americans from a diminishing Soviet

Union, including such sublime "crackpottery" as the Star Wars program, while cutting taxes for the wealthy and leaving America's infrastructure to crumble—all of this to the hushed promise that it was "Morning in America."

Reagan, noted the Black studies scholar George Lipsitz, found that he could do anything if he presented it as Americanism. "The new patriotism," he wrote, "serves vital purposes for neoconservative economics and politics; it provides psychic reparations for the damage done to individuals and groups by the operation of market principles." Give a man a gun, tell him that he belongs to the greatest nation on earth, and he might not notice that he has been robbed. Patriotism was the opium of the people: a beguiling compensation for the power we have lost.

"In place of a love for the historical rights and responsibilities of the nation, instead of creating community through inclusive and democratic measures, the new patriotism has emphasized public spectacles of power and private celebrations of success," lamented Lipsitz. It was bread and circuses without the bread. The new patriots glorified war as uplift and catharsis, and their heart was in the flag, not the Constitution. Most of us, observed Lipsitz, get more upset by students and antiwar protesters who "wrap themselves in the Constitution to trash the flag" than by those like Oliver North who "wrap themselves in the flag in order to trash the Constitution."

Oliver North was a central figure in the Iran-contra scandal that dominated the second term of Reagan's presidency: a scheme to arm insurgents against the Sandinista government in Nicaragua by selling missiles to Iran. Appalled that the United States was arming death squads in Central America, Congress passed the Boland Amendment to prohibit all "aid" to the contras. The Reagan administration simply ignored it until a plane crammed with supplies and CIA agents came crashing down in 1986. North, who looked more handsome than the actor who would have played him in a movie, offered one defense as he appeared before Congress: He was doing what was best for America. North, reported an article in *Time*, "plucked the patriotic heartstrings perhaps more musically than even the President." He lectured his interrogators on the communist menace, implying that he knew better than they did how to protect the nation against the danger. Far from issuing an apology, North demanded the resumption of aid to the contras: "for the love of God and for the love of country."

This prompted a stunning rejoinder from Senator George Mitchell of Maine. "Now, you've talked a lot about patriotism and the love of our country," he began. What did that mean? Most nations derived from a single tribe, or race. Many practiced a single religion. But the United States was different: "We have all races, all religions. We have a limited common heritage. The glue of nationhood for us is the American ideal of individual liberty and equal justice. The rule of law is critical in our society." To invoke patriotism against the law, to say that the end justifies the means, was to dissolve that bond. As was the appeal to God-as-higher-law. "Although he's regularly asked to do so, God does not take sides in American politics," advised the senator, "and in America disagreement with the policies of the government is not evidence of lack of patriotism." Indeed, the fact that Americans could criticize their leaders without fear of reprisal was "the essence of our freedom." This was no tirade. It was the lecture Jefferson would have given Lincoln for suspending habeas corpus and banishing his critics during the Civil War. And for a moment, the message seemed to land. As Mitchell described his pride in a nation built on equal justice before the law, North returned a nod of approval.

Yet someone missed the memo. Issuing a complete and unconditional pardon to Secretary of Defense Caspar Weinberger and five of his co-conspirators, some of whom had already pleaded guilty, President George H. W. Bush offered the timeless extenuation: "Caspar Weinberger is a true American patriot." His heart was in the right place. "I have also decided to pardon five other individuals for their conduct related to the Iran-contra affair," Bush continued, explaining that "the common denominator of their motivation—whether their actions were right or wrong—was patriotism." It was the love that covered all sins. Samuel Johnson had been a little timid in declaring patriotism the last refuge of the scoundrel, suggested George Lipsitz. It was clearly the first.

These pardons, complained Molly Ivins, do "real damage to the Constitution." And if patriotism was the excuse, it certainly wasn't the motive. Love of country was becoming a name for brutal partisanship and an aimless love of power. Ivins noted the disdain with which neoconservative thinkers dismissed the Constitution's constraints on the executive branch as "the parchment regime," and she was disturbed by the habit of tarring opponents as enemies of America. Ivins was appalled by Pat Buchanan's incendiary "cultural war" speech at the Republican National Convention in 1992, joking that it "probably sounded better in the original German." But she responded more sternly when culture war became the substance of politics. In 1994, Newt Gingrich had told a group of lobbyists that his election strategy was to portray Clinton Democrats as "the enemy of normal Americans" and proponents of "Stalinist measures." A training memo issued to GOP congressmen in 1995 encouraged Republicans to brand their opponents with words like "corrupt," "sick," "pathetic," "liberal," "welfare," and "traitors," while reserving terms like "freedom," "courage," "strength," "truth," "crusade," and "family" for themselves. Because "language matters," intoned the authors, without a flicker of irony. It is a vital "mechanism of control."

"I'm fond of hyperbole myself," confessed Ivins. "But when politicians start talking about large groups of their fellow Americans as 'enemies,' it's time for a quiet stir of alertness. Polarizing people is a good way to win an election, and also a good way to wreck a country."

Political partisanship was an example of what George Orwell termed "transferred nationalism," in which a party or a creed becomes a proxy for the nation. Like the traditional nationalist, the political zealot is often uninterested in what happens in the real world, just as long as he can feel that his own side is winning. Crimes committed by his tribe have a way of bouncing off his consciousness. For there are "no neutral areas in his mind." In a speech delivered at Brandeis University in 2000, the Hollywood legend and NRA president, Charlton Heston, exemplified the problem, even as he lamented it. "More and more we are fueled by anger, a fury fed by those who profit from it," he bemoaned in a husky, wounded baritone. "Democrats hate Republicans. Gays hate straights. Women hate men. Liberals hate conservatives. Vegetarians hate meat eaters. Gun banners hate gun owners." There was some truth to the charge, but every example involved the left attacking the right, feeding the sense of an authentic America, besieged by pretenders. Heston spoiled his rather brilliant definition of political correctness as "tyranny with manners" by likening his own critics to the rebels and Copperheads of the Civil War. Concluding a speech at Harvard with a quotation from the Gettysburg Address, he thundered: "Those words are true again. I believe that we are again engaged in a great Civil War, a cultural war that's about to hijack your birthright to think and say what lives in your heart." All we can do is fight.

This was what Orwell meant by transferred nationalism. That burning pride has gone intramural, and lost none of its appetite for destruction. Heston has claimed the "miracle" of America for his own partisan cause and cast the liberal as a Benedict Arnold. Liberals could be equally contemptuous, and the nature of a culture war was to sow distrust on all sides. Yet there is no doubt that the political right was the primary vehicle of transferred nationalism, building arsenals of resentment and inspiring much of the period's physical violence. The Oklahoma City bombing of 1995 was committed by a Gulf War veteran and former NRA member called Timothy McVeigh. This was the extreme case, but McVeigh's history of antigovernment activism reveals a startlingly conventional animus. As a resident of New York, McVeigh had written to his congressman to express his "shock" at the state's draconian "firearms restrictions," saying he "strongly believe[d] in a God-given right to self-defense." His letter brimmed with the classic terminology of the "law-abiding citizen," vexed to distraction by the overreach of the state. The envelope was stamped with the words "I'm the NRA."

The journalist and historian Godfrey Hodgson, who had coined the phrase "liberal consensus" in a study on America from World War II to Nixon, sensed an ominous shift in the tone of public life at the turn of the century. Hodgson noted that some of George W. Bush's admirers had carried posters at the 2004 Republican convention asking "how they were to shoot liberals if their guns were taken from them." Everyone knew that this was a joke in bad taste, not the portent of American fascism, Hodgson conceded. But these were not healthy signs. In a bizarrely candid op-ed, the Fox News executive Scott Norvell mocked the "institutionalized leftism" of the BBC, volunteering that "we at Fox News manage to get some lefties on air occasionally, and often let them finish their sentences before we club them to death and feed the scraps to Karl Rove and Bill O'Reilly." Where does a metaphor end?

Explaining why conservatives began to purchase the AR-15 assault rifles that were so recently off-limits, the right-wing pundit Grover Norquist proudly adduced, "It was an f-you to the left." The fight was the game. Partisanship was policy. No less than Thomas Jefferson had seen it coming. He once complained that he had been "dished up . . . as an antifederalist," maintaining that he was neither federalist nor antifederalist but a man of independent opinions. To surrender one's mind to a party, he warned, was "the last degradation of a free and moral agent." It is the mark of a declining state, wrote Jean-Jacques Rousseau, when the people vote by "acclamation" rather than reflection, when the electorate "has ceased to deliberate, and either worships or damns" as instructed from above. That kind of "unanimity" is normal in an empire, disastrous in a democracy, he warned: a "slavery" of the mind.

From the launch of *National Review* in 1955, a misnamed "conservative" movement had trained its votaries to regard liberals as shallow, un-American, and less than fully human. In so doing, they attacked more than their political adversaries. Government, wrote Thomas Paine, is the badge of lost innocence: It is an attempt to bring peace to a fractured and fallen world. "Why has government been instituted at all?" wondered Alexander Hamilton. "Because the passions of men will not conform to the dictates of reason and justice, without constraint." The U.S. Constitution is a product of that tradition of civil liberty and balanced powers: a coalition of mortals. Any philosophy that ascribed purity to itself and darkness to its detractors was going to frustrate the project. Much of what offended conservative ideas of sovereignty was fundamental to the American political creed. When you can be branded "as part of the lunatic left" for raising a voice for gun control, protested Molly Ivins, liberty is in trouble. The problem reached crisis proportions after 9/11.

II

The attacks on New York and Washington on that clear September morning created a surge of national unity and a temporary truce between the parties. The audacity of the operation, in which symbols of American power and prosperity were turned into instruments of mass murder, achieved exactly what was intended: an uncontrollable rage. Rarely had an enemy seemed more completely malevolent. But who was the enemy? The war on terror was, from the outset, a war against an abstraction: a perfect evil, imperfectly located. Screaming for vengeance, America took a hammer to the Bill of Rights.

There were few more deeply shared convictions among the founders, noted Lincoln in 1848, than the necessity of "giving the war-making power to Congress." Allow a president to invade another country "whenever he shall deem it necessary," warned Lincoln, "and you allow him to make war at pleasure." Such a power the founders regarded as "the most oppressive of all Kingly oppressions; and they resolved to so frame the Constitution that no one man should hold the power of bringing this oppression upon us." To argue otherwise, he told his old friend and law partner, William Herndon, was to destroy "the whole matter" and to place "our President where kings have always stood."

Of course Lincoln, as we have seen, breached this principle with spectacular aplomb, running to Congress long after he had committed the nation to war in 1861. But as Daniel Ellsberg remarked in the context of Vietnam, once a war begins, it is easy to make it popular, because you're telling people what they want to believe—"that we're better than other people, we are superior in our morality." And that is usually enough to deal with the legalities. That sentiment was understandable after 9/11, and the outcome was a virtual surrender of popular sovereignty to the executive branch. Within days of the attacks, Congress granted vast and unspecified powers to the president, with unanimous support in the Senate and a stunning 420–1 majority in the House. In a solitary word of dissent, Representative Barbara Lee expressed her concern that military action would not prevent further acts of terrorism, and her hope that we do "not become the evil that we deplore." It was like a butterfly circling a tank.

With a fig leaf of international cooperation, the United States duly deposed the Taliban in Afghanistan, without finding the perpetrators of the attacks, beginning a twenty-year war that concluded with the Taliban's return to power in 2021. This was followed by a disastrous war in Iraq launched on a sea of falsehoods. By the time U.S. forces found Osama bin Laden in 2011, these wars of redress had caused 900,000 direct casualties, according to the Costs of War Project at Brown University, creating a new generation of adversaries along the way. As a group of disenchanted veterans defined the problem in a *New York Times* op-ed, "Democracy doesn't come in a box." You cannot build peace by "shooting at people." Yet such was the belief of a nationalism that swallowed a nation.

Abu Ghraib. Torture memos. Waterboarding. Extraordinary rendition. Guantánamo Bay. Liberty was in remission. The Patriot Act of 2001, hurried through the Senate by a vote of 98–1, vitiated constitutional protections against arbitrary detention, unreasonable searches, and the right to a swift and fair trial. The Bush administration created what one scholar termed a "law-free zone," accusing those who would fret over "phantoms of lost liberty" of giving aid and comfort to the enemy. It was a powerful, and devastating, response. The Fifth Amendment's demand for due process, or the Eighth Amendment's protection against cruel and unusual punishment, were effectively declared unpatriotic. It was the repeat of a pattern that started with the arrest of "Copperheads" during the Civil War and continued with the incarceration of "subversives" such as Eugene Debs in World War I. It was the failure of democratic nerve that Randolph Bourne named as the cost of nationalism in the same era. And journalism, the piercing conscience of democracy, as Jefferson and Tocqueville saw it, followed the crowd.

In February 2003, the Fox News anchor Sean Hannity predicted that "the left" would have egg on its face for doubting whether Saddam Hussein possessed weapons of mass destruction. "We're going to go in and we're going to liberate this country in a few weeks," he said, and "We're going to open up those . . . those gulags and those prisons and you're going to hear stories of rape and torture and misery, and then we're going to find all of the weapons of mass destruction that all of you guys on the left say don't exist." Perhaps he hadn't been watching the competition. The liberals made the war.

In March 2002, *The New Yorker* published an imploring, saber-rattling entreaty by Jeffrey Goldberg titled "The Great Terror"—a phrase typically reserved for Stalin's atrocities of the 1930s. The author made repeated comparisons with the Holocaust, teasing links between Iraq and September 11, and speculating that Saddam's despicable treatment of the Kurds was the prelude to foreign aggression—because "the Kurds were for practice." Experts now believed that "Iraq will have an atomic bomb in three years," Goldberg added with untempered certainty. So we have to act. He quoted an Israeli general who justified an attack on Iraq's nuclear facilities on the theory that "preemption is always a positive," when you're dealing with this kind of adversary. Never mind the fact that the judges at Nuremberg defined "a war of aggression" as "the supreme international crime"—a guiding principle of international law. Like many of his peers in the fourth estate, Goldberg substituted a fantasy of deliverance for the obligations of international law. He described a people panting for liberation and dreaming of the sight of "American tanks coming down across this plain going to Baghdad." One man apparently told him, "The U.S. is the lord of the world."

This was propaganda masquerading as journalism; militarism sold as compassion. To understand the present, wrote Thompson in his Cold War lecture, we must "first resist the great suggestive-power of memory"—that is, the simple transfer of remembered images to our own very different times. The moment we invoke Hitler or Stalin as compelling analogies, all judgment is lost. Such "lessons of history" are actively unhelpful in dealing with the present, because they substitute monsters and demons for the people and circumstances we need to understand. And that is what nationalism does.

In all but a handful of cases, American news media relinquished their independence and joined a crusade to slay a Hitler who was not. Days after the 9/11 attacks, the CBS anchor Dan Rather appeared on the *Late Show with David Letterman,* where he pledged unconditional loyalty to the administration: "George Bush is the president. He makes the decisions, and, you know, as just one American, wherever he wants me to line up, just tell me where, and he'll make the call." The result was a breathless innocence that failed to scrutinize the administration's rhetoric about anthrax and mushroom clouds, and a reluctance to publish evidence of American atrocities at Abu Ghraib prison, when it first appeared. As Rather flatly confessed in an interview with CNN's Larry King, "Look, I'm an American. I never tried to kid anybody that I'm some internationalist or something. And when my country is at war, I want my country to win, whatever the definition of 'win' may be." NBC's Tim Russert offered a similar disclaimer: "Yes, I'm a journalist, but first,

I'm an American. Our country is at war with the terrorists, and as an American, I support the effort wholeheartedly."

To follow the flag was to inflame the nation and betray the Constitution. A *Time* article of April 2003 now reads like a satire, saluting George W. Bush as a "great man" who "now owns a bit of history to prove it." "The President's ability to decide when and where to use America's military power is now absolute," gushed the writer. This was "not what the Constitution says, and it's not what the War Powers Act says," he granted. And it flew in the face of the UN Charter. "But who cares? And who cares what America's allies think either?"

Those who did care, or dared to question the "intelligence" behind the invasion, paid with their careers. The country music band the Dixie Chicks endured death threats and virtual annihilation from the airwaves for the crime of saying "We do not want this war" at a concert in London, and the actor Pamela Anderson recalled how a man assaulted her on a plane yelling, "Do you know what this country's done for you?" until staff put him in handcuffs. The cause of the commotion? "He thought I was a Dixie Chick."

III

"What we do with civilization," said the Vietnam veteran and author Karl Marlantes, "is that we learn to inhibit and rope in these aggressive tendencies, and we have to recognize them. I worry about a whole country that doesn't recognize them." Patriotism muddled that aspiration. It valorized what it should have contained. As Dan Rather ruminated in an interview with the BBC, "I worry that patriotism run amok will trample the very values that the country seeks to defend." This surge of patriotism, he now admitted, had paralyzed his profession, leaving journalists in a fog of passivity: "I know the right questions," they would think, "but you know what, this is not exactly the right time to ask them." Wouldn't it be more patriotic, he now surmised, "to stand up, look them in the eye, and ask the questions they don't want to hear"? It depends what you mean by patriotism.

When the actor Jane Fonda heard reports of torture and "free fire zones" in Vietnam, while she was working in Paris, she initially refused to believe them. Friends lent her a book called *The Village of Ben Suc* by Jonathan Schell, and she was radicalized. "I was one person before I read it, and I was another person after I finished," she recalled, deciding at once to move back to the States to protest the war. She had no choice. "The more staunchly patriotic you are, when you realize that your country has betrayed your belief in it, you become angrier than most other people who don't care one way or the other."

When patriotism means exceptionalism, it is nationalism before it has left the room. Patriotism as unconditional love—my country right or wrong—is the love that kills. Patriotism as a humble and qualified affection, anchored to a clear set of values, brings different results. In the movie *Chariots of Fire,* based on the fierce rivalry of two athletes at the Paris Olympics of 1924, the girlfriend of one of the protagonists, Harold Abrahams, asks his genial teammate Lord Lindsay how he can carry himself with such ease. Don't you want to be the best, the fastest in the world? she wonders. "To be *a* fastest, yes, but not *the* fastest," he responds. What about fame, immortality? "I don't need that," he says. He runs for pleasure, not praise. When the devout Christian Eric Liddell finds that he cannot compete in the hundred meters, because the heat is scheduled for a Sunday, Lindsay—who has already won a silver in the hurdles—gives up his spot in the four hundred: "Just to see you run." Abrahams and Liddell take home the golds, but Lindsay is the real hero of the story. He is the only character who is truly free.

Coming after what was, by then, the abject failure of the war in

Iraq, the Obama presidency offered something resembling a patriotism of humility. In his remarks at the National Prayer Breakfast in 2015, President Obama used the words "humble" and "humility" no fewer than ten times, counseling Americans not to look down on other faith traditions when we, "in our home country," justified slavery and Jim Crow "in the name of Christ." Later that year, Obama described the Selma march of 1965 as an act of patriotic devotion, led by those who "believed that America is a constant work in progress; who believed that loving this country requires more than singing its praises." For patriotism can look forward, as well as back. Men like the fearless John Lewis, or the young mother of five who followed him into the batons and tear gas, found greatness not by honoring the past but by transcending it. "That's what it means to love America. That's what it means to believe in America." Indeed, Obama wondered, "What greater expression of faith in the American experiment than this, what greater form of patriotism is there than the belief that America is not yet finished, that we are strong enough to be self-critical?"

Yet this was too profound, too searching for a public that had celebrated Martin Luther King Day, earlier in the year, by helping Clint Eastwood break box-office records with *American Sniper,* a gruesome apologia for American brutality in Iraq. "America," Obama had reasoned, "is not some fragile thing," incapable of self-critique. But *that* America was fragile, in the extreme. The fury that greeted his mild and thoughtful remarks at the National Prayer Breakfast presaged the performative rage of the Trump years. And Obama's failure to arrest the U.S. war machine in the Middle East, where he clung to the older narrative of innocence, left an ambiguous and combustible legacy: a symbolic challenge to a white, racist America with little attention to the guns and the militarism that sustained it. Obama managed to poke the bear of white Christian nationalism just by being who he was, and to feed it by perpetuating his predecessor's disastrous wars. A new dawn for America turned into a new age of nationalism. The conspiracy surrounding his birth certificate was a perfect storm of racism, xenophobia, and media-assisted malice. As Obama drolly remarked of the "swamp of crazy" now flooding American homes, "If I watched Fox News, I wouldn't vote for me [either]." Many Republicans were incredulous that Donald Trump earned the presidential nomination in 2016, he noted. But if you build a house on lies, hoaxes, bile, and exaggeration, "this is the nominee you get."

In that sense, Trump was the terminus of a conservative movement that passed from red-baiting to liberal-baiting without pausing for breath: the transferred nationalism of mindless partisanship. Trump is also the face of a more traditional patriotism, argues Jeffrey Sachs: a populist variant of American exceptionalism. We should be shocked by Trump's America, not surprised, urges the economist. "America First" is a symptom, not a cause. If anything positive can come out of this age of vitriol, he suggests, it might be for Americans to reject a cult of self-aggrandizement that is really self-harm. This state-sanctioned narcissism, writes Sachs, in homage to a French proverb, "is worse than a crime, it is a mistake." Suspicion of foreigners, contempt for the United Nations, a child-like faith in military solutions—these are fruits of the same tree. It is, he confesses, unfathomable that a nation as wealthy and sophisticated as America can sit as low as 114 on the Global Peace Index, which ranks countries by such criteria as homicide rates, military expenditure, and access to small arms. That was 2017. We currently sit at 128 out of 163 nations on the Peace Index, between Kenya and Ecuador. Our annual contribution to the United Nations—a source of distress to penny-pinching nationalists—amounts to a mere seven hours of Pentagon spending. We are addicted to force—a philosophy rooted in the alluvial soil of exceptionalism. Sachs finds an antidote in the blossoming internationalism of John F. Kennedy, and it is there that I conclude this book.

EPILOGUE

Patriotism Spelled Humanity

> I hope we shall prove how much happier for man the Quaker policy is, and that the life of the feeder is better than that of the fighter.
>
> —THOMAS JEFFERSON TO JOHN ADAMS, JUNE 1, 1822

John F. Kennedy was no Gandhi. He was no King. But he cast off his nationalism to serve his country and the world. Kennedy's transition from cold warrior to peacemaker is one of the stories of modern times, and it deepens the tragedy of his sudden and violent death. Kennedy had been no less terrified by the belligerence of his own generals than by that of the Soviets during the Cuban missile crisis of 1962, a distrust that had been building since the Bay of Pigs fiasco of the previous year, when the CIA and Joint Chiefs of Staff persuaded him to authorize a harebrained scheme to invade Cuba and overthrow Castro. As the enormity of the Bay of Pigs disaster registered, Kennedy told one of the highest officials of his administration that he wanted "to splinter the C.I.A. in a thousand pieces and scatter it to the winds." Having won the presidency on promises of standing up to communism, Kennedy began to worry about the enemy within: the all-powerful, ever-blundering military machine.

Kennedy might also have been influenced by a delegation from the Friends Committee on National Legislation, who visited him in the White House in May 1962, to protest a plan to name a nuclear submarine after William Penn. When the Quakers explained that this would be like naming a battleship the USS *Gandhi* or a jet bomber the *Saint Francis of Assisi*, the Catholic Kennedy grinned and told them that it wouldn't happen. He then listened intently as the visitors pressed the finer points of their philosophy, letting the meeting run over. When a secretary interrupted to say that his next appointment was due, Kennedy chirped, "Tell them to wait, I'm learning something from these Quakers." Voltaire and Benjamin Lay would have been proud.

Whether it was reason or experience that forced the epiphany, Kennedy adopted a new approach to the Soviet Union in the last year of his presidency. Instead of a monster, bent on destruction, Kennedy began to see Nikita Khrushchev as someone like him: a reasonable man, surrounded by zealots. Rather than play to his own gallery of nationalists and risk another escalation, Kennedy launched a charm offensive toward the Soviets, calling for nothing less than "comprehensive disarmament" as a condition of "world peace." This was delivered not from the White House or the Pentagon, in a show of strength, but from the campus of American University, in the billowing gown of a professor.

What kind of peace did he mean? "Not a *Pax Americana* enforced on the world by American weapons of war"—weapons "which can only destroy and never create." "Not the peace of the grave," the bitter fruit of war. But a genuine and lasting peace, which makes life worth living. There could be no freedom without this kind of peace, and it could start with a new attitude toward the Russians. "No government or social system is so evil that its people must be considered as lacking in virtue," he contended. And while we recoil from the dogmas of communism, "we can still hail the Russian people for their many achievements—in science and space, in economic and industrial growth, in culture and in acts of courage." Kennedy went on to praise the bravery and sacrifice of the Russians during World War II, hailing this as a more profound reality than the cycle of suspicion in which both nations were trapped. He humanized them. And if we cannot end our differences, he said, "we can help make the world safe for diversity. For, in the final analysis, our most basic common link is that we all inhabit this small planet. We all breathe the same air. We all cherish our children's future. And we are all mortal." It was a master class.

Kennedy announced that he, Khrushchev, and the British prime minister, Harold Macmillan, had begun discussions toward a comprehensive test ban treaty, conscious that this would be no substitute for disarmament, but a vital step toward that goal. And then he addressed his own nation: "My fellow Americans, let us examine our attitude toward peace and freedom here at home. The quality and spirit of our own society must justify and support our efforts abroad." Ultimately, he argued, peace will flow not from the signatures of statesmen but from an attitude of generosity and hope among the people. "Confident and unafraid," he concluded, "we labor on—not toward a strategy of annihilation but toward a strategy of peace."

Khrushchev was said to have been deeply moved by the speech, especially the parts acknowledging the immense suffering of the Russian people during World War II. He called it "the greatest speech by any American President since Roosevelt," and he took the unprecedented step of ordering a Russian translation of the entire speech to be published in the major Soviet newspapers, *Pravda* and *Izvestia*. This was diplomacy, the moving of minds. As the historian Adrian Hastings has written, "The factor of personality is not something to be ignored if one wishes to make sense of human history."

The following month, Kennedy hailed the test ban treaty as "the end of one era and the beginning of another," honoring the Soviet leader as an equal partner in the project. In any nuclear exchange, "Chairman Khrushchev" had warned, "the survivors would envy the dead." Two months later, Kennedy stood before the United Nations and extolled the "new rays of hope" breaking through the clouds of fear and distrust that had too long darkened the international horizon. Preaching to his own nation as much as to the Soviets, he said that if we want "our countries to be fully secure, we need a much better weapon than the H-bomb—a weapon better than ballistic missiles or nuclear submarines—and that better weapon is peaceful cooperation." To that end, he proposed a collaboration between the United States and the Soviet Union "in the field of space," mooting the possibility of "a joint expedition to the moon." Why, he challenged, "should man's first flight to the moon be a matter of national competition"? Surely, we should "explore whether the scientists and astronauts of our two countries—indeed of all the world—cannot work together in the conquest of space."

This was revolutionary. Competition between East and West would continue, but a competition of ideas, not weapons. And to fight for democracy was not to claim perfection for ourselves, Kennedy insisted. "We are working to right the wrongs of our own country," he acknowledged. Peace, like freedom, was a process, and small steps were the levers that could move the world. "My fellow inhabitants of this planet," he concluded, "let us take our stand here in this Assembly of nations. And let us see if we, in our own time, can move the world to a just and lasting peace." Kennedy was not trying to end the arms race, remarked a British politician; he was calling off the Cold War. Two months later, he was assassinated.

America has a way of destroying its visionaries—even when the visionary is only a messenger, pointing placidly to the nation's ideals. The dubious achievement of patriotic ardor has been to make ideas fundamental to the Declaration of Independence sound foreign and utopian. From Henry Wallace calling for "the century of the common man" as an alternative to the aching pomp of "the American Century" to those who counseled Lincoln against the chimera of union by conquest, the skeptics have been closer to the democratic values of reason and consent than the priests of exceptionalism. They knew what many of the antifederalists knew: that appeals to providence and destiny cannot cheat the laws of political attraction and trust. It was not that they were any less patriotic, in the deeper sense of loving their country, but they knew that an asserted, theological unity was no substitute for the real thing, and not something that could be manufactured by war. That is why Randolph Bourne regarded Americanism as a mortal threat to the American promise, and Martin Luther King felt the need to probe the civil religion as vanity and amnesia. "America has not yet changed because so many think it need not change," he observed in a late essay, "but this is the illusion of the damned."

The irony, for Bourne and King, was that theocratic arrogance was the ultimate holdover from colonial Europe—something that should have been left behind in 1776. America has changed profoundly since King issued that warning, but we have also witnessed the return of providentialist audacity with wars of aggression in the

Middle East and Christian nationalism at home. If King remains the antidote to such delusions, Kennedy's evolution from anxious militarist to prophet of peace may be the more workable template. "Let our great role in history be that of peace makers," he said. It is never too late.

ACKNOWLEDGMENTS

Having completed this book on January 6, 2026, I find it hard not to think of Kurt Vonnegut and his tragicomic reflections on the life of a writer in a time of war. In the sixties, he recalled, every self-respecting artist in the country spoke out against the Vietnam War, and did so with the clarity of a laser beam. But the power of this weapon turned out to be "that of a custard pie dropped from a step-ladder six feet high." Don't expect to change history when you write a book, he warned. The best you can hope for is to make a few new friends.

I will take that. Writing this book has been a pleasure from beginning to end, and I have my editor, Kevin Doughten, to thank, first and foremost, for entrusting me with the task and for the (almost total) freedom in which he has encouraged me to write it. Huge thanks are also due to Jess Scott for her unfailing precision and patience during the editorial process, and to all the production team at Crown. As ever, I am deeply grateful to my agent, Laurie Bernstein, for her shrewd and generous counsel. I'm an independent scholar, but I feel immensely supported by those around me.

Among them, I'd like to mention Patrick Allitt, whose relentless good humor is matched only by his knowledge of this vast and vexing country. Thanks also to Mike Vorenberg for encouraging me to do for patriotism what I tried to do for the Second Amendment in *One Nation Under Guns,* and to bring a light touch to a serious topic. I'm also grateful to Joe Crespino and Yanna Yannakakis for inviting me to teach a course on war and democracy in the history department at Emory, which allowed me to road test some of this material and gave me hope that some of the ideas could fly. Among the students in that enjoyable class, I would like to thank Josh Rankin for sustained brilliance in discussion and for introducing me to the world of Aimé Césaire. Thanks are due, as ever, to the wider community of scholars who made this book possible, especially Richard Slotkin, Colin Woodard, Abram C. Van Engen, Nicholas Guyatt, and Stephen Kinzer. I would also like to thank Larry Miller, James Rissler, Marilyn McGinnis, and Sasha Swinson for suffering my conversation on *The Big Country* and for generally keeping me on the straight and narrow in 2025.

I owe more than the usual debt of thanks to my children, Connie, George, and Emma. What for me is a book and research project is for them a life and reality—a point made indirectly by Connie when she was interviewed as a witness and survivor of the shooting at Brown University in December 2025. Time and again, they show me what it means to engage rather than retreat, and I count my time serving as a judge for the Midtown High School debate club, better known as the Jesters, among my most precious in the United States. Eternal thanks to my wife, Meara, who handles everything and is the closest thing I know to Howard Zinn's memorable description of Stokely Carmichael as one who "would stride cool and smiling through hell, philosophizing all the way." Minus the philosophizing, that is her. I dedicate this book to all the friends who have shown me the best of this country, and to one in particular, Emanuele Di Lorenzo.

NOTES

A note on the notes: This book draws on a wide range of material, and I have erred on the side of obscurity in citing my sources. I have omitted references to presidential statements or iconic speeches that are easily accessible online.

Prologue: Americanism or the American Promise?

1 **"pregnant" with "the fate of the world":** Jefferson to Roger Weightman, June 24, 1826, www.loc.gov/exhibits/jefferson/214.html.

2 **"All eyes are opened":** Jefferson to Weightman, June 24, 1826.

2 **"the power of a superior agent":** John B. Boles, *Jefferson: Architect of American Liberty* (Basic Books, 2017), 477.

3 **"Much as I hate slavery":** *Collected Works of Abraham Lincoln,* vol. 2 (Rutgers University Press, 1953), name.umdl.umich.edu/lincoln2.

4 **audacious and "interested" pieties:** Jefferson to Margaret Bayard Smith, Aug. 6, 1816, founders.archives.gov/documents/Jefferson/03-10-02-0186.

4 **the "American promise":** Randolph Bourne, *Untimely Papers* (B. W. Huebsch, 1919), www.gutenberg.org/cache/epub/68626/pg68626-images.html.

5 **"Gentlemen of the jury":** Emma Goldman, Address to the Jury, July 9, 1917, awpc.cattcenter.iastate.edu/2017/03/21/address-to-the-jury-july-9-1917/.

5 **"abrogates the principles":** Emma Goldman, *Anarchism and Other Essays* (Mother Earth Publishing Association, 1910), 139.

5 **"terrible solidarity":** Max Eastman, "The Religion of Patriotism," *Masses,* July 1917.

6 **"can analyze nationalism":** Devere Allen, *The Fight for Peace* (Macmillan, 1930), 231.

Chapter 1: Chosen

7 **Harriet Beecher Stowe:** Vernon Louis Parrington, *Main Currents in American Thought: An Interpretation of American Literature from the Beginnings to 1920,* vol. 1 (Harcourt, Brace, 1927), 12–13.

8 **"French bastard landing":** Thomas Paine, *Common Sense* (1776), 9, www.google.co.uk/books/edition/Common_Sense/PE8UAAAAQAAJ?hl=en.

8 **"groaned beneath a much larger number":** Paine, *Common Sense,* 9.

8 **"an ass for a lion":** Paine, *Common Sense,* 50.

8 **"than all the crowned ruffians":** Paine, *Common Sense,* 11.

9 **"the loving heresy":** Donald J. D'Elia, "The Republican Theology of Benjamin Rush," *Pennsylvania History: A Journal of Mid-Atlantic Studies* 33, no. 2 (1966): 188, www.jstor.org/stable/27770405.

9 **"no respecter of persons":** *Tracts on Liberty by the Levellers and their Critics,* vol. 4 (1647), oll.libertyfund.org/pages/leveller-tracts-4.

9 **"This thing called *prerogative*":** *Tracts on Liberty,* oll.libertyfund.org/pages/leveller-tracts-4.

9 **"out of the pawes":** William Walwyn, "Englands Lamentable Slaverie" (1645), quoted in Michael Kent Curtis, "In Pursuit of Liberty: The Levellers and the American Bill of Rights," *Wake Forest University Legal Studies Paper,* no. 956931, papers.ssrn.com/abstract=956931.

9 **"of a quick, ingenious":** John Milton, *Areopagitica* (1644), www.econlib.org/library/Essays/miltA.html.

10 **"a mutual bond":** John Milton, *The Tenure of Kings and Magistrates* (1650), milton.host.dartmouth.edu/reading_room/tenure/text.shtml.

10 **"One's country":** David Masson, *Life of John Milton* (Macmillan, 1880), 502.

11 **"enemies of pomp":** Voltaire, *Toleration and Other Essays,* trans. Joseph McCabe (G. P. Putnam's Sons, 1912), oll.libertyfund.org/?option=com_staticxt&staticfile=show.php%3Ftitle=349&chapter=28219&layout=html&Itemid=27.

11 **"never bow to anybody":** Voltaire, *Letters on England* (Penguin, 1980), 26.

11 **"If I were forty":** "'A Dying Testimony, to the Abbé Gaultier,' 21 February, 1778," www.whitman.edu/VSA/letters/21.2.1778.html.

11 **Benjamin Lay:** Jill Lepore, *These Truths: A History of the United States* (W. W. Norton, 2018), 74–75.

11 **"The Revolution was in the Minds":** Adams to Jefferson, Aug. 24, 1815, founders.archives.gov/documents/Jefferson/03-08-02-0560.

12 **"contending for pre-eminence":** Federalist No. 10.

12 **"The eyes of all people":** John Winthrop, *A Modell of Christian Charity* (1630), history.hanover.edu/texts/winthmod.html.

13 **"sin boldly":** Jane E. Strohl, "Luther's Spiritual Journey," in *The Cambridge Companion to Martin Luther,* ed. Donald K. McKim (Cambridge University Press, 2006), doi.org/10.1017/CCOL0521816483.

13 **"Preachers are the greatest":** Martin E. Marty, *Martin Luther* (Penguin, 2004), 98.

13 **"By predestination":** *Institutes of the Christian Religion,* www.ccel.org/ccel/calvin/institutes.v.xxii.html.

14 **"It is impossible":** Jean-Jacques Rousseau, *The Social Contract and Other Later Political Writings* (Cambridge University Press, 1997), 151.

14 **"a special overvaluing":** Winthrop, *Modell of Christian Charity.*

15 **"Voted, that the earth":** Francis Jennings, *The Invasion of America: Indians, Colonialism, and the Cant of Conquest* (University of North Carolina Press, 2010), 83.

15 **"our title to what we possess":** Winthrop to Nathaniel Rich, May 22, 1634, www.gilderlehrman.org/history-resources/spotlight-primary-source/john-winthrop-describes-life-boston-1634.

15 **"a sweet sacrifice":** William Bradford, *Of Plymouth Plantation: Sixteen Twenty to Sixteen Forty-Seven* (Rutgers University Press, 1952), 296.

15 **"We had sufficient light":** John Underhill, *Newes from America; or, A New and Experimentall Discoverie of New England; Containing, A Trve Relation of Their War-like Proceedings These Two Yeares Last Past, with a Figure of the Indian Fort, or Palizado,* ed. Paul Royster (London, 1638), name.umdl.umich.edu/A14203.0001.001.

15 **"too furious, and slaies":** Underhill, *Newes from America.*

15 **"God so disposed":** Increase Mather, *History of King Philip's War* (Boston, 1862), 131.

16 **"they are in the Hands":** Cotton Mather, *Souldiers Counselled* (1689), name.umdl.umich.edu/N00394.0001.001.

16 **"The dealings of God":** Sacvan Bercovitch, *The Puritan Origins of the American Self* (Yale University Press, 1975), 55.

16 **"the Apple of God's eye":** Bercovitch, *Puritan Origins of the American Self,* 53.

16 **"Our Rulers, Officers, and Councellors":** Edward Wharton, *New-England's Present Sufferings* (London, 1675), name.umdl.umich.edu/A65574.0001.001.

17 **"If God be pleased":** Jonathan Edwards, "God's People Tried by a Battle Lost," in *Sermons and Discourses, 1743–1758,* ed. Wilson H. Kimnach (Yale University Press, 2006).

17 **"GOD BE PRAISED!":** Ralph Henry Gabriel, *The Pageant of America* (Yale University Press, 1927), 103.

17 **"Leah," the plain and homely:** Bercovitch, *Puritan Origins of the American Self,* 156.

17 **"the beloved children":** Bercovitch, *Puritan Origins of the American Self,* 156.

18 **"God pleads his own":** Abraham Keteltas, "God Arising and Pleading His People's Cause," *Political Sermons of the American Founding Era,* vol. 1 (1730–1788), 2nd ed. (Liberty Fund, 1998), oll.libertyfund.org/titles/sandoz-political-sermons-of-the-american-founding-era-vol-1-1730-1788-5.

18 **"The Dominion of Providence":** John Witherspoon, *The Dominion of Providence over the Passions of Men* (1776), oll.libertyfund.org/pages/1776-witherspoon-dominion-of-providence-over-the-passions-of-men-sermon.

18 **"Cousin America has run off":** Kevin Phillips, *1775: A Good Year for Revolution* (Viking, 2012), 215.

19 **"We have it in our power":** Paine, *Common Sense.*

19 **"second, far more":** Bercovitch, *Puritan Origins of the American Self,* 113.

19 **a basic tenet:** John F. Berens, *Providence & Patriotism in Early America, 1640–1815* (University Press of Virginia, 1978), 71.

19 **"four separate Wars":** David Hackett Fischer, *Albion's Seed: Four British Folkways in America* (Oxford University Press, 1989), 827.

20 **"detested the people of Virginia":** Fischer, *Albion's Seed,* 821.

20 **"nasty people":** Colin Woodard, *American Nations: A History of the Eleven Rival Regional Cultures of North America* (Penguin Books, 2012), 128.

20 **"was their common loathing":** Fischer, *Albion's Seed,* 821.

20 **"savages and barbarians":** Fischer, *Albion's Seed,* 821.

20 **"to force us":** Barry Alan Shain, *The Declaration of Independence in Historical Context: American State Papers, Petitions, Proclamations, and Letters of the Delegates to the First National Congresses* (Yale University Press, 2014), 361.

21 **"its citizens did not rally":** Lorenzo Sabine, *The American Loyalists* (1847), 32, archive.org/details/americanloyalist00sabiuoft.

21 **The "leaven" of the revolution:** Sabine, *American Loyalists,* 30.

21 **"whether their slaves":** John Adams, "Notes of Debates on the Articles of Confederation, Continued," University of Virginia Press, July 30,

1776, founders.archives.gov/documents/Adams/01-02-02-0006-0008-0003.

21 **"A republican government":** John Adams, *Notes of Debates, Continued,* Oct. 12, 1775, founders.archives.gov/documents/Adams/01-02-02-0005-0004-0006.

21 **"The cry from these States":** *Charles Sumner: His Complete Works,* vol. 7 (1900), 28, www.gutenberg.org/files/48077/48077-h/48077-h.htm.

21 **"jarring interests":** Berens, *Providence & Patriotism,* 73.

21 **"The real wonder":** Federalist No. 37.

22 **"cruel war against human nature":** Thomas Jefferson, "Jefferson's 'Original Rough Draft' of the Declaration of Independence," June 11–July 4, 1776, founders.archives.gov/documents/Jefferson/01-01-02-0176-0004.

22 **"was struck out":** Notes of Proceedings in the Continental Congress, June 7–Aug. 1, 1776, founders.archives.gov/documents/Jefferson/01-01-02-0160.

22 **"these gentlemen continued":** Thomas Jefferson, "Anecdotes of Benjamin Franklin," ca. Dec. 4, 1818, founders.archives.gov/documents/Jefferson/03-13-02-0407.

22 **"Does it follow":** *The Collected Political Writings of James Otis,* ed. Richard Samuelson (Liberty Fund, 2015), oll.libertyfund.org/titles/collected-political-writings.

23 **"with a false hypothesis":** Thomas Hutchinson, *Strictures* (1776), oll.libertyfund.org/pages/1776-hutchinson-strictures-upon-the-declaration-of-independence.

23 **"gloomy doctrines":** Federalist No. 21.

23 **"distempered imaginations":** Federalist No. 8.

23 **"whose sagacity":** Federalist No. 21.

24 **"airy phantoms":** Federalist No. 8.

24 **"more ardent than enlightened":** Federalist No. 26.

24 **"It is impossible":** Herbert J. Storing, *The Complete Anti-Federalist* (University of Chicago Press, 1981), 76.

24 **"The plan of government":** Storing, *Complete Anti-Federalist,* 226.

24 **"Different laws, customs":** Storing, *Complete Anti-Federalist,* 230.

24 **like "Prussian soldiers":** Storing, *Complete Anti-Federalist,* 160.

24 **"the chains of despotism":** Storing, *Complete Anti-Federalist,* 165.

25 **"for every cargo":** Storing, *Complete Anti-Federalist,* 379.

25 **"bargain with sin":** Joseph E. Ellis, *The Quartet: Orchestrating the Second American Revolution, 1783–1789* (Alfred A. Knopf, 2015), 145.

25 **"notwithstanding their aversion":** Storing, *Complete Anti-Federalist,* 61.

25 **"We scarcely had risen from our knees":** Storing, *Complete Anti-Federalist,* 61.

25 **"render us contemptible":** Storing, *Complete Anti-Federalist,* 61.

25 **"It seems to have been reserved":** Federalist No. 1.

26 **"Happily for America":** Federalist No. 14.

26 **"genius" of the American people:** Brian James Burchett, "American Exceptionalism in *The Federalist*" (master's thesis, Central Michigan University, 1994), www.proquest.com/docview/230847885/abstract/7A4121B275AC4CE2PQ/10.

26 **"If it be asked":** Federalist No. 57.

26 **"free and gallant citizens":** Federalist No. 46.

27 **"Hearken not to the unnatural voice":** Federalist No. 14.

27 **"This country and this people":** Federalist No. 2.

27 **"You may solace":** Storing, *Complete Anti-Federalist,* 364.

27 **"the bayonet":** Storing, *Complete Anti-Federalist,* 371.

27 **"in the ardour":** Storing, *Complete Anti-Federalist,* 143.

27 **"the adoption":** Storing, *Complete Anti-Federalist,* 263.

29 **"unconditional Election":** John Adams to Samuel Quincy, April 22, 1761, founders.archives.gov/documents/Adams/06-01-02-0039.

29 **"America," he wrote in the heat:** Adams to Nathanael Greene, March 18, 1780, founders.archives.gov/documents/Adams/06-09-02-0041.

29 **"There is no special providence":** *Works of John Adams,* vol. 4 (Boston, 1851), oll.libertyfund.org/titles/adams-the-works-of-john-adams-vol-4.

29 **"the virtue of Americans":** Mercy Otis Warren to John Adams, July 28, 1807, founders.archives.gov/documents/Adams/99-02-02-5198.

29 **"There is no Special Providence for Us":** Adams to Rush, Oct. 22, 1812, founders.archives.gov/documents/Adams/99-02-02-5883.

30 **"an Arena of gladiators":** Jefferson to Adams, Jan. 11, 1816, founders.archives.gov/documents/Jefferson/03-09-02-0219.

30 **"The Morality of Tacitus":** Adams to Jefferson, Feb. 2, 1816, founders.archives.gov/documents/Jefferson/03-09-02-0285.

31 **"A nation which makes *greatness*":** Abraham Bishop, *An Oration, on the Extent and Power of Political Delusion* (1800), name.umdl.umich.edu/N27748.0001.001.

31 **"naturalizes" something that is unnatural:** Roland Barthes, *Mythologies* (Hill and Wang, 1972), 131.

31 **Barthes likened the effect to "inoculation":** Barthes, *Mythologies,* 150.

32 **"a strongly developed":** Berens, *Providence & Patriotism,* 61.

33 **"more fictional fiction":** Edmund S. Morgan, *Inventing the People: The Rise of Popular Sovereignty in England and America* (W. W. Norton, 1988), 153.

33 **"Madison," writes Morgan, "was inventing a sovereign":** Morgan, *Inventing the People,* 267.

Chapter 2: Who Were Your Daddies?

35 **"Pray gentlemen":** *Boston Gazette,* Jan. 8, 1770.

35 **"Where did you learn":** *Boston Gazette,* Jan. 8, 1770.

35 **was a "contagion":** Bernard Bailyn, *The Ideological Origins of the American Revolution* (Belknap Press of Harvard University Press, 1992), 230.

35 **"If slavery":** Samuel Johnson, *Taxation No Tyranny* (1775), oll .libertyfund.org/titles/johnson-taxation-no-tyranny-an-answer-to-the -resolutions-and-address-of-the-american-congress.

36 **"a very ill grace":** Levi Hart, *Liberty Described* (1775), name.umdl .umich.edu/N11133.0001.001.

36 **"It always appeared":** Abigail Adams to John Adams, Sept. 22, 1774, founders.archives.gov/documents/Adams/04-01-02-0107.

36 **Early modern thinkers:** Laurie M. Bagby, *Thomas Hobbes* (Lexington Books, 2009).

37 **"drawn from the political folkways":** Fischer, *Albion's Seed,* 781.

37 **"no one provokes me":** Woodard, *American Nations,* 137.

37 **"sown in the nature of man":** Federalist No. 10.

38 **"Another clause secures us":** James Madison, "Slave Trade and Slaveholders' Rights," June 17, 1788, founders.archives.gov/documents/ Madison/01-11-02-0091.

39 **"science of politics":** Federalist No. 9.

39 **"the art of committing":** In Wendell Phillips, *Can Abolitionists Vote or Take Office Under the United States Constitution?* (New York, 1845), 38.

39 **"tears away his fellow creatures":** Paul Finkelman, "Garrison's Constitution," National Archives, Aug. 15, 2016, www.archives.gov/ publications/prologue/2000/winter/garrisons-constitution-1.

39 **"march their militia":** Finkelman, "Garrison's Constitution."

39 **"We have obtained":** Jonathan Elliot, ed. *The Debates in the Several State Conventions on the Adoption of the Federal Constitution as Recommended by the General Convention at Philadelphia, in 1787* (Lippincott, 1888), 280.

40 **"without trembling for bread or life":** Finkelman, "Garrison's Constitution."

40 **"Our Revolution":** "The Unholy Alliance," *New York Times,* Jan. 22, 1861.

40 **"Northern Indians":** Thomas Jefferson to George Rogers Clark, Jan. 1, 1780, founders.archives.gov/documents/Jefferson/01-03-02-0289.

40 **"If it be the design":** *Autobiography of Benjamin Franklin* (1791), www.gutenberg.org/files/20203/20203-h/20203-h.htm.

41 **"glory and honor":** Ezra Stiles, *The United States Elevated to Glory and Honor* (1783), name.umdl.umich.edu/n14363.0001.001.

41 **"wild wish":** Mary Wollstonecraft, *A Vindication of the Rights of Woman*

(J. Johnson, 1792), oll.libertyfund.org/titles/wollstonecraft-a-vindication-of-the-rights-of-woman.

41 **"accustomed to hearing":** Nicholas Guyatt, *Providence and the Invention of the United States, 1607–1876* (Cambridge University Press, 2007), 186.

42 **"the most popular":** Guyatt, *Providence and the Invention of the United States,* 184.

42 **"We [would] rather die in Maryland":** C. Peter Ripley, ed., *The Black Abolitionist Papers: The United States, 1830–1846*, 5 vols. (University of North Carolina Press, 1985), 3:99.

42 **"this wicked distinction":** Natalie Joy, "The Indian's Cause: Abolitionists and Native American Rights," *Journal of the Civil War Era* 8, no. 2 (2018), dx.doi.org/10.1353/cwe.2018.0026.

42 **sent "back" to Holland:** Guyatt, *Providence and the Invention of the United States,* 207.

42 **"The American Colonization Society":** Joy, "Indian's Cause," 218.

43 **"Shall we put":** Guyatt, *Providence and the Invention of the United States,* 184.

43 **"called us to colonize":** Guyatt, *Providence and the Invention of the United States,* 193.

43 **"liberated from her black population":** Guyatt, *Providence and the Invention of the United States,* 193.

44 **"like snow beneath the beams":** Guyatt, *Providence and the Invention of the United States,* 197.

44 **"the withered leaves":** Guyatt, *Providence and the Invention of the United States,* 199.

45 **"clothed in white":** Philip F. Gura, *The Life of William Apess* (University of North Carolina Press, 2015), 20–21.

45 **"Death never seemed":** Gura, *Life of William Apess,* 21.

45 **Apess was writing at a time when providential narratives:** Abram C. Van Engen, *City on a Hill: A History of American Exceptionalism* (Yale University Press, 2020).

45 **"the elect martyrs":** George Bancroft, *An Oration Delivered on the Fourth of July, 1826,* 5, www.loc.gov/item/03022582/.

45 **"a more beautiful maturity":** Bancroft, *Oration Delivered on the Fourth of July, 1826,* 9.

45 **"the dearest interests":** Bancroft, *Oration Delivered on the Fourth of July, 1826,* 24.

46 **"a few scattered tribes of feeble barbarians":** George Bancroft, quoted in Drew Lopenzina, *Through an Indian's Looking-Glass: A Cultural Biography of William Apess, Pequot* (University of Massachusetts Press, 2017), 23.

46 **"The doctrines of the pilgrims":** William Apess, *Eulogy on King Philip* (1836), digitalcommons.unl.edu/zeaamericanstudies/39/.

46 **"the greatest man that ever lived":** Apess, *Eulogy on King Philip.*

46 **"the first footsteps":** Daniel Webster, "A Discourse, Delivered at Plymouth, December 22, 1820," 6, digitalcommons.unl.edu/zeaamericanstudies/40/.

47 **"a most sorry and wretched doctrine":** Apess, *Eulogy on King Philip.*

47 **"red Canaanites":** Apess, *Eulogy on King Philip.*

47 **"not overly malevolent":** Sean Wilentz, quoted in Gary Scott Smith, "Andrew Jackson: Providentialist President," in *Religion in the Oval Office* (Oxford University Press, 2015).

48 **"The democratic idea":** William J. Watkins, "The Day We Celebrate," *Frederick Douglass' Paper,* Aug. 18, 1854, libraries.udmercy.edu/archives/special-collections/index.php?record_id=1&collectionCode=baa.

48 **"America! America!":** Watkins, "Day We Celebrate."

49 **"but patriotism may be a vice":** William R. Newby, quoted in Ripley, *Black Abolitionist Papers,* 4:356.

49 **"treats us like dogs":** "Spirited Meeting of the Colored Citizens of Philadelphia," *Liberator,* April 10, 1857.

49 **"our manifest destiny":** John O'Sullivan, "Annexation," *United States Magazine and Democratic Review* 17, no. 85 (1845): 6.

49 **"the extension and preservation":** Garrison to Richard D. Webb, July 1, 1847, teachingamericanhistory.org/document/letter-on-the-mexican-american-war/.

50 **"When a sixth of the population":** Henry David Thoreau, *On the Duty of Civil Disobedience* (1849), www.gutenberg.org/ebooks/71.

50 **"Now, what are they?":** Thoreau, *On the Duty of Civil Disobedience.*

51 **"Patriotism," he asserted:** Henry David Thoreau, *Walden* (1854), archive.org/details/waldenorli00thor.

51 **"annual splendor":** Henry David Thoreau, *October, Or Autumnal Tints* (W. W. Norton, 2012), 97.

51 **"This people must cease":** Thoreau, *On the Duty of Civil Disobedience.*

51 **"I didn't go in the kitchen":** David Blight, *Frederick Douglass: Prophet of Freedom* (Simon & Schuster, 2018), 114.

51 **"Do not misunderstand":** Frederick Douglass, "Love of God, Love of Man, Love of Country" (1847), frederickdouglasspapersproject.com/s/digitaledition/item/10276.

52 **"This is your 'land of the free' ":** Douglass, "Love of God, Love of Man, Love of Country."

53 **"It has been said":** Frederick Douglass, "The Fugitive Slave Law," Aug. 11, 1852, rbscp.lib.rochester.edu/4385.

54 **"Our country":** George Bancroft, *The Necessity, the Reality, and the Promise of the Progress of the Human Race* (1854).

54 **"in the course of human events":** William J. Watkins, "Our Influence Abroad," *Frederick Douglass' Paper,* Dec. 22, 1854.

55 **"the great object":** Watkins, "Our Influence Abroad."

55 **"trampled beneath their feet":** "The Great Crisis!" *Liberator,* Dec. 29, 1832.

55 **"lies in northern bayonets":** "The Liberator and Slavery," *Liberator,* Jan. 7, 1832, link.gale.com/apps/doc/GT3005833826/SAS?sid=bookmark-SAS&xid=99bb5d20.

55 **"that it is solely":** "Liberator and Slavery."

56 **"Just so soon as the bonds":** "Speech of Mr. J. R. Underwood . . . 27th of January, 1842," hdl.handle.net/2027/hvd.hx2w5b?urlappend=%3Bseq=5.

56 **"What madness in the South":** Madison to Clay, June 1833, founders.archives.gov/documents/Madison/99-02-02-2762.

57 **"a Pro-Slavery Compact":** Wendell Phillips, ed., *The Constitution a Pro-Slavery Compact* (1845), www.google.com/books/edition/The_Constitution_a_Pro_slavery_Compact/z3F6EEw4_fsC?hl=en.

57 **"blood-cemented union":** "Liberty Party 'Patriotism,'" *Liberator,* March 19, 1847.

57 **"impractical for tyrants":** "No Union with Slaveholders," *Liberator,* May 31, 1844.

57 **"a covenant with death":** Finkelman, "Garrison's Constitution."

57 **"You know":** "Speech of James W. Walker of Ohio," *Liberator,* June 7, 1850.

57 **"Whoever strengthens":** Melinda Lawson, "'Dedicated to the Proposition': Principle, Consequence, and Duty to the Egalitarian Nation, 1848–1865," in *Contested Loyalty: Debates over Patriotism in the Civil War North,* ed. Robert M. Sandow (Fordham University Press, 2018), 27.

58 **"There is no safety":** Lawson, "'Dedicated to the Proposition,'" 27.

58 **"If I am to love":** Lawson, "'Dedicated to the Proposition,'" 28.

58 **"The reason why":** William Lloyd Garrison, *No Compromise with Slavery* (1854), www.gutenberg.org/cache/epub/24194/pg24194-images.html.

59 **"self-evident lie":** "Slavery a Blessing—Freedom a Curse," *Liberator,* March 13, 1857.

59 **In a subsequent article:** George Fitzhugh, "Revolutions of '76 and '61 Contrasted," *De Bow's Review* (1867).

59 **"the dangerous error":** John C. Calhoun, "Speech on the Oregon Bill,"

June 27, 1848, teachingamericanhistory.org/document/speech-on-the-oregon-bill-3/.

59 **"branding-irons and bloodhounds":** William Lloyd Garrison, *Letter to Louis Kossuth* (R. F. Wallcut, 1852), archive.org/details/ASPC0001979700.

60 **"Thirty thousand escaped":** Garrison, *Letter to Louis Kossuth.*

60 **"While . . . the Union is preserved":** Garrison, *No Compromise with Slavery.*

60 **"the dissolution of the present":** Douglass, "Love of God, Love of Man, Love of Country."

60 **"principles and purposes, entirely hostile to the existence of slavery":** "The Meaning of July Fourth for the Negro," speech given at Rochester, New York, July 5, 1852, https://masshumanities.org/files/programs/douglass/speech_complete.pdf.

61 **"Judge [a] people not by what they are":** Fyodor Dostoevsky, *The Diary of a Writer* (Scribner, 1919).

Chapter 3: The War That Never Ended

62 **"there was light":** Jon Meacham, *And There Was Light: Abraham Lincoln and the American Struggle* (Random House, 2022).

63 **"day of mourning":** Edmund Wilson, *Patriotic Gore, Studies in the Literature of the American Civil War* (W. W. Norton, 1994), ix–xxxii.

63 **"We have," Wilson said, "accepted the epic":** Wilson, *Patriotic Gore,* ix–xxxii.

65 **"Our republican robe":** *Collected Works of Abraham Lincoln,* vol. 2 (Rutgers University Press, 1953), https://quod.lib.umich.edu/l/lincoln/lincoln2/1:282.1?rgn=div2&view=fulltext.

66 **"you impair the object":** *Burke's Speech on Conciliation with America* (1775), www.gutenberg.org/files/5655/5655-h/5655-h.htm.

67 **"appeals to arms":** Jefferson to Madison, March 24, 1793, www.let.rug.nl/usa/presidents/thomas-jefferson/letters-of-thomas-jefferson/jefl103.php.

67 **"the scourge of the Old World":** Federalist No. 8.

67 **"the least militaristic":** Alexis de Tocqueville, *Democracy in America* (Penguin, 2003), 324.

67 **"All those who seek to destroy":** Tocqueville, *Democracy in America,* 756.

67 **"a delinquent state":** "Records of the Federal Convention: Article 1, Section 8, Clause 15," press-pubs.uchicago.edu/founders/documents/a1_8_15s5.html.

67 **"The more he reflected":** "Records of the Federal Convention."

68 **"force against the unconstitutional":** James Madison, "Debates in the

Federal Convention of 1787," June 8, 1787, teachingamericanhistory.org/document/friday-june-8-debates-in-the-federal-convention-of-1787/.

68 **"the people of each State":** John Quincy Adams, *The Jubilee of the Constitution* (1839), archive.org/details/jubileeofconst1839adam.

69 **"pretext" or "provocation":** James Buchanan, "Message on Threats to the Peace and Existence of the Union," Jan. 8, 1861, millercenter.org/the-presidency/presidential-speeches/january-8-1861-message-threats-peace-and-existence-union.

69 **"By what principle":** Michael Burlingame, *Abraham Lincoln: A Life,* vol. 2 (Johns Hopkins University Press, 2013), 5.

69 **"breathed of war":** Burlingame, *Abraham Lincoln,* 5.

69 **"foolish" and "unfortunate":** Burlingame, *Abraham Lincoln,* 5.

69 **"to regain lost forts":** Burlingame, *Abraham Lincoln,* 6.

71 **"more atrocious":** "Probable Commencement of the Civil War at Last," *New York Herald,* April 11, 1861, www.historians.org/sixteen-months/probable-commencement-of-the-civil-war-at-last/.

71 **"It cannot be denied":** "The Future of Secession," *New York Times,* March 21, 1861, www.nytimes.com/1861/03/21/archives/the-future-of-secession.html.

72 **"re-enforce Fort Sumter":** Arnold M. Shankman, *The Pennsylvania Antiwar Movement, 1861–1865* (Fairleigh Dickinson University Press, 1980), 53.

72 **"public opinion in the North":** Shankman, *Pennsylvania Antiwar Movement,* 53.

72 **"that the military":** Shankman, *Pennsylvania Antiwar Movement,* 53.

72 **"The idea of fighting":** Shankman, *Pennsylvania Antiwar Movement,* 51.

73 **"a long, bloody":** Thomas Low Nichols, *Forty Years of American Life,* vol. 2 (Applewood Books, 2007).

73 **"War for the Union!":** Thomas Low Nichols, *Forty Years of American Life,* vol. 1 (Applewood Books, 2007).

73 **"clearly in the wrong":** "Going to Go," *New-York Daily Tribune,* Nov. 9, 1860.

73 **"If the cotton States":** *New-York Daily Tribune,* Nov. 26, 1860.

74 **"Is it not self-evident":** William Lloyd Garrison, *The Letters of William Lloyd Garrison, 1861–1867* (Belknap Press of Harvard University Press, 1971), 11.

74 **"let the Union perish":** Eric Foner, *Fiery Trial: Abraham Lincoln and American Slavery* (W. W. Norton, 2010).

74 **"That cotton fibre":** Wendell Phillips, *Speeches, Lectures, and Letters of Wendell Phillips,* vol. 1 (Lea and Shepard, 1891).

74 **"opiate speeches":** Wendell Phillips, *Disunion* (1861), www.google.com/books/edition/Disunion/HfQSAAAAYAAJ?hl=en.

74 **"to surrender anything":** Phillips, *Disunion.*

74 **"Is Abraham Lincoln capable":** William Schouler, *A History of Massachusetts in the Civil War,* 2 vols. (E. P. Dutton, 1868–71), 1:46.

75 **"Wayward sisters, depart":** Burlingame, *Abraham Lincoln,* 99.

75 **"Let the South go":** Burlingame, *Abraham Lincoln,* 102.

75 **"There is no attachment":** Burlingame, *Abraham Lincoln,* 105.

76 **"the Deep South":** Burlingame, *Abraham Lincoln,* 105.

76 **"the evacuation of Fort Sumpter":** Burlingame, *Abraham Lincoln,* 108.

76 **"The public mind":** Burlingame, *Abraham Lincoln,* 108.

76 **"They attacked Sumter":** *Diary of Orville Hickman Browning* (Trustees of the Illinois State Historical Library, 1927), 476.

76 **"a sham," "a mockery":** David Williams, *A People's History of the Civil War: Struggles for the Meaning of Freedom,* ed. Howard Zinn (New Press, 2006), 65.

76 **"With the facts before us":** Williams, *People's History of the Civil War,* 65.

77 **"I frankly say":** Shelby Foote, *Civil War: A Narrative,* 3 vols. (Alfred A. Knopf, 1958), 1:48.

77 **"deluded masses":** Elizabeth R. Varon, *Armies of Deliverance: A New History of the Civil War* (Oxford University Press, 2019).

78 **"no greater calamity":** Andrew Glass, "Robert E. Lee Resigned His Commission in Army, April 20, 1861," *Politico,* April 20, 2012, www.politico.com/story/2012/04/robert-e-lee-resigned-his-commission-in-army-april-20-1861-075369.

78 **"You went with your people":** Howard Jones, introduction to Robert Penn Warren, *The Legacy of the Civil War* (Random House, 1961; repr., Bison Books, 2015).

78 **a scathing article in *The Atlantic Monthly*:** Nathaniel Hawthorne, "Chiefly About War Matters," *Atlantic Monthly,* July 1, 1862, www.theatlantic.com/magazine/archive/1862/07/chiefly-about-war-matters/306159/.

78 **"What do I care":** Williams, *People's History of the Civil War,* 161.

79 **"What are you fighting for":** *The Civil War,* season 1, episode 2, "A Very Bloody Affair," written by Ken Burns, directed by Ken Burns, aired Sept. 24, 1990, video.alexanderstreet.com/watch/a-very-bloody-affair.

79 **"unwelcome presence upon us":** Jane Howison Beale, *The Journal of Jane Howison Beale of Fredericksburg, Virginia, 1850–1862* (Historic Fredericksburg Foundation, 1979), 73.

79 **William Thompson Lusk in a letter:** "War Letters of William Thompson Lusk," *Daily Observations from the Civil War,* Aug. 20, 2013, dotcw.com/category/war-letters-of-william-thompson-lusk-74/.

80 **"If the objective":** Burlingame, *Abraham Lincoln.*

80 **"The death which":** *Collected Works of Ambrose Bierce,* vol. 1 (Neale, 1909), www.gutenberg.org/files/13541/13541-h/13541-h.htm#shiloh.

81 **"It has come that man has":** *The Civil War,* season 1, episode 6, "Valley of the Shadow of Death," written by Ken Burns, directed by Ken Burns, aired Sept. 26, 1990, video.alexanderstreet.com/watch/valley-of-the-shadow-of-death.

81 **from a "limited" to a "total-war philosophy":** James M. McPherson, *Battle Cry of Freedom: The Civil War Era* (Oxford University Press, 2003), 333.

81 **"I gave up all idea":** Lance Janda, "Shutting the Gates of Mercy: The American Origins of Total War, 1860–1880," *Journal of Military History* 59, no. 1 (1995): 13, doi.org/10.2307/2944362.

81 **"I shall not surrender":** Daniel E. Sutherland, "Abraham Lincoln, John Pope, and the Origins of Total War," *Journal of Military History* 56, no. 4 (1992): 580, doi.org/10.2307/1986161.

81 **"I'm tired of the sickening":** *The Civil War,* season 1, episode 3, "Forever Free," written by Ken Burns, directed by Ken Burns, aired Sept. 24, 1990, video.alexanderstreet.com/watch/forever-free.

81 **"no regard for life":** "Valley of the Shadow of Death."

81 **"War is cruelty":** Sherman to the Mayor and Council of Atlanta, Sept. 12, 1864, cwnc.omeka.chass.ncsu.edu/items/show/23.

81 **"We are not only fighting":** Janda, "Shutting the Gates of Mercy," 15.

82 **"Our men now believe":** Sutherland, "Abraham Lincoln, John Pope, and the Origins of Total War," 582.

82 **"cast mankind two centuries back":** Sutherland, "Abraham Lincoln, John Pope, and the Origins of Total War," 582.

82 **"hard war tactics":** Varon, *Armies of Deliverance,* 381.

82 **"Instances are reported":** Ethan S. Rafuse, ed., *The American Civil War* (Routledge, 2017).

82 **"they had better sew up":** Nora Williams, "They Done a Very Bad Act: Rape in the Civil War and Reconstruction" (honors thesis, Wofford College, 2021).

82 **"a tale of horror":** Varon, *Armies of Deliverance,* 28–29.

82 **"Submission has been":** Varon, *Armies of Deliverance,* 321.

83 **"start anew with a new set":** Foner, *Fiery Trial.*

83 **"I rejoice," he said:** "The Rebellion," *New York Times,* April 28, 1861.

83 **"abolitionist is merged":** Foner, *Fiery Trial.*

83 **"the muskets of Illinois":** "Rebellion."

83 **"If I could save the Union":** Lincoln to Greeley, Aug. 22, 1862, www.abrahamlincolnonline.org/lincoln/speeches/greeley.htm.

84 **"the most disgraceful":** Foner, *Fiery Trial.*

85 **"I never saw joy before":** Frederick Douglass, *The Life and Writings of Frederick Douglass,* 5 vols., ed. Philip S. Foner (International Publishers, 1975), 3:337.

85 **"These are the times":** Ben Wright and Zachary W. Dresser, eds., *Apocalypse and the Millennium in the American Civil War Era* (Louisiana State University Press, 2013), 163.

85 **"an abomination":** "Our National Fast," *Douglass' Monthly,* Oct. 1861, 531.

85 **"the manifest destiny of this war":** Frederick Douglass, "Mission of the War," https://blackpast.org/african-american-history/1864-frederick-douglass-mission-war/.

85 **"handed over to judgment":** Charles Sumner, "Emancipation! Its Policy and Necessity as a War Measure for the Suppression of the Rebellion," Oct. 6, 1862, archive.org/details/emancipationitsp00sumn.

86 **"Lincoln legend":** H. L. Mencken, *Prejudices* (Alfred A. Knopf, 1922), 171–75.

87 **"The humble but true":** Benjamin Rush, *The Selected Writings of Benjamin Rush,* ed. Dagobert D. Runes (Philosophical Library, 1947).

87 **"War is the health":** Bourne, *Untimely Papers.*

87 **"When victories mean nothing":** Harry S. Stout, *Upon the Altar: A Moral History of the Civil War* (Viking, 2006), 274.

88 **After the battle:** Edward F. Leddy, *Magnum Force Lobby: The National Rifle Association Fights Gun Control* (University Press of America, 1987), 55.

88 **"Rarely," writes Williams, "has any nation":** Williams, *People's History of the Civil War,* 192.

88 **In a speech delivered:** Clement Vallandigham, "Speech on the Great Civil War in America," House of Representatives, Jan. 14, 1863, sesquicentenary.wordpress.com/2012/03/04/clement-vallandigham-congressman-from-ohio-january-14-1863-u-s-house-of-representatives/.

89 **"Whoever may be benefitted":** Hawthorne, "Chiefly About War Matters."

89 **"You cannot possibly":** Gordon Hutner, "Nathaniel Hawthorne's Civil War," *J19: The Journal of Nineteenth-Century Americanists* 9, no. 1 (2021): 142.

90 **"almost impossible for a respectable":** Williams, *People's History of the Civil War,* 346.

90 **"'The Negroes were the cause'":** Frederick Douglass, "The Race Problem," Oct. 21, 1890, hdl.handle.net/2027/yale.39002003186195?urlappend=%3Bseq=5.

90 **"we are different races":** "Address on Colonization to a Committee of Colored Men," *New-York Daily Tribune,* Aug. 15, 1862, www.loc.gov/item/sn83030213/1862-08-15/ed-1/.

91 **"Where," wondered an appalled Union soldier:** Williams, *People's History of the Civil War,* 345.

91 **"monsters of virtuous pretension":** William Gilmore Simms, *A City Laid Waste: The Capture, Sack, and Destruction of the City of Columbia,* ed. David Aiken (University of South Carolina Press, 2005), doi.org/10.2307/j.ctvwcjdr0.7.

92 **"The real war will never":** David R. Goldfield, *Still Fighting the Civil War: The American South and Southern History* (Louisiana State University Press, 2013), 336.

92 **"by dictatorial power":** *Congressional Globe,* 1864, digital.library.unt.edu/ark:/67531/metadc30859/m1/525/.

93 **"He that is slain":** Thomas Hobbes, *Leviathan* (1651), www.gutenberg.org/files/3207/3207-h/3207-h.htm.

93 **"All governments rest":** Federalist No. 49.

93 **"If the successors of Roger Williams":** Lysander Spooner, *No Treason,* no. 1 (1867), en.wikisource.org/wiki/No_Treason/1.

94 **"they have 'Saved the Country!'":** Lysander Spooner, *No Treason,* no. 6 (1870), en.wikisource.org/wiki/No_Treason/6.

94 **"refusing to surrender":** Lysander Spooner, *No Treason,* no. 2 (1867), en.wikisource.org/wiki/No_Treason/2.

94 **"have been abolished":** Spooner, *No Treason,* no. 6.

94 **"It is very difficult":** Stout, *Upon the Altar,* 274.

95 **"They first cut our throats":** Simms, *City Laid Waste,* 1.

95 **"an event without temporal boundaries":** Goldfield, *Still Fighting,* 1.

95 **"As the war for the Union":** David Blight, *Race and Reunion: The Civil War in American Memory* (Belknap Press of Harvard University Press, 2003), 307.

95 **If the "cornerstone" of the Confederacy:** Alexander H. Stephens, "Cornerstone Speech," March 21, 1861, www.battlefields.org/learn/primary-sources/cornerstone-speech.

95 **"his almost chosen people":** *Collected Works of Abraham Lincoln,* vol. 4, (Rutgers University Press, 1953) name.umdl.umich.edu/lincoln4.

96 **"white people inflicted torture":** Edward E. Baptist, *The Half Has Never Been Told: Slavery and the Making of American Capitalism* (Basic Books, 2016), 466.

96 **"The problem after a war":** Noam Chomsky, *Masters of Mankind* (Haymarket, 2020), 55.

96 **"There is little difference":** Ida B. Wells, *Southern Horrors: Lynch Law in All Its Phases* (New York Age Print, 1892), www.gutenberg.org/files/14975/14975-h/14975-h.htm#THE_SOUTHS_POSITION.

96 **"leading citizens":** Wells, *Southern Horrors.*

97 **"is worse off, in many respects":** *Washington National Republican,*

April 17, 1888, www.historyisaweapon.com/defcon1/douglassfraud.html.

97 **"The South was more conquered":** Blight, *Race and Reunion,* 311.

97 **"a crime of monstrous inhumanity":** Warren, *Legacy of the Civil War.*

97 **"the biggest lie any nation":** Gloria L. Cronin and Ben Siegel, *Conversations with Robert Penn Warren* (University Press of Mississippi, 2005), 102.

97 **Julia Ward Howe:** Allen, *Fight for Peace,* 277–78.

97 **"the military method":** Laura E. Richards, *Julia Ward Howe* (Boston, 1915), 307.

Chapter 4: A Nation of Nations

99 **"to burn incense":** William Lloyd Garrison, "Centennial Reflections," *Independent,* July 6, 1876.

100 **"the country from the curse":** Garrison, *Letters of William Lloyd Garrison,* 412.

100 **The patriarch was unmoved:** Garrison to Wendell Phillips Garrison, July 21, 1876, usingessexhistory.org/documents/william-lloyd-garrison-centennial-letter-boston-1876/.

101 **"If a village is attacked":** Janda, "Shutting the Gates of Mercy," 21.

101 **"We must act":** Janda, "Shutting the Gates of Mercy," 23.

101 **"practical reenslavement":** W. E. B. Du Bois, *The Souls of Black Folk* (1903), www.gutenberg.org/files/408/408-h/408-h.htm.

102 **"calico dresses":** Du Bois, *Souls of Black Folk.*

103 **"I always bet on sunshine":** Henry W. Grady, *Life and Labors of Henry W. Grady* (H. C. Hudgins, 1890), www.google.com/books?id=nl10lyxl21MC.

103 **"Our whole history":** Ralph Waldo Emerson, quoted in Grady, *Life and Labors of Henry W. Grady,* 241.

103 **"trusts Georgia alike":** Grady, *Life and Labors of Henry W. Grady,* 273.

103 **"the wounds of war":** Grady, *Life and Labors of Henry W. Grady,* 274.

103 **"an ignorant and inferior race":** Grady, *Life and Labors of Henry W. Grady,* 267.

103 **"the right of the whites":** Grady, *Life and Labors of Henry W. Grady,* 263.

103 **"If there is any human force":** Grady, *Life and Labors of Henry W. Grady,* 266.

103 **"It is the inalienable right"**: Grady, *Life and Labors of Henry W. Grady,* 266.

104 **"Never did oratory cover up":** "Henry W. Grady's Boston Speeches," *Pilot,* Dec. 1889.

104 **"white aliens":** "The Disfranchisement of the Negro," *Atlanta Weekly Constitution,* Dec. 17, 1878.

104 **"Because it is":** Michael Rogin, "*Ronald Reagan," the Movie and Other Episodes in Political Demonology* (University of California Press, 1988), 192.

105 **"till men in New York":** Wells, *Southern Horrors.*

105 **"special abhorrence":** "American Swagger," *Independent,* April 27, 1871.

106 **"even scanter patience":** Theodore Roosevelt, *The Strenuous Life* (P. F. Collier & Son, 1901), www.gutenberg.org/files/58821/58821-h/58821-h.htm.

106 **"Thank God for the iron":** Roosevelt, *Strenuous Life.*

106 **"Wonderfully has God":** Albert Beveridge, *March of the Flag* (1898), archive.org/details/marchofflagbegin00beve.

107 **a crisis of patriotism:** Jonathan M. Hansen, *The Lost Promise of Patriotism: Debating American Identity, 1890–1920* (University of Chicago Press, 2003).

107 **"Is our national character":** "Bryan's Views of the War: It Must Not Be a War of Conquest and Aggrandizement," *New-York Tribune,* June 15, 1898.

108 **"the swaggering, bullying":** William Jennings Bryan, *Life and Speeches of Hon. Wm. Jennings Bryan* (R. H. Woodward, 1900).

109 **"I call this sentimental nonsense":** William Everett, *Patriotism* (1900), www.google.com/books/edition/Patriotism_An_Oration_Delivered_Before_t/yg0tvgAACAAJ?hl=en.

109 **"I've lost my country":** Hansen, *Lost Promise of Patriotism,* 1.

110 **"God damn the U.S.":** Robert L. Beisner, *Twelve Against Empire: The Anti-Imperialists, 1898–1900* (McGraw-Hill, 1968), 48.

110 **" 'Duty and Destiny' ":** *Annual Meeting of the New England Anti-Imperialist League, November 30, 1901,* 21, archive.org/details/reportofannualme0305anti.

110 **"Phrases repeated have a way":** *Annual Meeting of the New England Anti-Imperialist League,* 24.

110 **"We used to believe":** *Annual Meeting of the New England Anti-Imperialist League,* 25.

111 **"American section":** *Annual Meeting of the New England Anti-Imperialist League,* 26.

111 **"the essence of nationality":** William James, *Works of William James,* 19 vols., ed. Frederick H. Burkhardt (Harvard University Press, 1975) 11:166.

111 **"Dead men tell no tales":** *Works of William James,* 11:164.

112 **"Some of us":** *Chicago Liberty Meeting,* April 30, 1899, www.google.com/books?id=EDsyOouc-hQC.

112 **"We are driven to the rather":** Jane Addams, *Newer Ideals of Peace*

(Macmillan, 1906), www.gutenberg.org/cache/epub/69879/pg69879-images.html.

112 **"unity with all human beings":** Addams, *Newer Ideals of Peace.*

113 **"the new nation, guide and lawgiver":** Ralph Waldo Emerson, *Complete Works of Ralph Waldo Emerson,* 12 vols., ed. Edward Waldo Emerson (Houghton, Mifflin, 1903),11:646.

113 **"When I see the emigrants":** *Complete Works of Ralph Waldo Emerson,* 11:645.

113 **"the superstition of Travelling":** Bercovitch, *Puritan Origins of the American Self,* 175.

113 **"The man who loves":** Theodore Roosevelt, *American Ideals and Other Essays, Social and Political* (G. P. Putnam, 1903).

113 **"not a polyglot boarding house":** Theodore Roosevelt, *Works of Theodore Roosevelt,* vol. 21 (Charles Scribner's Sons, 1925).

113 **"to naturalize the bewildered immigrant":** Addams, *Newer Ideals of Peace.*

115 **"If we don't prepare":** *Masses,* Sept. 1916, "Logic," drawn by Boardman Robinson.

116 **"All armor plate":** Amy Aronson, *Crystal Eastman: A Revolutionary Life* (Oxford University Press, 2020), 146.

116 **"a new kind of world":** Aronson, *Crystal Eastman,* 135–36.

116 **"the brutal use":** Jane Addams, *The Long Road of Woman's Memory* (Macmillan, 1916), www.gutenberg.org/ebooks/69234.

116 **"human sacrifice":** Addams, *Long Road of Woman's Memory.*

117 **"Foolish? These are the first sensible":** "Address of Miss Jane Addams," *Christian Work,* July 31, 1915, 145–48.

117 **"The Revolt Against War":** "Address of Miss Jane Addams."

118 **"once shot his gun":** "Address of Miss Jane Addams."

118 **"the weakness and silliness":** "Jane Addams Comes Home," *New York Times,* July 6, 1915.

118 **"credit of his sacrifice":** James Cracraft, *Two Shining Souls: Jane Addams, Leo Tolstoy, and the Quest for Global Peace* (Lexington Books, 2012), 84.

118 **"poor foolish Jane Addams":** Cracraft, *Two Shining Souls,* 83.

119 **"the sacred nationalist myth":** Cracraft, *Two Shining Souls,* 84.

119 **"mass psychology":** Sherry R. Shepler and Anne F. Mattina, "Paying the Price for Pacifism: The Press's Rhetorical Shift from 'Saint Jane' to 'the Most Dangerous Woman in America,'" *Feminist Formations* 24, no. 1 (2012): 166, dx.doi.org/10.1353/ff.2012.0002.

119 **"pacifist in wartime":** Jane Addams, *Peace and Bread in Time of War* (University of Illinois Press, 2010), 80.

119 **"becomes almost a sport":** Bourne, *Untimely Papers.*

119 **"The only man":** Theodore Roosevelt, *Americanism* (1915), www.gutenberg.org/files/68152/68152-h/68152-h.htm.

120 **"If I did not believe":** "The Real Wilson Revealed on Stump," *New York Times,* Oct. 6, 1912.

120 **"essentially theological":** John Maynard Keynes, *The Economic Consequences of the Peace* (Harcourt, Brace and Howe, 1920), oll.liberty fund.org/titles/keynes-the-economic-consequences-of-the-peace.

121 **"not only cheered":** "President Calls for War Declaration," *New York Times,* April 2, 1917.

121 **"that nations do not declare war":** Bourne, *Untimely Papers.*

122 **"democratic and antiseptic war":** Bourne, *Untimely Papers.*

122 **"Nothing could be more calamitous":** Eastman, "Religion of Patriotism," 8–12.

123 **"Liberty and Union":** "Religion of Patriotism."

123 **three "heretics" of the national religion:** "Religion of Patriotism."

123 **"They have always":** Glenn V. Longacre, "Free Speech on Trial: Eugene Debs at Canton, Ohio," *Prologue Magazine* 49, no. 4 (2017–18), www.archives.gov/publications/prologue/2017/winter/debs-canton.

124 **"the most stringent":** *Schenck v. United States,* 249 U.S. 47 (1919).

124 **"an unwritten law":** Adam Hochschild, *American Midnight: The Great War, a Violent Peace, and Democracy's Forgotten Crisis* (Harper Collins, 2022).

124 **"He is an indifferent patriot":** Thorstein Veblen, *An Inquiry into the Nature of Peace and the Terms of Its Perpetuation* (Macmillan, 1917), brocku.ca/MeadProject/Veblen/Veblen_1917/Veblen_1917_01.html.

125 **"derangement of values":** Bourne, *Untimely Papers.*

125 **"this feeling for country":** Bourne, *Untimely Papers.*

126 **"Country is a concept of peace":** Bourne, *Untimely Papers.*

126 **"Men are told simultaneously":** Bourne, *Untimely Papers.*

126 **Bourne turned the tables:** Randolph S. Bourne, "Trans-National America," *Atlantic Monthly,* July 1916.

127 **"Americanizing" meant "Anglo-Saxonizing":** Bourne, "Trans-National America."

127 **"vivid American university":** Bourne, "Trans-National America."

128 **"composite nation":** Frederick Douglass, "The Composite Nation," 1867, www.blackpast.org/african-american-history/1867-frederick-douglass-describes-composite-nation/.

128 **"The failure of the melting-pot":** Bourne, "Trans-National America."

128 **"this blind and deaf Don Quixote":** Keynes, *Economic Consequences of the Peace.*

128 **"a peace with wars already":** "What Kind of Peace?," *Liberator,* April 1918.

129 **"There are few episodes in history":** Keynes, *Economic Consequences of the Peace.*

129 **"Malcontentedness may be the beginning":** Bourne, *Untimely Papers.*

129 **"I am only a citizen":** Ernest Freeberg, *Democracy's Prisoner: Eugene V. Debs, the Great War, and the Right to Dissent* (Harvard University Press, 2008), 299.

Chapter 5: Playing God

133 **"most powerful and vital":** "The American Century," *Life*, Feb. 17, 1941.

134 **freedom from "freedom":** Peter Viereck, *Conservatism Revisited* (Routledge, 2005), 155.

134 **"One prod to the nerve":** George Orwell, "Notes on Nationalism," *Polemic*, May 1945, orwell.ru/library/essays/nationalism/english/e_nat.

134 **"an infantile disease":** Stephen Nathanson, *Patriotism, Morality, and Peace* (Rowman & Littlefield, 1993), 187.

134 **"I am by heritage":** Paul Ratner, "Why Einstein Thought a World Government Was a Good Idea," Big Think, Oct. 23, 2016, bigthink.com/the-past/should-we-have-a-world-government-einstein-thought-so/.

135 **"a country where civil liberty":** Maria Popova, "Albert Einstein's Little-Known Correspondence with W. E. B. Du Bois About Equality and Racial Justice," *The Marginalian*, Jan. 6, 2015, www.themarginalian.org/2015/01/06/albert-einstein-w-e-b-du-bois-racism/.

135 **"The world was promised":** Albert Einstein, Address at the Fifth Nobel Anniversary Dinner, New York, Dec. 10, 1945, www.americanrhetoric.com/speeches/alberteinsteinpostwarworld.htm.

135 **"the imaginary war":** Mary Kaldor, *The Imaginary War: Understanding the East-West Conflict* (Blackwell, 1990).

135 **"one who has inadvertently":** John Lewis Gaddis, *George F. Kennan: An American Life* (Penguin Press, 2012), 272.

136 **"the original sin of American exceptionalism":** Andrew J. Bacevich, "Kennan Kvetches," *Harper's Magazine*, April 2014, harpers.org/archive/2014/04/kennan-kvetches/.

136 **"How do American actions":** Henry A. Wallace, "Achieving an Atmosphere of Mutual Trust and Confidence," History Matters, July 23, 1946, historymatters.gmu.edu/d/6906/.

136 **"Surely to announce to the world":** Jawaharlal Nehru, *Jawaharlal Nehru: An Anthology*, ed. Sarvepalli Gopal (Oxford University Press, 1980), 395.

137 **"To sound off":** Hannah Arendt, *On Revolution* (Penguin Books, 1990), archive.org/details/OnRevolution.

139 **"priestly nationalist":** Leilah Danielson, *American Gandhi* (University of Pennsylvania Press, 2014), 248.

139 **"policy of boldness":** John Foster Dulles, "A Policy of Boldness," *Life*, May 19, 1952.

139 **"appearance that the West":** "How Dulles Averted War," *Life,* Jan. 16, 1956.

140 **"Not unless our automobiles collide":** Stephen Kinzer, *The Brothers: John Foster Dulles, Allen Dulles, and Their Secret World War* (Henry Holt, 2013), 179.

140 **"the classic Communist maneuver":** "How Dulles Averted War."

140 **"behind an iron curtain":** "United States Has No Choice but to Get Along with Castro," *Dayton Daily News,* July 28, 1959.

140 **"the art" of bringing your opponent:** "How Dulles Averted War."

140 **"I'm not bloodthirsty":** John D. Wilsey, *God's Cold Warrior: The Life and Faith of John Foster Dulles* (William B. Eerdmans, 2021), 188.

140 **"Foster Dulles," he growled:** Kinzer, *Brothers,* 201.

141 **"decrease the likelihood":** Jeffrey Sachs, host, *Book Club with Jeffrey Sachs,* podcast, season 3, episode 2, "Lindsey A. O'Rourke, Covert Regime Change: America's Secret Cold War," Dec. 5, 2023, podcasts.apple.com/us/podcast/season-3-episode-2-lindsey-a-orourke-covert-regime/id1555300202?i=1000637557208.

141 **"When he saw a dead body":** Graham Greene, *The Quiet American* (Penguin, 2004), 24.

141 **"crackpot realism":** C. Wright Mills, *The Causes of World War Three* (Ballantine Books, 1960), 94.

141 **"We have warned":** "Behind the 'Spy' Panic," *New Masses,* March 5, 1946.

141 **"Americanism with its sleeves rolled up":** Clay Risen, *Red Scare: Blacklists, McCarthyism, and the Making of Modern America* (Scribner, 2025), 172.

142 **"hangs ultimately on recognition":** Federation of American Scientists, NSC-68, irp.fas.org/offdocs/nsc-hst/nsc-68-cr.htm.

143 **"I feel that we're looking at":** Arendt to Jaspers, May 13, 1953, brooklynrail.org/2006/03/express/a-letter-from-hannah-arendt-to-karl-jaspers/.

143 **"the banality of evil":** Hannah Arendt, *Eichmann in Jerusalem* (Penguin, 1994).

143 **"guarantee today who they will be":** Hannah Arendt, *The Human Condition,* 2nd ed. (University of Chicago Press, 1998).

143 **"clear and present":** Arendt to Jaspers, May 13, 1953.

143 **"There is so much":** Louis Menand, *The Free World: Art and Thought in the Cold War* (Farrar, Straus and Giroux, 2021).

144 **"beautiful book":** Roger Berkowitz, "Democracy and Dissent," *Amor Mundi,* March 16, 2025, hac.bard.edu/amor-mundi/democracy-and-dissent-2025-03-16.

144 **"lost treasure":** Arendt, *On Revolution.*

144 **"monstrous falsehood":** Arendt, *On Revolution.*

144 **"breathtaking speed":** Arendt to Jaspers, May 13, 1953.
145 **"we suffer from a dearth":** Alfred Kazin, *New York Jew* (Syracuse University Press, 1996).
145 **"but the power":** Arendt to Jaspers, May 13, 1953.
145 **"Public opinion is the death":** Arendt, *On Revolution.*
145 **"but the thinking is typically American":** Arendt to Jaspers, May 13, 1953.
145 **"the German calamity":** John J. Simon, "Albert Einstein, Radical: A Political Profile," *Monthly Review,* May 2005, monthlyreview.org/2005/05/01/albert-einstein-radical-a-political-profile.
146 **"What ought the minority":** "Refuse to Testify," *New York Times,* June 12, 1953.
146 **"the spirit of the Constitution":** "Refuse to Testify."
146 **"enemy of America":** "Einstein Criticized," *New York Times,* June 14, 1953.
146 **letters arrived at Princeton:** History Working Group, Institute for Advanced Study, "Einstein, Plumbers, and McCarthyism," 2017, www.ias.edu/ideas/2017/einstein-mccarthyism.
147 **"a Southern plantation":** "Paul Robeson's Column," *Freedom,* Nov. 1950.
147 **"singing the songs":** Paul Robeson, *Here I Stand* (D. Dobson, 1958).
148 **"hysterical raving":** Hudson River Maritime Museum, "Paul Robeson and the Peekskill Riots," *History Blog,* Jan. 18, 2021, www.hrmm.org/2/post/2021/01/paul-robeson-and-the-peekskill-riots.html.
148 **"in complete human dignity":** "Paul Robeson's Column," *Freedom,* Nov. 1950.
148 **"Paul, were you born in Russia?":** "Paul Robeson's Column," *Freedom,* Nov. 1950.
148 **"the masters of the press":** "Paul Robeson's Column," *Freedom,* Nov. 1950.
149 **"Because of my beliefs":** Kimberly Juanita Brown, *Black Elegies: Meditations on the Art of Mourning* (MIT Press, 2025), 121.
149 **"Are you now a member":** Paul Robeson, *Paul Robeson Speaks: Writings, Speeches, and Interviews, a Centennial Celebration* (Citadel Press, 1978).
150 **"It is a sad":** *Paul Robeson Speaks.*
151 **"dues-paying F.B.I. contingent":** Peter Kihss, "1,500 Informants for the F.B.I. Reported in Communist Party," *New York Times,* Oct. 18, 1962, www.nytimes.com/1962/10/18/archives/1500-informants-for-the-fbi-reported-in-communist-party.html.
151 **"the anti-liberal, anti-Negro":** Kihss, "1,500 Informants for the F.B.I. Reported in Communist Party."

151 **"highly valued":** Arendt, *On Revolution.*

152 **"Nobody fucks with J. Edgar":** Lerone A. Martin, *The Gospel of J. Edgar Hoover: How the FBI Aided and Abetted the Rise of White Christian Nationalism* (Princeton University Press, 2023), 238.

152 **"Yesterday," he said, "this committee":** Ivan Greenberg, *Surveillance in America* (Lexington Books, 2012), 15–16.

153 **"You're still in law school":** Martin, *Gospel of J. Edgar Hoover,* 57.

153 **As early as 1946, Hoover was lecturing:** J. Edgar Hoover, "We of the FBI Need Your Help," 1950, n2t.net/ark:/85335/m5vt1kz5b.

153 **"There is room only":** Beverly Gage, *G-Man: J. Edgar Hoover and the Making of the American Century* (Viking, 2022), 334.

154 **"We are at war":** *Congressional Record,* www.google.com/books?id=MdSDRlS8EAAC.

154 **"Ours is the greatest republic":** *Congressional Record,* www.google.com/books?id=MdSDRlS8EAAC.

155 **"It can be plausibly argued":** Orwell, "Notes on Nationalism."

155 **"Real love of country":** John Lukacs, ed., *Through the History of the Cold War: The Correspondence of George F. Kennan and John Lukacs* (University of Pennsylvania Press, 2010), 141.

155 **"King's America was less a redeemer":** Jonathan Rieder, *The Word of the Lord Is upon Me: The Righteous Performance of Martin Luther King Jr.* (Belknap Press of Harvard University Press, 2008), 5.

155 **"militant middle ground":** Peniel Joseph, *The Sword and the Shield: The Revolutionary Lives of Malcolm X and Martin Luther King Jr.* (Basic Books, 2020).

156 **"the prodigal son":** Martin Luther King Jr., *Strength to Love* (Harper, 1963), 112.

156 **"I think the people":** "Rock Hits Dr. King," *New York Times,* Aug. 6, 1966.

156 **"isn't actually Mississippi":** "Fannie Lou Hamer and Malcolm X Speak in Harlem, NY, 1964," *Harlem World,* Nov. 9, 2018, www.harlemworldmagazine.com/fannie-lou-hamer-malcolm-x-speak-harlem-ny-1964-video.

156 **"We didn't land":** Richard Kurin, *The Smithsonian's History of America in 101 Objects* (Penguin, 2016), 69.

156 **"We see America":** Malcolm X, "The Ballot or the Bullet," April 3, 1964, www.rev.com/transcripts/the-ballot-or-the-bullet-speech-transcript-malcolm-x.

157 **"boomerang effect":** Aimé Césaire, *Discourse on Colonialism* (NYU Press, 2000), 41.

157 **"witnessing how the enslavement":** Malcolm X, "The End of White

World Supremacy," 1963, www.digitalhistory.uh.edu/disp_textbook.cfm?smtID=3&psid=3619.

157 **"Miss Jackson," she protested:** Emily J. Lordi, *Black Resonance: Iconic Women Singers and African American Literature* (Rutgers University Press, 2013), 272.

158 **"The only weapon":** Martin Luther King Jr., MIA Mass Meeting at Holt Street Baptist Church, Dec. 5, 1955, kinginstitute.stanford.edu/king-papers/documents/mia-mass-meeting-holt-street-baptist-church.

161 **"one of America's founding fathers":** Jonathan Eig, *King: A Life* (Farrar, Straus and Giroux, 2023).

161 **"the liberal elephant":** Richard Lischer, *Preacher King: Martin Luther King Jr. and the Word That Moved America* (Oxford University Press, 1995), 154.

161 **"still far behind":** Martin Luther King Jr., *Where Do We Go from Here: Chaos or Community?* (Harper & Row, 1967).

161 **"Here, in the life":** King, *Where Do We Go from Here.*

162 **"Let us not pay tribute":** King, *Where Do We Go from Here.*

162 **"arrogant assertion that one race":** King, *Where Do We Go from Here.*

163 **"Our nation was born":** Martin Luther King Jr., *Why We Can't Wait* (Harper & Row, 1964).

163 **"Now a nation that got started":** Lischer, *Preacher King,* 154.

163 **"I would submit":** Martin Luther King Jr., *The Radical King,* ed. Cornel West (Beacon Press, 2015), 253–64.

164 **"guided missiles":** King, *Radical King,* 80.

164 **"Ultimately, a great nation":** Martin Luther King Jr., Nobel Lecture, Dec. 11, 1964, www.nobelprize.org/prizes/peace/1964/king/lecture/.

164 **"self-preservation is the first law":** King, *Radical King,* 75–96.

165 **These ideas came together:** King, *Radical King,* 201–17.

166 **"What is that goddamned":** Gary May, "A Revolution of Values: Martin Luther King Jr. and the Poor People's Campaign," *Moyers,* Jan. 18, 2015, billmoyers.com/2015/01/18/revolution-values.

166 ***The New York Times* thought the speech:** "Dr. King's Error," *New York Times,* April 7, 1967.

166 **"Hate America" movement:** Eig, *King.*

167 **"demagogic slander that sounded like":** "Dr. King's Disservice to His Cause," *Life,* April 21, 1967.

167 **King believed in the idea:** Joseph, *Sword and the Shield.*

167 **"The whole future":** Vincent G. Harding, "The Legacy of Martin Luther King: Making Real the Promises of Democracy," *Sojourners,* April 23, 2010, sojo.net/articles/legacy-martin-luther-king-making-real-promises-democracy.

Chapter 6: The Flag and the Constitution

168 **"bondage of nationalism":** Ramachandra Guha, "Traveling with Tagore," introduction to Rabindranath Tagore, *Nationalism* (Penguin Books India, 2009), ramachandraguha.in/archives/traveling-with-tagore-penguin-classics.html.

169 **"To worship my country":** Rabindranath Tagore, *The Home and the World* (Macmillan, 1919), 20.

169 **"rid the world":** Guha, "Traveling with Tagore."

169 **"the colourless vagueness":** Tagore, *Nationalism* (1917), www.gutenberg.org/files/40766-h/40766-h.htm.

169 **"hide the fact that the Nation":** Tagore, *Nationalism* (1917).

169 **"The whole world is suffering":** Guha, "Traveling with Tagore."

170 **"I hope I am":** "English Learning," *Young India,* June 1, 1921.

170 **"a beggar or a slave":** "English Learning."

170 **"to dwarf the Indian body":** Guha, "Traveling with Tagore."

170 **"we surrender our reason":** "The Great Sentinel," *Young India,* Oct. 13, 1921.

170 **"altering the meaning":** "English Learning."

170 **"Untouchability for me is more insufferable":** Ramachandra Guha, *Gandhi: The Years That Changed the World, 1914–1948* (Alfred A. Knopf, 2018).

170 **"interminable parody of providence":** Tagore, *Nationalism.*

171 **"complaisance to South Carolina":** Notes of Proceedings in the Continental Congress, June 7–Aug. 1, 1776.

171 **"identified with extremism":** King, Nobel Lecture.

172 **"survival of our nation":** King Institute, "Goldwater, Barry M." *King Encyclopedia,* kinginstitute.stanford.edu/goldwater-barry-m.

172 **Rick Perlstein:** Rick Perlstein, *Before the Storm: Barry Goldwater and the Unmaking of the American Consensus* (Hill and Wang, 2001); Rick Perlstein, *Nixonland: The Rise of a President and the Fracturing of America* (Scribner, 2008).

173 **"We are all equal":** Barry Goldwater, *The Conscience of a Conservative* (Victor, 1960), www.gutenberg.org/ebooks/74319.

173 **"Which is it":** Peter Viereck, "The New Conservatism," *New Republic,* Sept. 1962, 17–19.

173 **"a bigger and better Welchism":** Viereck, "New Conservatism."

174 **"thought-controlling nationalism":** Viereck, "New Conservatism."

174 **"This country is going":** "Mitchell Assails 'Stupid' Students," *New York Times,* Sept. 19, 1970.

174 **"Our Nation is moving":** *National Advisory Commission on Civil*

Disorders (1968), belonging.berkeley.edu/sites/default/files/kerner_commission_full_report.pdf?file=1&force=1.

175 **"I know it may not be fashionable":** Richard Nixon, Address on the Vietnam War, Nov. 3, 1969, teachingamericanhistory.org/document/address-on-the-vietnam-war/.

175 **"the boomerang effect":** Hannah Arendt, "Home to Roost: A Bicentennial Address," *New York Review of Books,* June 26, 1975, www.nybooks.com/articles/1975/06/26/home-to-roost-a-bicentennial-address/.

175 **"I played only villains":** Fred Frommer, "G. Gordon Liddy," *Britannica,* Nov. 26, 2025, www.britannica.com/biography/G-Gordon-Liddy.

176 **It reflected a "market":** Arendt, "Home to Roost."

176 **"I don't know of any place":** "Handguns and the American Psyche," *Boston Globe,* June 7, 1981.

177 **"The market has changed":** J. Joseph Curran Jr., "A Farewell to Arms: The Solution to Gun Violence in America," Maryland Attorney General's Special Report, Oct. 20, 1999, www.generalstaff.org/Firearms/A_Farewell_to_Arms.pdf.

177 **"I have crossed the Atlantic":** E. P. Thompson, *Beyond the Cold War* (Pantheon Books, 1982), digitalarchive.wilsoncenter.org/document/113717.pdf?v=7fb1c480d8c2cad310bd9b1dc7ed01ea.

177 **"government was the problem":** Molly Ivins, *Nothin' but Good Times Ahead* (Alfred A. Knopf, 1994), 105.

178 **including such sublime "crackpottery":** Ivins, *Nothin' but Good Times Ahead,* 103.

178 **"The new patriotism":** George Lipsitz, "Dilemmas of Beset Nationhood: Patriotism, the Family, and Economic Change in the 1970s and 1980s," in *Bonds of Affection: Americans Define Their Patriotism,* ed. John Bodnar (Princeton University Press, 1996).

179 **"plucked the patriotic heartstrings":** "The Fall Guy Fights Back," *Time,* July 20, 1987.

179 **"for the love of God":** Luke Hill, "The Day George Mitchell Saved American Patriotism from Oliver North," *Commonweal,* Oct. 14, 2014, www.commonwealmagazine.org/day-george-mitchell-saved-american-patriotism-oliver-north.

179 **"Now, you've talked a lot":** Hill, "Day George Mitchell Saved American Patriotism from Oliver North."

180 **"Caspar Weinberger is a true":** "The Pardons," *New York Times,* Dec. 25, 1992.

180 **Samuel Johnson:** Lipsitz, "Dilemmas of Beset Nationhood."

180 **"real damage to the Constitution":** Ivins, *Nothin' but Good Times Ahead,* 191.

180 **"the parchment regime":** Molly Ivins and Lou Dubose, *Bill of Wrongs: The Executive Branch's Assault on America's Fundamental Rights* (Random House, 2007), xvii.

180 **"probably sounded better":** Ivins, *Nothin' but Good Times Ahead,* 136.

180 **"the enemy of normal":** Molly Ivins, "Geek Show," *Dallas Observer,* Nov. 16, 1994.

180 **A training memo issued:** "Language: A Key Mechanism of Control," users.wfu.edu/zulick/454/gopac.html.

181 **"I'm fond of hyperbole":** Ivins, "Geek Show."

181 **"transferred nationalism":** Orwell, "Notes on Nationalism."

181 **"More and more we are fueled":** Scott Melzer, *Gun Crusaders: The NRA's Culture War* (New York University Press, 2009), 102.

181 **"Those words are true again":** Charlton Heston, "Winning the Cultural War," Feb. 16, 1999, www.americanrhetoric.com/speeches/charltonhestonculturalwar.htm.

182 **McVeigh had written to his congressman:** "Letter from Bomb Suspect Released," UPI, May 2, 1995, www.upi.com/Archives/1995/05/02/Letter-from-bomb-suspect-released/3139799387200/.

182 **"how they were to shoot liberals":** Godfrey Hodgson, *Myth of American Exceptionalism* (Yale University Press, 2009), 174.

182 **"institutionalized leftism":** "An Aunt with an Attitude," *Wall Street Journal,* May 20, 2005, Europe edition.

183 **"It was an f-you":** Todd C. Frankel et al., "The Gun That Divides a Nation," *Washington Post,* www.washingtonpost.com/nation/interactive/2023/ar-15-america-gun-culture-politics/.

183 **"dished up . . . as an antifederalist":** Jefferson to Francis Hopkinson, March 13, 1789, oll.libertyfund.org/title/jefferson-the-works-vol-5-correspondence-1786-1789.

183 **when the people vote by "acclamation":** Jason Stanley, *How Propaganda Works* (Princeton University Press, 2015), 35.

183 **That kind of "unanimity":** Jean-Jacques Rousseau, *The Social Contract* (Wordsworth Editions, 1998), 107.

183 **"Why has government":** Federalist No. 15.

183 **"as part of the lunatic left":** " 'Crazy' Ideas on Drugs and Arms," *San Francisco Chronicle,* Dec. 16, 1993.

184 **"giving the war-making power to Congress":** Lincoln to William Herndon, Feb. 15, 1848, in *Collected Works of Abraham Lincoln,* vol. 1, quod.lib.umich.edu/l/lincoln/lincoln1/1:458.1?rgn=div2;view=fulltext.

184 **"our President where kings":** Lincoln to Herndon, Feb. 15, 1848.

184 **"that we're better":** Norman Solomon, *War Made Invisible: How America Hides the Human Toll of Its Military Machine* (New Press, 2024).

185 **"not become the evil":** Barbara Lee, Statement in Opposition to H.J.

Res. 64, Sept. 14, 2001, www.americanrhetoric.com/speeches/barbaraleeagainstinvasion.htm.

185 **"Democracy doesn't come in a box":** Lyle Jeremy Rubin et al., "Democracy Doesn't Come in a Box," *New York Times,* Nov. 11, 2019, www.nytimes.com/2019/11/11/opinion/veterans-afghanistan-war.html.

185 **"law-free zone":** Elaine Cassel, *The War on Civil Liberties: How Bush and Ashcroft Have Dismantled the Bill of Rights* (Lawrence Hill Books, 2004).

186 **"We're going to go in":** Eric Hananoki, "Where Are the Media's Iraq War Boosters 10 Years Later?," *Media Matters for America,* March 19, 2013, www.mediamatters.org/war-iraq/where-are-medias-iraq-war-boosters-10-years-later.

186 **an imploring, saber-rattling entreaty:** Jeffrey Goldberg, "The Great Terror," *New Yorker,* March 25, 2002.

186 **"the supreme international crime":** John Pilger, "We See Too Much. We Know Too Much. That's Our Best Defence," *Independent,* April 6, 2003, www.independent.co.uk/voices/commentators/john-pilger-we-see-too-much-we-know-too-much-that-s-our-best-defence-113929.html.

187 **"American tanks coming down":** Goldberg, "Great Terror."

187 **"first resist the great suggestive-power":** Thompson, *Beyond the Cold War.*

187 **"George Bush is the president":** David Dadge, *The War in Iraq and Why the Media Failed Us* (Praeger, 2006), 41.

187 **"Look, I'm an American":** Norman Solomon, "Look, I'm an American," in *Tell Me Lies: Propaganda and Media Distortion in the Attack on Iraq,* ed. David Miller (Pluto, 2004), 157.

187 **"Yes, I'm a journalist":** Dadge, *War in Iraq and Why the Media Failed Us,* 44.

188 **"now owns a bit of history":** "The Power of One," *Time,* April 21, 2003, time.com/archive/6668576/the-power-of-one-2/.

188 **"We do not want this war":** Erin Keller, "The Chicks Have No Regrets Being Canceled for Bush Remark: 'Set Us Free,'" *New York Post,* May 4, 2023, https://nypost.com/2023/05/04/the-chicks-have-no-regrets-being-canceled-for-bush-remark-set-us-free/.

188 **"Do you know what this country's done for you?":** Sean Mandell, "Pamela Anderson 'Almost Got Killed' by Man Who Thought She Was a Dixie Chick," *New York Post,* January 6, 2025, https://nypost.com/2025/01/06/entertainment/pamela-anderson-almost-got-killed-by-man-who-thought-she-was-a-dixie-chick/.

188 **"What we do with civilization":** Lyle Jeremy Rubin, "The Vietnam War Was Worse Than Just a Tragic Miscalculation," *Christian Century,*

Jan. 17, 2018, www.christiancentury.org/review/books/vietnam-war-was-worse-just-tragic-miscalculation.

188 **"I worry that patriotism run amok":** BBC, "Veteran CBS News Anchor Dan Rather Speaks Out on BBC Newsnight Tonight," press release, May 16, 2002, www.bbc.co.uk/pressoffice/pressreleases/stories/2002/05_may/16/dan_rather.shtml.

189 **"I was one person":** Clara Bingham, *Witness to the Revolution* (Random House, 2016), 275.

191 **"swamp of crazy":** Ryan Teague Beckwith, "Read President Obama's 'Swamp of Crazy' Speech About Republicans," *Time,* Oct. 14, 2016, time.com/4531245/barack-obama-swamp-crazy-speech-transcript/.

191 **"is worse than a crime":** Jeffrey Sachs, *A New Foreign Policy: Beyond American Exceptionalism* (Columbia University Press, 2018), 5.

191 **We currently sit at 128:** Institute for Economics and Peace, *Global Peace Index 2025: Identifying and Measuring the Factors That Drive Peace,* June 2025, www.visionofhumanity.org/wp-content/uploads/2025/06/Global-Peace-Index-2025-web.pdf.

Epilogue: Patriotism Spelled Humanity

193 **"to splinter the C.I.A.":** "C.I.A.: Maker of Policy, or Tool?," *New York Times,* April 25, 1966.

194 **"Tell them to wait":** Terry Messman, "A Quaker's Ceaseless Quest for a World Without War," Street Spirit, Sept. 7, 2014, thestreetspirit.org/2014/09/07/a-quakers-ceaseless-quest-for-a-world-without-war/.

195 **"the greatest speech":** James M. Lindsay, "TWE Remembers: JFK's 'Strategy of Peace' Speech," *The Water's Edge* (blog), Council on Foreign Relations, June 10, 2013, www.cfr.org/blog/twe-remembers-jfks-strategy-peace-speech.

196 **"The factor of personality":** Adrian Hastings, *A History of English Christianity 1920–2000* (SCM Press, 2001), 519.

197 **"the century of the common man":** Henry A. Wallace, "The Century of the Common Man," May 8, 1942, www.americanrhetoric.com/speeches/henrywallacefreeworldassoc.htm.

197 **"America has not yet changed":** Martin Luther King Jr., *A Testament of Hope: The Essential Writings of Martin Luther King, Jr.,* ed. James M. Washington (Harper & Row, 1994), 328.

198 **"Let our great role":** Remarks of Senator John F. Kennedy at the Cow Palace, San Francisco, Nov. 2, 1960, www.jfklibrary.org/archives/other-resources/john-f-kennedy-speeches/san-francisco-19601102.

INDEX

Q

R

S

ABOUT THE AUTHOR

Dominic Erdozain is a writer and historian with a passion for bringing the past into dialogue with the present. Erdozain has written widely on the intellectual origins of democracy and published articles with CNN and *Time*. He is the author of *One Nation Under Guns* and a graduate of Oxford and Cambridge. He is currently a visiting professor at Emory University.